Captaining the
Corps d'Afrique

Captaining the Corps d'Afrique

The Civil War Diaries and Letters of John Newton Chamberlin

JOHN NEWTON CHAMBERLIN
Edited by John Bisbee

McFarland & Company, Inc., Publishers
Jefferson, North Carolina

The copyright of all material in this manuscript, with exceptions noted below, including preface, introduction, chapters, bibliography, appendices, figures, and any other materials, is owned by the editor, John W. Bisbee. Typescripts of many letters belong to Marilyn Young and others to Jim Goodin. Photos from John Chamberlin's album and typescripts of Chamberlin's 1865 diary belong to Lelia and Paul Klear. Young, Goodin, and the Klears have given me express permission to use these documents in this book. None of these materials may be copied or used in any way without the express written permission of the editor or owner.

LIBRARY OF CONGRESS CATALOGUING-IN-PUBLICATION DATA

Names: Chamberlin, John Newton, [1837]–1880, author. | Bisbee, John (Retired professor), editor.
Title: Captaining the Corps d'Afrique : the Civil War diaries and letters of John Newton Chamberlin / John Newton Chamberlin ; edited by John Bisbee.
Description: Jefferson, North Carolina : McFarland & Company, Inc., Publishers, 2016. | Includes bibliographical references and index.
Identifiers: LCCN 2016021545 | ISBN 9781476664491 (softcover : acid free paper) ∞
Subjects: LCSH: Chamberlin, John Newton, –1880—Diaries. | Chamberlin, John Newton, –1880—Correspondence. | United States. Army. Colored Infantry Regiment, 97th (1864–1866) | United States. Corps d'Afrique. Engineer Regiment, 3rd (1863–1864) | United States—History—Civil War, 1861–1865—Personal narratives. | United States—History—Civil War, 1861–1865—Participation, African American.
Classification: LCC E492.94 97th .C46 2016 | DDC 973.7/415092 [B]—dc23
LC record available at https://lccn.loc.gov/2016021545

BRITISH LIBRARY CATALOGUING DATA ARE AVAILABLE

ISBN (print) 978-1-4766-6449-1
ISBN (ebook) 978-1-4766-2500-3

© 2016 John W. Bisbee. All rights reserved

No part of this book may be reproduced or transmitted in any form or by any means, electronic or mechanical, including photocopying or recording, or by any information storage and retrieval system, without permission in writing from the publisher.

Printed in the United States of America

McFarland & Company, Inc., Publishers
 Box 611, Jefferson, North Carolina 28640
  www.mcfarlandpub.com

To Carol
for unceasing support, genuine interest,
and common sense

Acknowledgments

I am indebted to many people who made this project possible. Marilyn Young, in addition to collecting and typing most of John Chamberlin's and Anna Bullock's letters, also did considerable research on the Chamberlin and Bullock families. Without her extensive and careful work and unselfish sharing of it, I would not know of my great-grandfather's legacy, and this book would not exist. My wife, Carol Bisbee, has provided critical editing, careful research, and useful organization for this book.

For more than two years during the planning and writing of this book, two friends, Madelyn and Brian Mihm, have provided strong support for this project and extensive editing for the manuscript; in addition, Madelyn has done a great deal of useful research in historical documents. There would not be a book without Marilyn, Carol, Madelyn and Brian. However, I am responsible for any mistakes or errors.

Lelia and Paul Klear provided a typescript of part of Chamberlin's diary of 1865, and Paul skillfully scanned all the photos in the album (see fig. 6, chap. 5). James Goodin shared approximately twenty of Chamberlin's letters. Preservation and distribution of John Chamberlin's and Anna Bullock's documents by Anna Bullock Chamberlin, Mabel Bisbee, Marian Harris, Marge Kellin Goodin, Clarice Scheffler, and Margaret Bisbee were essential for this book (see Appendix A). Richard Holloway read parts of the manuscript and provided historical information and advice about publication. Megan Halsband found valuable newspaper articles. Cory Reinking helped scan document pages into Word, and Janet and Bruce Harshberger read sections of the manuscript.

I greatly appreciate the enthusiastic support and unselfish work that all of these people, and others unnamed, have provided for this project.

Table of Contents

Acknowledgments   vi
Preface   1
Introduction   5

1. Entering the Fray   7
2. The Union Takes Pensacola   15
3. New Orleans   23
4. Control of the Mississippi River   33
5. 3rd Engineers, Corps d'Afrique   46
6. Loneliness of War   56
7. The Red River Campaign   63
8. Coping with the Misery of War   70
9. Changes for the Black Soldiers   77
10. The Presidential Election and the War   87
11. Return to Florida   93
12. Camp Life   101
13. The Defeat of the Rebels   107
14. Victory at What Price?   114
15. Post-War Nation   125
16. Visit at Home   134
17. Final Military Days   139
18. Planning a Future Together   147

Table of Contents

Epilogue   157

Appendices:

    A. The Chamberlin and Bullock Documents:
        A Brief History   161
    B. Order for Service in the Corps d'Afrique   162
    C. Engineering Instructions, Duane's Manual   163
    D. Fort Gaines Orders   165
    E. Receipt for Clothing Issued in October 1864   166
    F. Stores Lost in Action, December 18, 1864   167
    G. Field Work Order, April 24, 1865   169
    H. Chronology of John's and Anna's Letters   170
    I. *Jennie Rogers* Orders   172
    J. Leave of Absence, October 18, 1865   173
    K. Soldiers in Black Companies Commanded
        by Capt. Chamberlin   173

Chapter Notes   176

Bibliography   192

Index   199

Preface

This book tells the story of John Newton Chamberlin's life during and immediately after the Civil War, 1861–1866. While serving in the Union Army, Chamberlin (1837–1880) wrote hundreds of pages of letters and diaries that provide the basis for this book. The documents cover wide-ranging topics: camp life, specific battles in the Department of the Gulf, the role of black soldiers, the landscape and geography of the South, views of fellow officers, and the national politics of slavery and Reconstruction. The letters and diaries reveal Chamberlin to be well-read, observant, and articulate, as well as a man of moral principle, strong religious faith, and intelligence, with a deep sense of duty and patriotism.

Chamberlin enlisted a few months after the war began and served through the entire war plus another year after hostilities ended. A native of Sennett, New York, he served the whole four-and-one-half long years in the Deep South. In 1863 he became the captain of an all-black company in the Corps d'Afrique (later the U.S. Colored Infantry). This book is one of very few narratives by white officers of black troops, and one of even fewer to record and discuss the work of a black engineering company. Chamberlin and his men participated both in major military actions and in raising sunken vessels and building dams, forts, bridges, and roads. More than just day-to-day accounts of his company's activities, his writings show a growing understanding of the war from the perspective of soldiers and civilians. In addition, he analyzed important national issues such as the impact of slavery (which he hated), the responsibility of both sides for the war, and the future of the country.

Amid the reports and reflections on war and politics, Chamberlin's letters also reveal a man of sensitivity, loneliness, anger, tolerance, love, and hope. At times he was thoroughly delighted by the natural beauty

Preface

of the South, even poetic in describing the moonlight on a river. He admitted to being homesick at times, and to being deeply touched by the black soldiers' requests for him to write love letters for them. In all these ways Chamberlain reveals a sensitivity often at odds with the brusqueness and drunkenness of fellow white officers. Many of Chamberlin's letters were written to his family, but beginning in 1864 he started exchanging letters with an old school-mate, Anna Bullock, who at that time lived in Waterloo, Iowa. Their letters trace their two-year burgeoning relationship, leading to their marriage after the war.

Chamberlin was an incessant writer whose handwriting was clear and at times elegant. His diaries for 1861–1865 and the 103 letters that he wrote or received are preserved in the original or in typescript copies that were prepared before the originals were lost. See Appendix A for a complete list of original letters and diaries, typescripts, photographs, and military documents. Because some materials are available now only in typescript, it is impossible to know whether occasional misspellings are Chamberlin's or unintentionally the product of those who prepared and copied the typescripts. I have made every effort to be as faithful to the original texts as possible.

In addition, I have used the following editorial principles: (1) I have preserved most of Chamberlin's nineteenth-century spellings and phrases without comment. He used a possessive "s" without an apostrophe. His capitalizations of some words and his abbreviations were not always consistent. Sometimes he used a straight quotation mark (") after a military unit or date, such as the 75" N.Y.V. (New York Volunteers), or March 3" to indicate "th," "rd," etc. To indicate misspellings of proper names, I have used [sic]. (2) Throughout his documents, Chamberlin spelled his name ending in "-lin," "-lain," and "-lan." Since he used Chamber*lin* more than 70 percent of the time, that is my preferred spelling when not quoting him. (3) I refer to African American soldiers not as *colored*, but as *black*, in keeping with twenty-first-century practice, except when quoting Chamberlin, other sources, or other Civil War documents that use "colored." (4) To help distinguish between the story I am writing and the quoted nineteenth-century letters and diaries, I have indicated long quotes by indenting them and using a smaller font. (5) Diary entry dates are listed in **boldface**. (6) Many times I have used selected excerpts from letters rather than the full letters.

Preface

This is not a complete story of the Civil War, but the story of John Chamberlin's Civil War experiences, told mostly in his own words. I have selected many of his letters, diary entries, military records and orders, the map of a redoubt he built, and some of Anna Bullock's and others' letters, and I have also included several photographs from Chamberlin's album to show his life during and shortly after the war. My choice of documents was based on their relevance to Chamberlin's life during the Civil War and his views of it. Thus I have minimized descriptions of the weather and references to extended family, family acquaintances, and events at home in upstate New York. The book has been organized basically as a chronological account, except when it seemed appropriate to bring together writings on the same theme from slightly different time periods. One benefit of this chronological approach is to trace Chamberlin's changing views of blacks and black regiments, the idea of war and this war in particular, Southerners, the North's responsibility for slavery, and the future of the country.

I have given information relating to some of the letters and diaries to put them in context. My research has been based on the *Official Records of the Union and Confederate Armies and Navies,* the *New York Times* and other newspapers from 1861 to 1865, primary sources from the 1800s, official New York State records, reference sources (encyclopedias and dictionaries) on the Civil War, and the writings of recent scholars like William Dobak, Eric Foner, Joseph Glatthaar, Doris Kearns Goodwin, and James McPherson.

On a personal note, it has been exciting to study these diaries and letters of my great-grandparents, as well as to research historical background and family history. My great-grandfather is no longer simply a fading photograph on the wall of relatives, nor an ancestor whose sword and uniform were handed down to me from the distant past. He has become a person with character, values, feelings, and aspirations. Though her submission to her husband made her very much a woman of her time, Anna Bullock ultimately showed herself to be very strong as she shepherded her family through difficult circumstances. Perhaps for the reader, too, this story will bring to life this principled captain of a regiment in a "U.S. Colored Inft."—the phrase on his tombstone—and his beloved wife.

Introduction

John N. Chamberlin was born on October 23, 1837, in Windsor, Vermont. He grew up working on the family farm near Sennett, Cayuga County, New York. Chamberlin patriotically volunteered to join the 75th New York Volunteers in September 1861 and served until a year after the war was over. He trained in New York and on Santa Rosa Island, Florida, then went to the Pensacola area in December 1861. After nine months there, in September 1862 he moved with his regiment to New Orleans where he encountered the complex cultural and racial mixture distinctive to this city.

Chamberlin's military activity increased in 1863 with skirmishes in central Louisiana and the siege of Port Hudson. In September, he was commissioned captain of a new company of black soldiers who worked primarily as engineers. While still harboring vestiges of the racist views of his time, he demonstrated a growing appreciation of his soldiers. He wrote their love letters and taught them to read.

He and his engineers participated in the disastrous Red River Campaign in the spring of 1864. Also at this time, Chamberlin started writing to Anna Bullock, an old school mate who had moved to Waterloo, Iowa. This correspondence consisted of lengthy descriptions and analyses of military, political, and social events, as well as discussions of home and plans for the future. For the rest of 1864 Chamberlin's soldiers worked on engineering tasks in central Louisiana and along the Gulf coast in Florida and Alabama. Chamberlin offered extensive comments about the presidential election, slavery, and the future of the country.

In early 1865, he and his troops headed to the Mobile area to support the final battles of the Civil War. After the war ended in April,

Introduction

Chamberlin stayed in southern Alabama for another year. He spent several weeks north of Mobile, where his duty was to encourage white Southerners to renew their allegiance to the Union. He returned to Mobile for his final months in the service. There he had few responsibilities; he even had time to start a small business with an army friend. While in Alabama, he observed and described the destruction of homes and farms. He noted that while white society was breaking down, the blacks were celebrating their freedom.

After being mustered out in April 1866 with the longest-serving black regiment of the Civil War, Chamberlin visited Anna Bullock. He proposed to her and went back to New York with a ring on his finger. Over the summer, the couple pledged their love and planned a fall marriage, after which Chamberlin intended to become a "citizen farmer" in New York.

CHAPTER 1

Entering the Fray

The Journey to Santa Rosa Island

In September 1861, after the terrible storm of war broke over the land, John Chamberlin, a teacher and farmer in Sennett, Cayuga County, New York,[1] enlisted in the 75th New York Volunteers (N.Y.V.). His parents "thought this was a most preposterous idea, there were enough ruffians to go." Presumably he enlisted as a private, but was mustered in as a corporal and later was promoted to sergeant.[2] Chamberlin trained in Auburn, New York, which was so close to his home that he occasionally worked on the farm for a day. According to a regimental history published in 1873, after some of the recruits had to be quartered in hotels and private homes, Col. John A. Dodge soon saw to it that permanent barracks were erected, and on October 14 almost eight hundred men entered "Camp Cayuga" for training. Six weeks later, on Saturday, November 30, the 854 men of the 75th regiment left camp for New York City and ultimately, the Florida panhandle. The men sailed on the steamer *Baltic* on December 6.[3] Chamberlin described that experience in one of his early letters to his family.

> On board the Baltic Steaming down N.Y. Harbor,
> Dec. 6th, 11 o'clock A.M.
>
> Dear Father & Mother, Brothers & sisters,
>   We left Gov. Island last night at 4 o'clock in a Barge & steamer tug & went on board the Baltic at 7 ½.
>   We have just started down the Bay & when the Pilot Boat leaves us at the Narrows we can send letters & after that we don't know when we shall have another chance. I am well and have enjoyed our journey very much. We are bound direct to Fort Pickens. The Baltic is indeed a mighty vessel,

Captaining the Corps d'Afrique

being 300 feet long & carrying 2700 Tons. The machinery is really gigantic. It will probably take us from 7 to 9 days to make the voyage. On the Hurricane Deck 12 o'clock, we are moving majestically down the Bay. The day is Cloudy & warm. The Band is on deck playing. On the whole the scene is more spirited & picturesque than any which I supposed I should ever witness. We are now passing Statene [sic] Island which seems almost mountainous, the height being covered with evergreens. Away to the N.W. the Jersey shore glimmers faintly through the blue haze in the distance. The old paddle wheels verily make the deep to boil, as a pot. Far away to the N.W. is a United States mail Steamer, the black smoke rolling out in the distance for miles. We are now hailed by a Pilot boat & the Vessel is stopped, the Pilot inquires what Boat it is, the captain answers the Baltic, where is she bound, direct to Fort Pickens under Government Charter & we start again.

We are now passing through the Narrows, Fort Layfaette [sic] is built in the water & is quite a safe looking place, on the east shore is Fort Hamilton & on the West is Fort Griswold, both mounting a great many guns & formidable looking places. We shall have comfortable quarters & good fare on the vessel. We shall soon put our Pilot on shore & stand out to sea.

Direct all letters to Fort Pickens, Fla. untill further directions.

   Love to all,
   J. N. Chamberlain

Chamberlin was moving from a peaceful, patriotic scene to an unknown world full of new experiences and people. He was often seasick on the seven-day trip to Santa Rosa Island in the Florida panhandle (fig. 1). The island, as described in one contemporary account, was low and sandy, about forty miles long from west to east and a little more than a mile wide at its widest point. It extended across the southern end of Pensacola Bay, "one of the finest harbors of the world" and the location of "one of the largest navy yards of this country" before the war. The western tip of the island, overlooking the entrance to the bay, was protected by Fort Pickens, "a large, five-sided, bomb-proof stone work, mounting numerous and heavy cannon."[4] The 75th N.Y.V. settled into camp beside Fort Pickens. Although the men were suffering from heat and sickness, *Cayuga in the Field* reports that they laid out and set up Camp Seward, near the southern shoreline of the island and east of the fort.[5]

Drilling and picket guard duty kept the men occupied during late December. The commander of the fort, Col. Harvey Brown, of the 5th

1. Entering the Fray

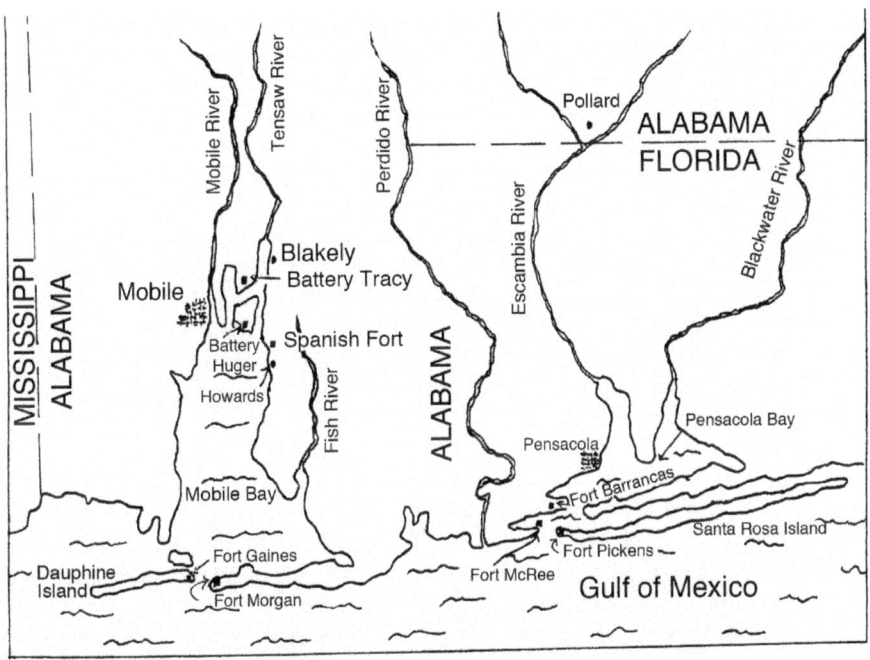

Figure 1. Map of southern Alabama and northwest Florida, 1860. Drawn by John Bisbee, based on Dobak, *Freedom by the Sword*, 90; O'Brien, *Mobile, 1865*, 136; and https://www.etsy.com/listing/155305836/pensacola-bay-map-c-1860-pensacola.

U.S. Artillery, wrote of the 75th: "This is a fine regiment, and will, I doubt not, do good service when they have the chance."[6] Chamberlin described some of the trip to Santa Rosa Island and his initial service to one of his sisters.

Camp Seward, Dec 28th, 1861

My Dear Sister Eleanor,

I have been quite unwell with a diarrhea but have got well now. It was caused (no doubt) by a general disarrangement of the stomach on board the Baltic & then poorly cooked food after we landed. A great many of our boys are troubled in the same way. We commenced drawing our rations of good fresh bread yesterday & we shall fare better & not be so liable to be sick. The bread is made at the Fort & although not exactly like home-made bread, is well baked & very good. Our other rations are cooked by the Camp cooks & as a general thing are pretty well cooked. We have potatoes & gravy, boiled meat, rice, beans & peas &c &c.

Yesterday morning there were three Contrabands came over from the Rebels.[7] One of them said he was the body servant of the Rebel Col. Jackson.[8] They were very communicative. Said that there had been an engagement on the Potomac. That the Rebel loss was 10,000 killed & wounded & 5000 prisoners which we hope is all so, but we have our doubts [no records of this engagement]. Also that Mobile was taken & all communication between Mobile & New Orleans cut off [Mobile was not taken until April 1865; see chap. 13]. That the Rebels were living in dayly & hourly dread that a fleet of gun-boats will arrive here & a general bombardment will commence, which last is no doubt true in the main. We have Battallion drill Tuesdays & Fridays from 2½ to 5 P.M. Other days we are drilled by Regulars from the Fort about 3 hours a day, the non-commishioned officers of each co. separately, but these Regulars are a lazy set & they let us rest most of the time. There was a National Vessel arrived in the Harbor yesterday & there was some firing which caused some excitement, but the trouble was that the vessel had a head wind & had to be towed in by a steamer.

Things remain in about the same state as usual on the Island. A strong Picket guard is kept & the usual activity is manifest in hauling ammunition to the Fort.

The improvements around the Fort & batterries go on as usual. We enjoy ourselves here much better than we should in Virginia, the weather being so much warmer & more pleasant. We don't have any mud here & not much rain.

Take good care of yourself & the rest of the Folks & don't do any more than you can help.

    Love to all,
    J. N. Chamberlin

Start of War

On **January 1**, 1862, in his diary, Chamberlin described his first experience of war: "One of our Batteries [at Fort Pickens] opened fire on a rebel steamer & the action soon became general. The roar of cannon & the bursting of bombs became almost incessant."[9] In a letter to his mother on September 24, 1862, he said, "The calm serenity of

1. Entering the Fray

Nature seemed turned into a perfect hell of confusion & strife by the wonderful appliances of artillery."

When life returned to normal, Chamberlin again wrote to a sister. This letter shows his political thinking to be ahead of his time:

Camp Seward, Santa Rosa, Thursday, Feb 5th 1862

Dear Sister,

I suppose you will like to hear from this out of the way place at almost any time whether anything happens or not, so I keep on writing down my conjectures & suppositions & what few things that happen from day to day & if they afford you any pleasure in the perusal I shall be repaid for all the trouble, for I assure you that all labor here is a weariness to the flesh. I have just been to the Sutlers & got 10 sheets of paper & this pen, which I think are very good, for a Soldier.[10] Our portfolio has proved to be a very convenient thing after all. Wilkins & I have been making some different arrangements about our tent,[11] I believe I wrote you that we had a double tent. Well Lick was on guard one night & we slept so comfortably that we made a plan to get the tent all to ourselves.

I have recd 4 letters, one which was directed to N.Y. while I was there & 3 others since, one by each mail & 2 tribunes & the Auburn Journal, & we expect another mail soon with great quantities of good news. I never before valued letters & papers as I do here. I tell you they are looked for anxiously by most of the boys. We are variously employed here but mostly in drilling. We drill from 3 to 5 hours daily when no other duty is required. One Co. is detailed daily to wheel sand to fill up a marsh near the Fort for a new parade ground for the Reg. Then about 2/3 of the time a company are on picket guard. Col. John A. Dodge is a very careful man of his Reg. No danger of his working them to death, although some of the boys complain bitterly of their treatment. The fact is we have so little to do that we don't want to do anything. It is probably necessary that some Reg. should be here to protect the Port & we are doing as important a duty as we could anywhere, perhaps, but it seems to us, away from the main scene of action as we are that the grand army of Northmen who are in the field today are comparatively doing nothing but idling away a precious winter. It seems as though a week wasted now in inaction may be the ruin of the Nation. This winter was the chosen time to crush out the Rebellion. It is the time for a Northern army to work in the South if ever.

I wish I knew what Congress is doing about the Slavery question. Are they at the same old shilly-shally business of trying to put down this accursed rebellion & at the same time to save its real cause—American Slavery? Why not strike a blow at the fountain head of all the mischief.

Captaining the Corps d'Afrique

With the same show of reason might Old Col. Brown make plans to take the Rebel forces on the other side of the bay & leave all their Batteries & intrenchments unharmed. The idea would not be half as preposterous as it is to try to leave Slavery in the place it occupied 12 months ago. The doom of American Slavery is sealed. Let no insane politician try to avert its just fate. In such an age as this events move with rapid strides.

 This year must mark many wonderful changes in the affairs of this Nation. Perhaps we are to suffer some more great defeat before we wake up to the fact that we are dealing with a wary & relentless foe. It may be that things are going on all right. What's the use of my talking, I don't know anything about it away down here on this sandy desert. God on his throne sits in judgement & takes note of all passing events & let us hope that ere long the dark cloud that lowers so heavily in our national horizon will give place to a radiant morning of peace & fraternity, liberty & law. But there is the call to drill & I must go.

 Evening, just had a beautiful shower! We are getting quite proficient in the manual of arms. Our instructor is a German, who has been almost ten years in the service. He drills all the Corporals of the Reg. He feels quite proud of us & well he may, for take us all together we are a fine looking set of men.

 We went up on the observatory, (a rude framework of logs) this A.M. & with Lieut Corning's glass we could see the other side about as clearly as if we had been there.[12] Had a plain sight of Pensacola which is 7 miles distant. The Rebel Steamer Time lay at the wharf & we could easily see the letters of her name.[13] The village appears to be a small collection of low roofed houses with verendahs running around them with here & there a house of considerable size. Only one church spire is visible & that looked very much like the Presbyterian church in Sennett. At the Navy Yard, mules, niggers & white men might be seen moving lazely about. All that could be seen at all inviting were some of the Government buildings which looked very comfortable & cozy. I presume the officers on the other side have more of the luxuries of life than ours as there is a railroad running in the vicinity of their works. We frequently hear the whistle of a locomotive & sometimes when the wind is North we hear the rumble of the cars, which reminds one forcibly of civilization & home.

 When I return home I hope to start on that railroad as one sea voyage is sufficient for me although under different circumstances I should like it very much.

   Love to all concerned,
   J.N.C.

1. Entering the Fray

Improving a Soldier's Life

Chamberlin reported in early 1862 letters to his family that he and his tent-mate Hartwell Wilkins spent considerable time on tent repair and improvement. They laid a floor in their tent soon after they arrived and put a bouquet of roses on the shelf. On **March 12**, according to his diary, Chamberlin "commenced making a chair out of an old barrel & got a soap box & made a cover to it." On **March 14** Chamberlin reported "heavy thunder showers at night. W [Wilkins] and I got a new tent & put it over our own which prevented leaking." On **March 25** they raised their tent fifteen inches off the ground, making a great deal more room. When forced to leave their much-improved tent, they feared that they would have to go into a tent with ten or twelve men. In a daring moment on **April 3**, Chamberlin ignored the chain of command and his own well-being and "went down to the Fort & had a talk with Gen. Arnold about keeping their tent.[14] The old scoundrel told me to go to my quarters or he would put me under arrest. I have yet to learn that I am not as good a man as he." The tent controversy turned out better than expected. "Through the common sense & kindness of our Capt. & the worthlessness to Uncle Samuel of our tents we have been allowed to keep the one we had."

In addition to worrying about protection from the elements, Chamberlin was concerned about food. It took two or three months for food boxes from home to reach them. However, in a **February 10**, 1862, entry in his diary, Chamberlin reported that a "schooner arrived from Havana with Tropical fruits & jellies. Oranges seem as common as cider apples at the North. They fulfill my expectations of what oranges should be. Very cheap. Many of the boys made themselves sick eating them." Two weeks later Chamberlin and his tent-mate found a new way to acquire food and to entertain themselves.

> Wilkins went on board the Yankee Blade & got 28 lbs. of butter, a cheese, a box of crackers, a box of Herring & a box of raisins. Also a package of tobacco for the boys & a barrel of apples which he sold for 3 dollars advance. We shall sell part of the butter & herrings & live on the rest. We made a pretty good day of it.

The two soldiers' entrepreneurial activities reappeared later. Chamberlin wrote on **April 11**: "Blew a perfect hurricane all day. Another

Captaining the Corps d'Afrique

Brig was stranded to-day, near the West end of the Isle." On the next day they "went down to the stranded vessel & bought 2 kegs of butter & a cheese & sold them again at a good profit." On the following day Chamberlin reported: "Wilkins & I have bought $130 worth of butter, cheese, pepper & condensed milk making 15 or 20 dollars profit." They also bought four cheeses for $10.75. In addition, the two soldiers finally got food from home: "Butter & dried apples &c, &c, &c. The butter was quite frothy & we sold it for 5 dollars, as we have a plenty of good butter." Wilkins received a "box containing 2 pails of butter, 15 lbs of dried apples, some pepper & lemons and also a package with a few raisins & figs & dates, some soap, photograph & postage stamps &c." What were they doing with all this butter?

In a March 2 letter to his brother, Chamberlin commented, "On the whole we are better off than we should be at home, for we have no cold storms to encounter, we don't have to work very hard & we live like kings. W & I especially. We have now a supply of good things sufficient to last us some time." Other soldiers, he noted, "who have to live entirely on their rations have enough to eat, but there is too much monotony about it."

Life on Santa Rosa Island was pretty easy for wartime, and life wasn't much harder at their next stop, Pensacola.

CHAPTER 2

The Union Takes Pensacola

Pensacola, Florida, a vital Gulf-coast seaport for either the North or the South, would be an entrance for supplies, and its well-protected Naval Yard would be beneficial for any warring party. After its fall to the Union in 1862, it was used as a center for initiating and supplying military engagements all along the Gulf Coast.

Pensacola was founded in 1698. At different times it was held by Spain, France, Britain, and the United States. By 1834 the Pensacola area was home to the Pensacola Navy Yard and three historic U.S. forts—Barrancas, Pickens, and McRee (fig. 1).[1] Pensacola was the state's largest city in 1860, with a population of 2,876.[2] The Confederates took control of the city in January 1861, when Florida seceded from the Union. But their failure to gain control of nearby Fort Pickens led to the eventual downfall of Pensacola.[3]

Union attempts to take the city began during late 1861 and early 1862 with a series of artillery battles. Union damage to Confederate fortifications in the city was much greater than the Confederate damage to Fort Pickens. On January 1, 1862, Chamberlin experienced his first artillery battle (see chap. 1), which led to extensive damage of Fort McRee. In late March most of the Rebel troops left Pensacola to battle Union invaders in Tennessee. By early May the remaining troops left with most of the Confederate artillery and supplies. On May 9 the last troops to leave set fire to the remnants of the Navy Yard and other Confederate defenses.[4] On **May 10,** 1862, Chamberlin reported in his diary that the Rebel Navy Base, Hospital, and Fort in Pensacola "burned to the ground amid a storm of shells from Ft. Pickens."

Captaining the Corps d'Afrique

Chamberlin described the Union forces' move to Pensacola in this excerpt from a May letter:

One mile in rear of Barrancas, Monday morn, May 12th 1862

Dear Brother,

We passed a very quiet day yesterday in a nice grove where there had been a rebel encampment. The Baracks were left standing but everything was destroyed that could be without burning. I am writing with a Rebel pen holder & ink & a union pen & they don't go very well together as you can very plainly see, I guess however that when they get a little more accustomed to each other they will go better. Only Co. Q & F are here. The remainder of the Regt. are over near Ft. Barrancas. We are to march to Pensacola soon. Don't know whether we shall get off or not today. Saturday night we slept on the brick pavement of the redoubt in the open air & slept pretty well. All day yesterday the boys were busy visiting the Rebel camps about here picking up what they could find. All manner of things were found. Great uncouth looking knives, plates, cups, clothing, knapsacks, canteens, marble topped tables, pitchers, Officers beds, & almost everything imaginable. They seemed to have lived in pretty good style. The 8th Battallion Miss. Cavalry were encamped near here & had good quarters & stables for their horses. They had good Officers. Their provisions seemed to consist mainly of corn meal & bacon. W & I had just a good a dish of mush & molasses from Rebel meal as ever any need have. We each went down to the Rebel Barracks last night & got each of us a good bunk & took them up to the redoubt where we stayed again last night & slept first rate, today we have gone to the grove again & are taking it cool in the shade of some trees which are very beautiful. There are some of the most beautiful flowers I ever saw.

In a May 13, 1862, letter from Pensacola, Chamberlin wrote to one of his brothers.

The Union soldiers marched down to this city & entered it at sundown with drums beating & the band playing Yankee Doodle, & formed a line on three sides of the Public Square & raised the stars & stripes by a large pole in the center of the square. There were many Union Citizens who seemed very much rejoiced to see us. We have been waiting for you almost a year they said & it seemed as if you would never come.

A day later, in a letter from Camp Arnold in Pensacola, Chamberlin described the city to his sister.

2. The Union Takes Pensacola

Probably ⅔ of the inhabitants had fled before we arrived. Those who remain are much disappointed in our appearance & behavior. Many of them really thought that the "damned Yankees" were perfect devils—ferocious wild beasts. Our Capt. was Officer of the day yesterday & at night the Spanish Consul—a quiet antediluviananted-looking old chap came & told him that some soldiers were trespassing on his grounds & his family were very much frightened. It seemed that two men in attempting to run the guard & get out into the city had got into the old gentleman's garden. He called lustily for his gun & they scadaddled but were arrested by our guards & confined in the Guard-house. The old fellow seemed to be very much pleased to think that they were so promptly arrested & that the guard was so efficient. He then went on to describe the ideas that many of the people had in regard to the Yankees. They supposed that as soon as the city was occupied by our troops the place would be pillaged & no person's life would be safe—in fact many who fled thought there would be an indiscriminate slaughter of all without regard to age or sex. Since the people have found out what we are like, that we have neither hoofs or horns, they began to return & occupy their houses. Last night two men came in & gave information to the Officer of the guard that there was a Rebel capt. in the City to see his family. The guard went immediately & arrested him. He at last owned up & it is said that he didn't seem to be very sorry that he was captured.

Chamberlin described more of the city in a letter to one of his sisters.

Pensacola, Fla., May 31 1862

My Dear Sister

In one of my former letters I spoke of the beauties of this place & now I will describe them a little more fully. The Cemetery covers something like 12 or 15 acres enclosed with a substantial board fence.[5] It is beautifully shaded with live-oak & hickory which seem to be a natural growth there being no regularity about them. The Cemetery is pretty filled with graves some of them it is said dating back 200 years. These are Spanish graves & are scarcely discernable. They were rudely arched over with brick & a few crumbling ruins alone mark the place where the early Spanish settlers buried their dead.

In one corner in a brick enclosure is the grave of the wife of Geo. Walton, one of the Signers of the Declaration of American Independence. There are some very splendid tombs & monuments of recent date, beautifully engraved describing the virtues of the deceased.

The grounds look as though they had been very much neglected for a

Captaining the Corps d'Afrique

year past as everything in the South does. On some parts the ground is covered with weeds & bushes. Some of the enclosures are beautifully covered with flowers & look as if they had some kind hand to care for them. There are about 75 newly made graves in one corner of the yard. They are said to be the graves of Rebel soldiers who died here during the winter. There were 12 or 15000 men quartered in & around Pensacola during the winter & the mortality was said to have been very great. The citizens say that 25 or 30 bodies were taken away on the rail-road daily. We also saw when we came over in the graveyard near the Marine Hospital, the graves of between 300 & 400 Rebels. There must have been a vast amount of sickness among them & probably they were deficient in proper medicines to combat the diseases, I must say if I am to die a soldier I hope it will be in a better cause than theirs.

I have about come to the conclusion that aside from the timber of Florida I wouldn't give 3 cts an acre for the whole state. Were it not for the good Harbors I believe it is hardly worth fighting for. The country so far as I have seen is very level & sandy & not strong enough to grow a decent crop of anything. Many parts are covered with swamp which is covered with an inpenetrable jungle of bushes & vines, which are supposed to harbor all manner of horrible reptiles. Although I have not seen any of them yet. The only truly grand sights are the almost boundless everglades covered with pine forests. No wonder it was a great job to hunt the Indians out of Fla, & that they gave the Government a mighty sight of trouble before they were conquered & I should judge that the population of the country away from the City was about ¹⁄₁₀ of a man to a square mile. I don't know hardly how the people live except it be on fish, as there [is] but very little growing around the City & there aint much that can be called a country anywhere near. I suppose they live on corn & pork, however as that is the principle food of the Southerners.

We are living very lazy lives as usual, although we have more guard duty than on Santa Rosa. It seems to me that the rebellion is pretty near played out. With all the seaports in our possession & the Rebels hemmed in on every side it is no wonder that the Southern Journals speak in a tone of discouragement in regard to their prospects. The hope of foreign intervention must have nearly died out by this time with the most hopeful of them. Were it not for the horror with which the Rebel leaders everywhere regard hemp & and the beastly ignorance of the lower classes this rebellion would have given up before this.[6] But now the longer they continue the contest the worse they are off. All the destruction of property is more of a damage to themselves than to the nation.

When you get this letter hope you will be luxuriating in strawberries & green peas. If you don't receive this letter write & let me know. Hope you

2. The Union Takes Pensacola

will all continue well & enjoy the summer, as I expect to have some good times although far away from home.

From your affectionate Brother
s/ J. N. Chamberlain

Chamberlin's correspondence alternated between discussion of the war with its ramifications and description of his surroundings and day-to-day life. In midsummer he wrote his mother, then later his father, from Camp Arnold.

Dear Mother,

It is difficult to imagine how stupendous this war is. It is really the business of the whole country. To it every other enterprise has to bow. Thousands lay down in death every week. And still the contest seems to thicken. It is evident that the war has nearly reached the culminating point & that a great change must soon take place. If there is no great blunder committed somewhere the two great armies of the Rebels must soon be scattered. It remains to be seen how many they can rally again. The Union sentiment of the South seems slow in manifesting its self & it seems that the rebels in some places have got to be knocked down & knocked after they are down before they give up. But terrible & heart rending as this war is, it will no doubt teach the American people a lesson that they will not soon forget. It will teach us that a national crime & sin, even though backed by the whole force of the Government cannot forever be continued in without bringing down upon the nation the just judgements of Heaven. [Chamberlin said this years before Lincoln expounded the same view in his Second Inaugural Address in March 1865.][7] This war is to end Slavery. The handwriting on the wall shows plainer & plainer everyday to all men. My opinion of the slaves is the same as it always has been & I still hold that they should be free. Then take the states of South Carolina, Georgia & Florida & colonize them with the negroes. So mote it be.

Some time ago I sent my diary home. Write & let me know whether it arrived. I have made a book of foolscap sheets & use it as a diary & keep track of passing events.

My Dear Father,

Although there is not much excitement here & not much to indicate that a tremendous struggle is going on in the nation, yet there may be enough to furnish material for another letter & so having nothing else to do just now I will commence (at least). The Steamer Rhode-Island arrived here on the 19" bringing quite a Heavy mail & N. York papers up to the

Captaining the Corps d'Afrique

10" of July.[8] I recd 4 letters—3 from home & one from Cousin Abbie. The latest was the 7" of July.

W. & I are both well & enjoying ourselves as much as soldiers are generally allowed to. We live in the same old tent & have things pretty nice for soldiers. Of course our tent is our dining room, sitting room, & bed room. Yet we have plenty of room & everything has its proper place & is generally to be found there. We have nice cups & saucers & white plates & a big coffee pot to make our own coffee & we live well enough for any one if they can't live better just as well as not. The curse of fleas has been stayed so that a fellow can sit down without wriggling out of his chair & can lay down at night & sleep without first having an exciting skirmish with the scoundrels & finally giving up in despair & settling down to scratch yourself to sleep. Indeed since we came here we have been troubled very little with fleas. I look back to those days & nights on Santa Rosa with feelings akin to horror.

The weather is still very hot, although it does not seem any hotter to me than summer weather at the North. We have had more rain for a week or two past than usual & the heat has been somewhat tempered thereby. Were it not for the sea breeze the heat would be very oppressive. A fine breeze blows from the sea nearly all the time during the day. We have the same duties to perform that we have ever since we came here, namely, building forts & intrenchments & doing guard duty. Picket guard is not very dangerous business here as we scarcely ever see or hear anything. When we are on picket we go out scouting 3 or 4 times about a mile outside the lines, but we don't see any thing but a few rabbits or snakes & it is very discouraging business. Contrabands continue to come in nearly every day. There are now about 70 over at Ft. Pickens, employed by the Government. They all bring in some sort of rumors, the last of which was that Richmond was burned & Jeff. Davis had escaped in a balloon,—a pretty well got up yarn.

On August 1, 1862, Chamberlin gave his brother a little broader view of life at Camp Arnold.

The same daily routine of duties has to be gone through with, drilling one hour each day & the intervening time spent in almost as many different ways as there are individuals, some in playing cards, some in reading or writing & in sleep, while others are discussing the probabilities or possibilities of the war. Then there is in each co. more or less of the universal Yankee genius which displays its-self in a great variety of ways. Here you may see a fellow industriously engaged in hammering out finger rings out of dimes & quarters & halves, there is another putting a new spring into a

2. The Union Takes Pensacola

revolver or gun-lock, yonder a man whittling away diligently at a miniature water-wheel to set running in the brook, another who has real genius as an artist taking sketches of everything about the camp & so absorbed as not to notice anything that is going on around him, men at work with saws & chisels, hammers, planes, files, scissors, needles & thread & above all with the universal jack-knife, so there is a clatter in camp from morning till night. Nearly all the trades & professions seem to have their representative & this gives some life & animation to our camp which would otherwise be insufferably monotonous. Many in the Regt. are better off here in many respects than they were at home. Some of them have now the best set of clothes that they ever had; in fact, we have new clothes oftener than we want them sometimes. On pay days, some will have more money than they ever saw together before.

On Tuesday the 29" Three companies of our Regt. went on an expedition up the bay & as our co. went along I will give you an account of our adventures & what we saw.

Company B had reported that some of the Rebel cavalry were up the East Bay (fig. 1, chap. 1); Chamberlin continued:

There was a fair prospect for us to catch some of them that night. Co. D. and Co. B. went on board the Steamer [*Creole*] & at about 8 o'clock we started up the Bay. The night was warm & still the stars shone brightly & as we glided swiftly over the smooth surface of the Bay, the foam glided by shining like silver. I sat on deck for an hour watching the shore on either side seen indistinctly in the dim light, but the shores are very monotonous & tired of gazing I lay down among the sleeping forms on deck with my cartridge box for a pillow & went to sleep. When I awoke we were coming up alongside the Meigs [the other steamer with the third company on board],[9] which was aground on a sand-bar. We worked away for some time trying to pull her off but at last had to give it up & took Co. A. on board from the Meigs & continued on up the Bay.

When we stopped again we had turned up the Black-Water River & were up along side an old wharf near the ruins of some saw mills. It was evident to me that we were in the immediate vicinity of the infernal regions. The water of the River was black & as motionless as though its surface had never been stirred, the stars were reflected in the water & the lonely old pines on the shore hung with sombre moss were reflected in the dark waters along the sides of the stream while all on shore looked dismal runious & unearthly to the last degree. It will ever remain in my memory as the most gloomy picture that I ever beheld. [With difficulty, companies A and D got off the steamer.]

Captaining the Corps d'Afrique

The Steamer continued on up the river until she ran aground & it was with some difficulty that she was got off again. There must have been scores of steam sawmills on the Bays & Rivers in this vicinity & millions of dollars worth of lumber was exported from here yearly, but the mills are now all burned. We waited for the Rebels all night but they didn't come & in the morning Co. A. came in with a drove of Secesh cattle, & soon after the Steamer came down the river, & we spent most of the forenoon in getting our cattle on board & some furniture which belonged to the Union men. We had an opportunity to see some of the ruin wrought by the Rebels. Here were two powerful steam sawmills each covering nearly a half an acre of ground, a large planing mill & a pail factory all burned to the ground & to make the ruin more complete it seemed that the castings had many of them been broken before the mills were set on fire. It was the most complete scene of destruction that I ever beheld. Nothing was left standing & machinery of the most powerful kind lay scattered about in the greatest confusion. The boilers & engines were all blackened & warped by the intense heat. In one place I counted side by side 12 large saws & near by a heap of 6 or 8 bushels of files & a little further on a large pile of circular & other saws warped into all imaginable shapes by the heat. Words cannot convey any idea of the scene of devastation which here presents its self. It is said by the citizens here that the property destroyed here was worth 375,000 dollars & these mills were not as extensive as many others in the vicinity. We started back a little before noon & had a very pleasant ride back to Pensacola.

We reached Pensacola at 3 o'clock without any particular incident worthy of notice. We hear rumors that we are to leave here for the north but like all other rumors we place no dependence on them until we know them to be true. In the faith of the good time coming when peace shall again brood over the land I remain as ever your affectionate brother, J. N. Chamberlin

In fact, instead of going north, the 75th N.Y.V. headed west to New Orleans in September 1862.

CHAPTER 3

New Orleans

The City

The Mississippi River was an essential lifeline for what was, in 1860, the western United States. The Southern economy, including that of New Orleans, depended on slave-produced cotton and sugar. The river was the road by which supplies for the planters moved in and out of their plantations. During the war, it was also the route for moving military supplies and troops. Whoever controlled New Orleans controlled much of the river activity.[1]

New Orleans was the Confederacy's leading port and largest city. In 1860, out of its heterogeneous population of 170,000, more than 13,000 were enslaved. In addition, approximately 11,000 free persons of color lived there, many of them prosperous and well-educated. Also, Dobak states that "northern-born white residents of New Orleans far outnumbered the entire population of Baton Rouge, the state capital."[2]

Once the Union decided to take this vital city in late February 1862, the conquest occurred quite fast, partly because the Rebels expected that the Union would attack from upriver. Instead the Union advanced up from the mouth of the Mississippi with Flag Officer David G. Farragut's fleet. When six days of bombardment failed to cause significant damage to the two forts protecting the mouth of the river, on April 24 Farragut ran his vessels past the forts up the river to New Orleans, experiencing only minor losses. In a few days, most Confederate troops withdrew from the city, leaving the mayor to offer its surrender. General Butler simultaneously forced the surrender of the river forts and sent his men to occupy New Orleans.[3] Thus, barely a year after the Civil War began, New Orleans became the second major city

Captaining the Corps d'Afrique

in the Confederate South (after Nashville on February 23, 1862) to be occupied by the Union Army.[4]

Chamberlin's regiment, the 75th N.Y.V., was transferred from Pensacola to New Orleans in September 1862. This period in Chamberlin's military career became more complex, as illustrated by his first letter from New Orleans.

U. S. Barracks, New Orleans, Sept. 6" [1862]

Dear Father & Mother,

After our journey to this place, my time has been so much occupied that I have only had time to write a short letter, but will now try to give you some information concerning our surroundings.

These Barracks are at the lower end of the city, near the river & are called the Marine Barracks.[5] They were built during the Mexican war & four large buildings were built for hospitals. The Barracks, Hospitals & the grounds attached comprise several hundred acres. There is a very beautiful grove in front of the hospitals & rows of china trees around most of the Barracks.[6]

The Barracks are of brick & the Hospitals are wooden buildings, The Rebels had troops here when Com. Farraget [sic] came to take the city & he sent some shells at their flag & burned one building, when the rebels found it very convenient to evacuate. All the copper pipes and eave gutters were torn off the buildings by the Rebels to make cannon & the windows taken out & the lead weights by which the windows were drawn up were taken out to make bullets. The water for cooking is not very good as the well is about as low as the river & of course very much like it.

Each building is supplied with several enormous tanks which are full of pure rain-water, so we have good water to drink. There are now here 2 Cos. of the 13" Connecticut—A Cavalry Regt. (the other companies being quartered in the City & above) & C Company of the 2" Louisiana Regt. who have been recruited in the City. The 1" Louisiana some 1100 strong were sent into the field last week.[7] There are also some Regt.s of negroes drilling somewhere about the city although I cannot find out exactly where.

Very few men in this country could have been made to believe that all these things would come to pass, (one year ago). The rough work here is done by the negroes & the soldiers drill. But I will write no more now as I was on guard last night & feel quite sleepy, besides I have a pass down to the City & in that way I can keep awake.

3. New Orleans

<u>Sunday Morn.</u>

Ten of us have taken up our quarters in the second story of an Observatory near where our Co. are quartered & have built bunks & have a very comfortable, quiet place.

Got up this morn. before reveille & got a pail of water & had a good bath. We had Co. Inspection as usual at 8 o'clock & now we are to have a quiet day with nothing to do only to go to dress parade. I went to the City yesterday P.M. & looked around the place considerable. The horse railroad runs up near our camp & for 5 cts a person can go up to the center of the city—to the custom house which is 5 miles. The main thoroughfare is Canal st. The st. is wide, well paved & will compare very favorable with the streets of N.Y. only the stores & warehouses are quite inferior compared with those of that City. There are other streets well-paved & cleanly-kept, but the greater part are either very rough or not paved at all & the sewers & alleys send up the most abomidable stinks that ever outraged the nasal organs of man.

There are (of course) many splendid private residences & the gardens & grounds are grand beyond description. The most gorgeous flowers bloom in the gardens & lemons, oranges, bananas &c seem to grow with almost tropical luxuriance. All kinds of business seems to be going on, although not very vigorously.

The stores & offices are nearly all open, but the streets do not present the busy apparance that they should. There seems to be something unnatural about the place, as if the people were all in their houses for fear of some plague. It seems strange to walk through the streets of the City & know that ⅔ of the people you meet are your bitter foes, but no insult is offered to a soldier & you scarcely see a sneer or a frown on the faces of any one. Gen. Butler has taught the people to use soldiers well as long as they behave themselves. I frequently heard the expression from children "there goes a yankee" but all civil questions asked are answered civilly. When I think of this City—8 miles long & 3 wide with all its manufacturies & machine shops & all the advantage it must have been to the rebels to hold the place it seems strange to me that they didn't make greater efforts to hold it & I begin to realize that it was a big thing to take the city & it is very important to hold it now. As near as I can find out there are from 12000 to 15000 union troops in this vicinity, the greater part of which are up the river about 12 miles at Carrolton, where they were expecting an attack some time ago but it is said the rebels have now withdrawn their forces. Our outposts are 20 miles out on the several approaches to the City & Gen. Butler has a system of signaling so that all operations are reported at head-quarters with great facility. In the day time the signals are made with flags from towers, steeples & other elevations & by night with rockets. None but the Officers of the Signal Corps understand anything about the signals... [letter ends in mid-sentence with no signature].

Gentleman Soldier

By the end of September, Chamberlin's military life in New Orleans once again offered a life of luxury and ease (fig. 2), as he told his sister Eleanor on September 26, 1862.

We received orders to go to the city as the body guard of Brig. Gen. Lewis G. Arnold. We were very busy in packing up everything ready to move. The distance that we had to march was about 5 miles & as I didn't fancy the idea of carrying a back-load that distance in the heat, with my characteristic brazen facedness I tucked my knapsack into the baggage-wagon & had it taken up to the city by mule-power. As I was not encumbered by my knapsack it was quite a pleasant walk to me.

Our new quarters are in a fine 4 story dwelling house at the corner of Rampart & Dauphin St's.[8] I occupy a splendid room about 15 X 20 together with 7 others of our men. I am now writing on a beautiful marble-topped stand. There is a drawer in it where I can keep my writing material & gloves &c &c & shelves beneath which I use as a cupboard. The table is mahogany finished in beautiful style. Then two other corporals & I occupy a splendid mahogany bed stead with a very thick matrass of spanish moss. We have a large mirror & everything in the most volupuous style imaginable. The room adjoining is a bath room with a pump for raising water from below so that we have a good chance to keep clean.

The other rooms are furnished equally as well as this & those that the Officers occupy are as splendid as any that I ever saw. All the furniture is of the most costly description. Very few of us ever lived amongst as much elegance & splendor as we do now. In the rear of the house is a paved yard with water tanks & a large kitchen for cooking & conveniences for washing clothes.

We have 12 men on guard all the time—4 in a relief one corporal & one Serjeant & in addition there must be 32 privates ready during a part of the day to turn out at a moment's warning at the approach of either Gen. Butler or Arnold. All that is required of us is to behave ourselves, do our duty & keep neat & clean & we shall have a very easy time. It was through the influence of Capt. Dwight that our Co. was detailed by the Gen so that you see he has an eye to the good of his old Co. yet.[9]

3. New Orleans

Figure 2, *top and bottom*: Suitcase belonging to Capt. J. N. Chamberlin. Labeled "Southern Express Company, New Orleans, LA." Courtesy James A. Goodin.

Captaining the Corps d'Afrique

Last week we all drew new black Infantry hats with black plumes & shoulder-scales, a kind of brass epaulette, & our Co. now make a very splendid appearance. We begin to think that we are to be gentlemen soldiers & most of the men take a commendable pride in their personal appearance. For the present we are to see nothing but the show & tinsel of war, but it may as well be us as anyone else.

Louisiana Native Guards

Early in the Union occupation, many slaves walked away from their owners and sought asylum with the Union Army. A number of them fled to Camp Parapet, originally a Confederate defensive work, near New Orleans. Heidler and Heidler state, "Some of the slaves were even directed to the camp by their owners, who no longer could feed them." Camp Parapet was commanded by the abolitionist Brig. Gen. John Wolcott Phelps. Phelps began organizing the former slaves, and equipping and training them for military service. When the War Department ordered him to stop, he resigned his commission and went home to Vermont. Gen. Benjamin Butler, commander of the Department of the Gulf, famous for his ingenious policy of confiscating slaves as contrabands of war, began to pay the blacks to work as servants and laborers for the Union Army.[10]

Chamberlin told his brother on September 22, 1862, that picket service in New Orleans brought the Union soldiers in contact with slaves and the planters' patrols.

> The Union guards go down to Jackson's old battle-ground & their instructions are to see fair play with the fugitives. The picket lines are on the borders of the plantations & the planters have a sort of patroll to catch negroes. Gen Butler don't recognize any such guard & our instructions are if we see any negroes coming within our lines to let them take their own course, but if the plantation guards try to stop them, to arrest them [presumably the plantation guards], & also to keep a sharp lookout for the enemy, but there is not much danger of any enemy in that direction.

Toward the end of 1862, when Butler needed reinforcements, according to Weaver, he "decided to call on Africa" and accepted the volunteers of the black Native Guards. Free black militia service already

3. New Orleans

had a long tradition in the city; soon after the fall of Fort Sumter in April 1861, free blacks in New Orleans had organized the Native Guards. In May, before the Union captured New Orleans, the Louisiana Confederate governor added a regiment of Native Guards to the state militia to help defend the city. The 1st Regiment of the Native Guards was mustered into service for the Union on September 27, 1862, making it, in Lawrence Lee Hewitt's words, "the first officially sanctioned regiment of black soldiers in the U.S. Army. Though the unit's designation remained the same, its Union composition differed dramatically from the earlier Confederate organization." Of the 906 free men of color from the pro–Confederate Native Guards, only 108 reenlisted. As the new regiment filled up, no one asked the enrollees if they were free or had been slaves. By November Butler had organized the 2nd and 3rd regiments of Louisiana Native Guards. In February 1863, the 4th Native Guards took to the field.[11] Some of these regiments, which were formed from the rising tide of slaves seeking to enlist in the Union Army, played a unique role in the siege of Port Hudson, as described in chap. 4. After that siege, some of these Native Guards would join a company commanded by Capt. John Chamberlin (see chap. 5).

According to historian Richard J. Sommers, "For the remainder of the war, General Butler continued to champion the use of African American troops, one of the few high-ranking generals who refused to consider black soldiers as 'uniformed ditchdiggers.'"[12] However, the black soldiers in the South lost Butler's support when in November 1862 he was replaced by Gen. Nathaniel Banks as the Union commander of New Orleans (fig. 3).[13] On February 22, 1863, Chamberlin wrote to his mother.

> You will probably hear of the meeting of Planters in N.O.[New Orleans] to consult with Banks in regard to the cultivation of the plantations.[14] They pretend to be Union men, but I believe that 2/3 of them are Rebels at heart. Banks seems anxious to gain the good opinion of these Planters. To that end [he] has issued an order returning the slaves of these so-called Loyal planters and forbidding the enlistment of any more negroes from the plantations. The negroes are to be free of course but whether it is more necessary to raise sugar cane or to whip the Rebels remains to be seen. I think that the immense business and responsibility of this Department is more than Banks is capable of. I believe that one of the greatest mistakes of the Administration in the conduct of this war was the

Figure 3. Gen. Nathaniel Banks and family. Original photograph given to John Chamberlin while he was in the Civil War, according to a note on the photograph written by Chamberlin's son-in-law (and husband of Mabel Bisbee), LeRoy Bisbee. Original in possession of John Bisbee.

3. New Orleans

removal of Gen. Butler. That he was a corrupt man and was making a princely fortune out of the war I have no doubt.

General Butler was reprimanded several times by the Secretary of War for abuse of authority, and mishandling of money or purchases during 1862. Dobak maintains that the cause of General Butler's "removal was not his management of racial issues," but that Butler and associated authorities were "so corrupt that they will take all means to make money." He also states that Butler had "alienated representatives of the European powers in New Orleans during a year when the State Department was working hard to assure that France and Great Britain did not enter the war on the side of the Confederacy."[15]

Chamberlin continued in his letter:

> He [Butler] was governing the rebels of this part of the State with an iron hand. There was very little of this half-way loyalty which in the presence of the blue coats of Uncle Sam, is all smiles and sweet words for the Union, but the moment their backs are turned are ready to perform any act of demonism as well as any other disciple of Jeff Davis. They couldn't get around old Butler,—hence the infernal howl that all rebeldom and rebel sympathizers set up at the high-handed acts of Butler in punishing treason when he took possession of the city. Banks is proving himself a mere political puppet, a man of straw to be handled about by anyone to their own advantage so long as he seems to gain credit thereby.

In a report dated December 28, 1862, a *New York Times* special correspondent gave a lengthy description of the assumption of power in New Orleans by Nathaniel Banks. Essentially he called it a "change from the severe regime of Gen. BUTLER to the milder and more indulgent rule of Gen. BANKS." He remarked that almost daily some new order was issued by Banks, "reversing the state of things that existed under his predecessor." These orders were seen by Secessionists, "jubilant over the change, ... [as] a restoration of their influence here." He commented that it was no wonder they extolled General Banks and condemned General Butler. Many questioned Banks' ability to handle such a large responsibility. The journalist suggested that a number of people in the community worried about Banks' ability to deal with the effect of the Emancipation Proclamation. General Banks reminded the people "that the State of Louisiana has not yet been designated by the President as in rebellion." Although this meant, legally, that slaves were

Captaining the Corps d'Afrique

not free, the reporter believed "that Slavery [was], at this moment dead and past all resurrection in the State of Louisiana."[16] In a letter to his mother on February 22, 1863, Chamberlin expressed his concern.

> Four Reg'ts of negroes have been organized or are in process of organization and they are more of a dread to the Rebels I believe than the same number of our white troops, but this new order of Banks will seriously impede the raising of these troops and discourage those who are trying to organize them.

A big question facing the Union was whether these black troops should fight, or continue as laborers. President Lincoln, in early 1863, still wanted to restrict black troops to noncombat roles; by March, the President had changed his mind. According to Eric Foner:

> The War Department authorized a massive recruiting effort in the occupied South. This decision may have been influenced by the battlefield success of the First and Second South Carolina Volunteers, nearly all of them former slaves, who occupied Jacksonville, Florida, early that month.... The performance of black soldiers in the spring and summer of 1863 at Port Hudson and Milliken's Bend in Louisiana and Fort Wagner in South Carolina dispelled lingering doubts about their abilities.[17]

Chamberlin was not yet personally affected by the controversy about the black soldiers. While the confusion continued, Chamberlin with the 75th N.Y.V. participated in a campaign to control the Mississippi River.

Chapter 4

Control of the Mississippi River

Bayou Teche Campaign

From the start of the Civil War, controlling the Mississippi River was a major part of the strategy of both the North and the South. At the end of 1862 the last stretch of the river controlled by the Rebels was bounded by Vicksburg on the north and Port Hudson on the south (fig. 4). General Banks' XIX Army Corps, with support from Admiral Farragut's naval forces, set out to secure the line of the Mississippi River as far north as possible, and coordinate an attack against Port Hudson. Later, General Grant was ordered to attack Vicksburg. In late February 1863, Banks launched a campaign against Port Hudson. When Admiral Farragut failed to get most of his seven gunboats past Port Hudson, Banks retreated and made other plans. In April he began an expedition up Bayou Teche in western Louisiana aimed at Alexandria. From there he would move against Port Hudson.[1]

Not until August 15, 1863, did Chamberlin describe this Bayou Teche Campaign, in a letter to an unknown family member from Camp Hubbard, Louisiana.

> I promised you in my last letter to give you a history of the last campaign in this Dept. I will begin with the evacuation of Brashear City by our Brigade [on **March 21**, according to Chamberlin's diary]. The Rebels had for several weeks been strengthening their forces on the Berwick side of the Bay and becoming more bold every day. From our own scouts and from Rebel deserters we recd information that they intended making a raid down the Bayou Beuff [Boeuf] 12 miles East of Brashear,[2] burning the R.R. bridge, and thus cut off our communications with N.O. The Rebel

Captaining the Corps d'Afrique

forces were under the command of Gen. Dick Taylor,[3] in whom they seemed to have considerable confidence. In conjunction with this movement the Rebel Gun-boats were to move down from the Achtafalaya [sic] River and Grand Lake—drive our Gun-boats out of the Bay and shell us out of Brashear and land a powerful force there. They had at that time some quite formidable Gun-boats—among them the Queen of the West,[4] captured by the Rebs from us below Vicksburg. There plans were well laid, and had they been successfully carried out we should have been left entirely at their mercy and would inevitably have been captured.

But the best laid schemes of men and mice often fail as will be seen in the sequel. On the 20" of March the whole Brigade recd orders to prepare to move at a moments notice. Accordingly every thing was packed up very quietly, and at night we struck our tents and were busy nearly all night in putting our baggage on board the cars. All our preparations being completed, in the gray of dawn on the morn of the 21" of March, 5 large trains heavily loaded moved out of Brashear, leaving only a picket guard to watch the enemy. We arrived at Bayou Beuff [Boeuf] without accident or any particular incident worthy of note, and immediately formed our camp along the shore of the Bayou in a large cane field. The enemy were wary enough not to attack us in our chosen position nor to attempt the occupation of Brashear City. Trains continued to run to Brashear to bring away lumber for tent floors and our bread was baked there.

We had very warm weather for the season and much rain and our position was rather an unhealthy one. All manner of reptiles and insects (Infernal) swarmed around our camp. The Bayou where we got all our water for drinking and cooking was full of huge alligators and sworms of musketoes and gnats tormented us day and night. This was a very unpleasant chapter in the history of the campaign. On the 23" Gen. Banks came from N.O. and went on to Brashear City with Gen Wetzel [sic],[5] and then and there, no doubt, the main features of the ensuing campaign were considered. It was this—an overwhelming force was to be hurled against the Rebs in the Attahapas [sic] country [presumably Attakapas, the present-day St. Martinville, Louisiana, area near Bayou Teche], and their fleet was to be destroyed in the Achtafaylaya [sic] River and the adjoining Lakes—all communications were to be cut off from Port Hudson and then the rebel stronghold was to be invested in earnest.[6]

On the 29" the Gun-boat Diana went up through Grand lake on a reconnoisance, and against positive orders from Gen. Weitzel attempted to return through the Bayou Teche. The Rebels had two Batteries planted on the shore, concealed in the bushes. They allowed the Boat to pass one of them and then a terrific fire. The upper works of the boat were reduced

4. Control of the Mississippi River

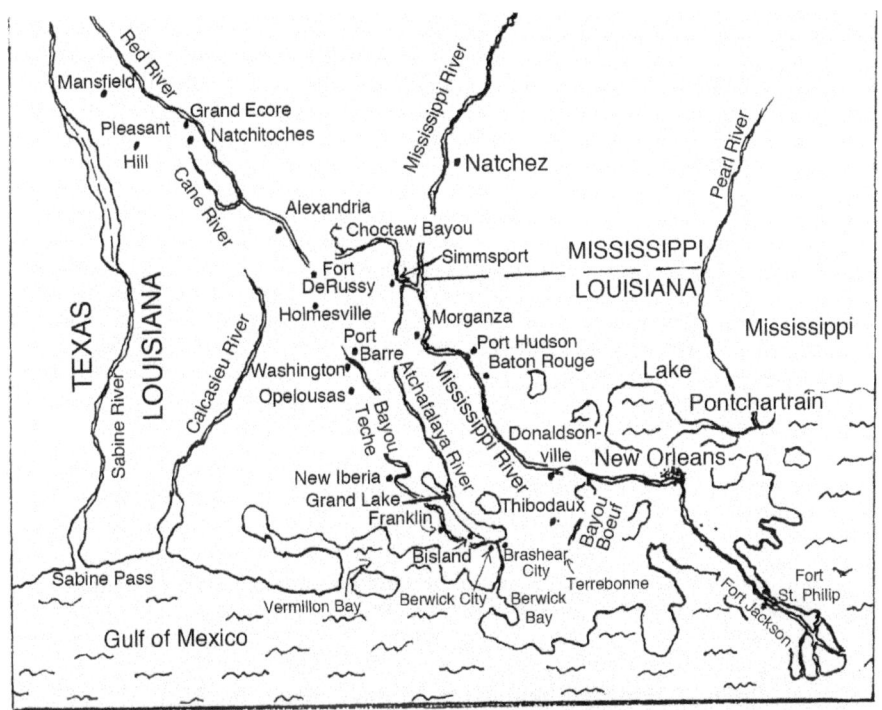

Figure 4. Map of central and southern Louisiana, 1860. Drawn by John Bisbee, based on Dobak, *Freedom by the Sword*, 90; Heidler and Heidler, *Ency. of the Am. Civil War*, 1617; Weaver, *Thank God My Regiment an African One*, before p. 1.

to a wreck—several men killed and wounded, and the boat forced to surrender.[7] There were 120 men on board who were paroled the next day. The pilot—a negro, and some others who escaped were hunted through the swamps with blood-hounds but escaped and came into camp the next morn having captured two reb. pickets on their way. The Diana was a good boat and her capture was quite a loss to us. The blame lay in the Capt. of the Boat.

In his diary of **March 31**, Chamberlin gave more details: "They [the released soldiers] gave quite an account of the Rebels. They live on Salt Beef and corn meal and have a great desire to get our Over coats and Rubber blankets &c." He told more of the story in a letter he wrote from Brashear City to a brother on April 5.

Captaining the Corps d'Afrique

Our loss on the gun boat Diana was not as serious as first reported. Nearly all the Officers were killed or wounded and several of the privates. All, excepting the Officers were Paroled and came back to Camp. They will be kept with their Regts untill an exchange is made. It is almost a miracle that so few were killed. The upper part of the vessel was completely riddled.

The Battle of Fort Bisland

Continuing his letter of August 15, Chamberlin described the next step in the military campaign.

On the 1" of April re-enforcements began to arrive from N.O. Several trains arrived with Artillery. On the 2" the Brigade marched back to Brashear City and went into camp again. Troops continued to arrive at Bayou Bueff [Boeuf] every day until on the 7" there was, at least 20,000 men there and the country was one vast camp along the Bayou. Several more powerful Gun-boats arrived in the Bay and on the morn. of the 9" we packed up all our baggage near the R.R. Depot. Our Brigade crossed the Bay in the A.M. and took the advance.

Chamberlin stayed behind, as he explained in an April 21, 1863, letter to his father.

On Monday the 6" of Apr. I started for N.O. to do some business for Capt. Corning and the Capt. of Co. A. Before I got to N.O. I found that I was going to have the mumps. However, I had a good time in the City, did my business satisfactorily and returned to Brashear on Wednesday. Well, my chops were pretty badly swollen by this time and as the Reg't were to leave the next day it was thought by the Sarg. that I had better remain behind, as our Reg't took nothing with them except each man his overcoat and rubber blanket.

The August 15 letter continued the story, as Chamberlin had heard it.

[Union] Troops now poured in from Bayou Beuff [Boeuf], as fast they could be transported across the Bay and the greatest activity everywhere prevailed. Gen. Banks was in immediate command and under him were Gens. Grover & Emory,[8] Comd'g Divisions and several Brigadiers. Troops continued to cross until the 11" and Gen. Grover, had a part of one Division on board of the transports to go up and effect a landing on the shore of Grand Lake to head off the Rebs and if possible, capture the greater

4. Control of the Mississippi River

part of them. The advance began on the 11" and as we [the regiment] proceeded one of our batteries occasionally shelled small parties of the enemie's pickets, but there was no General engagement.

Early on the morn. of the 12" we advanced and soon were within range of the guns of the Rebs. at there intrenched position at "Camp Bisland." This was a redoubt built on the bank of the Bayou Teche, with intrenchments running back to the almost impenetrable swamp with a deep and wide ditch in front partly filled with water. The armament of the Fort consisted of one heavy gun, mounted, and 3 light field Batteries. Word was sent to Banks that we were near enough for our long range guns to play upon the enemy with full effect and we recd orders to advance briskly until we drew the enemy's fire. This we did until we came within easy range of all the guns of the Fort, when they opened a tremendous fire of shot and shell upon us. They knew every inch of the ground—knew when we had advanced to the right position for their fire to be the most destructive in its effects, and then they opened upon us furiously.

We were all ordered to lay down & our Artillery came up and one of the most terrific Artillery fights on record took place. The awful crashing of Artillery, the bursting of shells and shrieking of solid shot and shell made one grand, continuous roar. The air seemed alive with shot and pieces of shell, and it seemed a miracle that so few of us were killed and wounded. The Rebels were quite essentially aided by the Gun-boat Diana which they captured from us and had fitted up for service. In the P.M. the 75th were ordered to make a movement to the left through the swamp and endeavor to out flank them if possible. It was a difficult task. The swamp was like all Southern thickets so nearly impassable that the men had to advance in single file—the Officers cutting their way through the thicket as best they could, and it was with the utmost difficulty that we reached the position to which we were ordered and then without any order. [Chamberlin's incomplete letter of August 15 ends at this point.]

 Contemporary accounts report that because of the artillery barrage described by Chamberlin, many of the Yankees "were hit by Rebel cannon fire, [and] fell back and camped for the night." On mid-morning of the next day (April 13), "the Union forces again advanced on Fort Bisland," and the fighting continued until dusk. "Later that night, Taylor learned that the Yankee division [General Grover's division, as Chamberlin mentioned above] that went up the Atchafalaya and landed in his rear was now in a position to cut off a Confederate retreat." Taylor began a major evacuation, and "the next morning, the Yankees found the fort abandoned."[9]

Captaining the Corps d'Afrique

The Battle of Irish Bend

The "Battle of Irish Bend" began on the morning of April 13, when Grover's division moved near Franklin and scattered the Rebel troops. That night his division crossed Bayou Teche and prepared to attack Franklin at dawn. In the morning Grover's lead brigade skirmished with the Rebels. During intense fighting, the Rebels forced the Yankees to fall back. The gunboat *Diana* approached and supported the Confederate right flank. Eventually the Confederates were outnumbered, so they left the field to the Union."[10]

Chamberlin gave his version of the story in a letter to his father from Brashear City on April 21.

> Grovers Division landed above Franklin and intercepted the Rebels whom our forces were chasing up. He had a pretty tough battle with them near Franklin but succeeded in whipping them thoroughly and captured a good many prisoners. The Rebel Steamer Garnie was near Franklin loaded with sick and wounded rebels. They were ordered by the rebels, to unload at Franklin and burn the boat. Lt. Allen of Gen. Weitzels Staff who was wounded and captured on the Diana was on the boat and as she reached Franklin he went ashore just as a squad of Perkins Cavelry rode into the place. Procuring a pistol from one of the men he hurried back to the boat and demanded the Capt. to surrender which he did with a good grace. She is now in our possession and is a really serviceable boat.
>
> They [the Union] have retaken the Steamer Diana and burned her. [According to a report in ORN, the Confederates destroyed the boat so it would not fall into Union hands.][11] The Famous Semmes Battery was on the vessel and was captured together with Capt. Semmes.[12] He is a piratical looking scoundrel. They brought him to Brashear on his way to N.O. The Rebel Gun-Boat Hart was also taken and destroyed together with 2 or 3 smaller boats.[13] Grovers Division went up the Atchafalaya and in the middle of Grand Lake encountered the famous Queen of the West which the rebels captured from us on the Miss. She was conveying a lot of rebel transports loaded with 3000 troops who were coming down to take Brashear City, The Queen of the West immediately made straight for the Estrella—one of our best Gunboats with the evident intention of running her down and sinking her. But the Estrella had no intention of giving up so she leveled her long 32 pr. and at a distance of 2 miles opened on the moniter and so well was the gun aimed that the third shot went plumb down through the smoke pipe and pierced the magazine blowing her into a thousand fragments. Seeing their pet ram demolished in such a summary

4. Control of the Mississippi River

manner, the Rebel Transports turned and fled while our men were picking up the surviverers of the Queen of the West. Capt. Fuller who formerly commanded the Cotton was in command and was captured. [ORN tells the identical story of this encounter.]¹⁴

According to Dobak, General Banks' troops (XIX Corps) moved up the Bayou Teche toward Opelousas looking for a route to the Red River without passing under the guns of Port Hudson. He hoped in this way to "cut off Confederate armies east of the Mississippi from their sources of rations to the west." By April 20, Union troops had reached Opelousas. Banks reported taking two thousand prisoners as he routed the Confederate force.¹⁵

Chamberlin offered this summary in his April 21 letter:

> So far the expedition has accomplished all that the most sanguine could have wished, and they are still moving on like a hurricane of fire somewhere beyond Opelousas. The Salt Works are captured so that the rebel supply of salt from West of the Miss. is cut off. I don't know where the destination of the troops is, but presume they will not stay this side of the Red River. With all the supplies cut off from the West side of the river, the rebels will not be able to hold long at Port Hudson and Vicksburg.
>
> I have been quite sick for 10 days, but I am better now and hope I shall be able to join the Regt in a few days. I will write more soon.
>
> From your Affectionate Son,
> J. N. Chamberlain

On April 26, 1863, Chamberlin began a three-day boat trip to rejoin the 75th N.Y.V. near Washington, Louisiana. There, he resumed picket duty although he still felt sick. The soldiers marched for three days and reached Alexandria, Louisiana, on May 7. He described this march and his arrival in a May 19 letter to a sister.

> I had just arrived, the troops having made a forced march from Opelousas to that place makeing the distance—78 miles in 75 hours. The last day our Brigade marched 33 miles.
>
> Well I got bushed and had to ride on one of the baggage wagons. We reached Alexandria late Thursday night and the next day marched up the river 2 miles and camped in a grove on the banks of the river. Saturday we recd orders to march the next morn at 6 o'clock and all those who were unable to march were sent to Alexandria. We stayed there in a store untill Tuesday P.M. when we were all ordered on board the little Steamer Union and started for Brashear City. Our course was down the Red River to the

Captaining the Corps d'Afrique

head of the Atchafalaya and then down that river to Brashear. There are some 75 of our Regt here, who were used up by the march. We live in tents and have enough to eat and are getting along very well. I have got pretty well rested up but I shall not go back to the Regt until I get tough again.

We hear that the 75th are coming down near the mouth of [the] Red River but I don't know what the next move will be. All our movements in this quarter have been very successful. I think the next movement will be against Port Hudson, although (of course) I don't know.

The country between Opelousas and Alexandria is the most magnificent that I have ever seen. The road lay along the banks of the Bayou Boeuf [a different one from that mentioned in the August 15, 1863, letter above]—the country where Solomon Northup was 12 years a slave.[16] The country is almost entirely level. The banks of the Bayou are very steep and from 15 to 23 feet high. There are great quantities of the last years crop of cotton on hand and for the first 30 miles of the way the Rebels had burned considerable all along the Bayou. After that we pressed them so closely that they had no time to do anything but get out of the way. This year the whole country is planted with corn. Here and there might be seen a plantation of cane and a few fields of cotton, but corn for the army is the great crop and I don't know but what they have enough planted in this State to supply the whole south. But we have rather knocked their plans in [the] head. It seems strange that the people of so splendid a country as this should have been so insane as to go into the foolish scheme of secession. The planters lived like kings having all that heart could wish and their slaves protected by the whole power of the Government—They have rebeled against the best Government on Earth and to-day they have no plantation and no nigger. Surely they are reaping the benefits of Secession.

We expect a mail to-night and I hope to get letters from home. Write often.

From your affectionate Brother
J. N. Chamberlain

The Siege of Port Hudson

The 75th N.Y.V., without Chamberlin, apparently headed to Port Hudson, Louisiana (fig. 4), to join General Banks' troops a few days after the above May 19 letter was written. Also in May 1863 General Grant's army began operations against Vicksburg. Initially, Grant had

4. Control of the Mississippi River

asked Banks to send troops to Vicksburg, but Banks chose an independent campaign of his own, an attack and siege of Port Hudson, Louisiana. On May 5 Union gunboats on the Mississippi shelled the town of Port Hudson. After fighting a few small engagements with the Rebels, General Banks scheduled a major infantry attack for May 27 with four different assault groups. After ineffective federal shelling, Gen. Godfrey Weitzel's forces attacked Port Hudson's northern defenses. Shortly thereafter Gen. Cuvier Grover's forces attacked from the northeast. Due to the lack of coordination of the assaults, and to the very rough terrain encountered by Weitzel's troops, the attack faltered. At this point the 1st and 3rd Louisiana Native Guards were called into battle. Their attack was also repulsed, but as Hewitt says, "Their baptism of fire came from an order to accomplish the impossible." Two other groups led by Thomas Sherman and Christopher Augur had no more success, and at the end of the day Banks' offensive had failed completely. The resulting siege of Port Hudson lasted until July 9 and turned out to be the longest such action in American military history.[17]

After being sick with the mumps in Brashear City and thus out of action in April and May 1863, Chamberlin's diary entries beginning May 29 tell about his first-hand involvement in the siege:

> **May 29:** A dispatch came from N.O. [New Orleans] calling for 200 Vols. to go to N.O. to take care of the wounded from Port Hudson. This looks ominous. 250 Volunteered. I am going.
>
> **May 31:** Terrible fighting is going on at Port Hudson and a great number are killed and wounded, but I think we are to do some guard duty here and the troops that are in the city are going to Port Hudson.
>
> **June 1:** Some of our boys went up to the city, but did not find out much in regard to our Regt. Heard that Capt. Corning was wounded. I think that the most terrible fighting of the war is now going on at Port Hudson and Vicksburg.
>
> **June 9:** Had a chance to go to Port Hudson to the Regt [which had gone to Port Hudson in late May]. Started at night on the Sallie Robinson.[18] Very heavily loaded and went very slow. Came near Sinking.
>
> **June 11:** Found ourselves 15 miles from our Regt. Found Charley Parker driving one Ambulance and got a ride with him 10 miles. Found our Regt in the P.M. The hardest looking place that I ever saw.

Captaining the Corps d'Afrique

June 12: Staid around all day and got somewhat rested up. One third of the Regt man the rifle-pits every day.[19] A continual firing of musketry and Artillery. Day and night. Don't get much sleep.

June 13: All firing ceased at noon and a flag of truce was sent in to demand the surrender of the place. They don't propose to do anything of the kind unless compelled to do so. We are to pitch into them tomorrow I suppose.

General Banks decided to try another assault, which Chamberlin described in his diary entries.

June 14: Started at 2 in the morn. Our Regt advanced [as] skirmishes to take the enemy works. The scenes and sights of today can never be forgotten. A terrible slaughter without any good results. Lost many killed and wounded.[20] Thank God! I am safe.

June 15: Our forces withdrew from the battle-field except enough to hold some rifle pits. Got back to camp a little before midnight—I am nearly used up today. Our Co. occupy the rifle pits today. Kept quiet.

June 16: 1000 volunteers called for as a storming column to take the enemy works. Very few will go from the 75". Had a heavy shower today. Terribly muddy and uncomfortable. Kept as dry as possible. A continuous firing day and night.

June 17: Stayed in the Ravine and dried our clothes as well as we could. Two men shot in the rifle pits today. A flag of truce was sent in this P.M. to bury the dead. Our loss must be 200 killed and 1000 wounded, many of the wounded slightly with buck-shot. Oh! the horrors of war.

June 18: Our Co. in the rifle-pits again today. A continual firing but no one hurt, fine cool day. What is to be done next, it is difficult to imagine. The Rebels say we might as well try to storm Hell as their intrenchments, and I think there is some truth in what they say.

June 19: Were relieved in the rifle-pits at 7 A.M. Very hot. Getting pretty near worn out. Nothing unusual occurred. Plenty of rumors, but nothing to be relied on.

June 20: Very heavy firing on the right. Recd orders to be in readiness to march at night. Don't know where we are going. [Most of the Union troops continued the siege.]

June 21: Were roused at 1 o'clock and fell in and started at 2. Marched in a N.E. direction 10 miles and halted in a piece of woods, had coffee made and bivowacked for the night in the open field in a rain-storm.

4. *Control of the Mississippi River*

June 22: Very cool day. Marched 5 miles and stopped in a forest of pine, oak, beech, &c. Any quantity of blackberries and green corn. The whole Brigade are feasting.

June 23: A most beautiful night. Our Co. were out as a picket. Slept in the woods and got pretty badly eaten with jiggers. No enemy to be seen or heard of. Rainy in the P.M. Marched back to where we encamped Sunday and bivowacked in the same place.

June 24: Returned to our old positions in the rifle pits. Very hot, tiresome march. Arrived at noon, were very nearly bushed. Washed my shirt in the P.M. and went to bed and let it dry. Many rumors are rife in camp, but not to be credited. Recd two letters from home.

June 25: Wrote a long letter home, but it is said that all mail from here is detained at N.O. Nothing of particular importance happened in camp. On the whole I feel better for the tramp that we have taken. Deserters from the Rebels say that they killed their last beef and are living on cow-peas [black-eyed peas].

According to Heidler and Heidler, the Union siege at Port Hudson resulted in Rebel shortages of virtually everything they needed, especially food. Illness increased because of malnutrition. At the same time, Banks received food, other supplies, and regular reinforcements.[21]

June 26: A terrific bomb bardment opened by the [Union] fleet at 3 P.M. which continued until midnight. Had a fine shower in the P.M.; deserters continue to come in.

June 27: Our Co. in the rifle-pits today. Very hot. About the same amount of firing as usual. Orders to have two days rations of hard-tack on hand and to lay on our arms, ready to move at a moments notice. It is expected that rebels will try to get out.

June 28: Beautiful day, and for the first time for many weeks our Co. have comparative quiet. No particular excitement along the lines. Our men are gradually approaching the lines. Very hot. Am somewhat afraid we shall not celebrate the 4" in Port Hudson.

June 29: Went down to camp and had a good ramble through the woods. I have got to take charge of the cooking again. A great amount of fault found. Moved the cook-tent from the open field into the woods. Worked pretty hard.

June 30: Gen. Banks has been making speeches to the troops all day. A movement is soon to be made without any doubt. Some fighting on the left last night. Two of our men were killed by a shot from one of our guns.

Captaining the Corps d'Afrique

July 1: All quiet today. Many rumors. Was busy helping the Capt. make out the muster-rolls.

July 2: Made some corn coffee for the boys who were very much pleased with it. The Rebels attempted to throw a lot of grenades at our men but they exploded in their own hands. About the same firing as usual.

July 3: 4 of our men who had been taken prisoners in Port Hudson escaped this morn. Got a mess of green corn for the Co.

July 4: The 87th anniversary of the Independence of the U.S. We are in no condition for a celebration here certainly. We should have been in Port Hudson today but it is very difficult to tell when we shall get in.

July 5: Everything goes on about as usual, some rebels came out this morning. They have very little to eat. I believe they have enough to eat, such as it is, however. We have tried the starving out process long enough.

July 6: Rather more firing than usual, and 12 deserters came out in one morning.

July 7: Official dispatches from Gen. Grant state that Vicksburg surrendered on the 4th. 27000 prisoners and over 200 guns and everything that they had.[22] Port Hudson may as well surrender now. All the Bands in the Dept. are out playing. A salute of 100 guns was fired at noon.

July 8: The Enemy have raised a flag of truce this morn. They say that if we send in the official report of the surrender of Vicksburg, they will "give in." P.M. The place is surrendered and we are to march in tomorrow morn at 7 o'clock.

July 9: Glory! We have got Port Hudson and 6100 prisoners. [Dobak says 6,408.][23] Marched in this morn and saw them lay down their arms. A rusty looking [Union] crew. Went on board the Laurel Hill[24] in the P.M. and started for Donaldsonville [fig. 4]. The Officers are having a high old drunk.

According to Winston Groom, the surrender of Port Hudson and Vicksburg had major impacts on both sides. Union warships could move freely on the Mississippi all the way to the Gulf of Mexico, and middle west states could resume their domestic and foreign trade. "The vital stream of Texas beef, corn, and grains that fed the armies of Lee and Bragg was reduced to a trickle, and any notion of reinforcing armies from one side to the other was out of the question." Early in the war, President Lincoln had apparently understood the importance of Vicksburg when he noted that the city was key to ultimate victory. Groom

4. Control of the Mississippi River

quotes Lincoln: "The war can never be brought to a close, until that key is in our pocket." Gallagher et al. state that Lincoln "had found in Grant a general unlike any he had in the Eastern Theater. 'He doesn't worry and bother me, ... and does the best he can with what he has got,'"[25] according to the president.

A major impact that the fighting at Port Hudson had on the Union Army was that the 1st and 3rd Louisiana Native Guards demonstrated there that black Union soldiers were ready for battle. These troops, as well as the 2nd Regiment, were originally mustered into service by General Butler in November 1862 in New Orleans (see chap. 3). As Noah Andre Trudeau notes, "In some cases, such as at Port Hudson and New Market Heights [Virginia, September 29, 1864], [the U.S.C.T.] were deliberately committed to a hopeless task—not for any strategic reason, but solely to test their mettle." Even though they faced terrible odds, the black troops demonstrated great fighting ability. People in and out of the army took notice. Smith quotes a soldier in the 156th New York, who said after observing the 1st and 3rd Louisiana Native Guards at Port Hudson,

> They charged and re-charged and didn't know what retreat meant. They lost in their two regiments some four hundred men as near as I can learn. This settles the question about niggers not fighting well. They, on the contrary, make splendid soldiers and are as good fighting men as any we have.[26]

Up to this point, Chamberlin had had no direct experiences with black soldiers; he had only heard about their bravery. Since he was about to become one of their leaders, soon his life might depend on their ability and perseverance.

Chapter 5

3rd Engineers, Corps d'Afrique

Glad to Change

Maj. Gen. Nathaniel Banks ordered the establishment of the Corps d'Afrique on May 1, 1863, although it was not recognized by the War Department as an official army corps. On July 27, 1863, shortly after Chamberlin left Port Hudson, Maj. George D. Robinson (fig. 5) of the 1st Louisiana Engineers offered him a position as a captain in Robinson's new regiment of black troops (Appendix B). On September 1, 1863, Chamberlin became captain of Company E of the 3rd Regiment Engineers Corps d'Afrique (hereafter designated as 3rd Engineers). His new regiment consisted of men transferred from the 1st Engineers, Corps d'Afrique, at New Orleans, Louisiana, on August 26, 1863.[1]

In a letter written in the fall of 1863 Chamberlin told his brother:

> I have never asked anyone for any promotion or Commission of any kind since I have been in the service. When the 75" were at Donaldsonville, Maj. Robinson (who was then at Port Hudson) sent a list of names to Mr. Knight—the commissary Sergt. of the 75", asking him to see those men and ascertain whether we would accept commissions in the Reg't. he was to organize. I went to Port Hudson the next day and made arrangements with the Maj. that I should have the man I wanted for 1" Lt. and went back and awaited the result.[2] I didn't have any objection to having Corning recommend me for a Commission, for I thought I might deserve one or the other at any rate.

In a mid–September 1863 letter, Chamberlin said he preferred a commission in a regiment of black troops rather than in the 75th N.Y.V. because:

5. 3rd Engineers, Corps d'Afrique

The men of the 75th have come to look upon a Commissioned Officer with jealousy if not with actual hatred, and the more an Officer tries to do for many of them, the more he is looked upon with distrust, and although I was liked as well as any Serg't in the company, still I could not look forward to a Commission with any great pleasure. Still another good reason, nearly all the Officers of the 75th spend their entire wages in dress and in dissipation and any Officer who is not "hale fellow well met" with them in all things don't amount to any particular sum. I could not drink as much whiskey as the majority of them and on that account I should have stood a very poor chance for promotion. Here I am Capt. of a Co. and have no one in the Co. to dictate to me at any rate. I have a 1st Lt. from my own Co. whom I have been with nearly two years and is a good sober fellow—a man whom I can depend upon.

Figure 5. Colonel George D. Robinson, commander of the 5th Corps d'Afrique and later its successor regiment, the 97th U.S.C.T. Original in John Chamberlin's photo album; see figure 6. Courtesy Lelia and Paul Klear.

Chamberlin's lifestyle was obviously different from that of many officers and soldiers. Chaplains of black regiments would have approved. They often stressed how important it was for those in authority to set a correct example for their soldiers. According to Keith Wilson, "Officers were criticized for failing to attend church, swearing, drinking, gambling, and failing to keep the Sabbath."[3] Chamberlin's negative views of his fellow white soldiers, which he expressed in the

Captaining the Corps d'Afrique

above letter, were not new. In a February 22, 1863, letter, he had told his mother:

> I grow more and more disgusted with the service every day. Not but the Government means well by us but to see the more than infernal actions of the Officers. Every Officer is bound to get rich out of this war and you may depend upon it if I can get out of this with honor I shall do it even if I go among a set of cannibals for I should be sure of finding more honor among them than among the Officers of the 75th Reg. N.Y.V. No Fiction.[4] But I had better stop right where I am for it does no good to swear about it.

His view of his former regiment had not changed a year later, as he described the regiment's situation to his brother in a letter of June 15, 1864.

> The Regt is a rabble without much dicipline about it. Several of the Officers have resigned and others would if they Thought their resignations would be approved. They have from 30 to 40 men under guard nearly all the time and in a word they are a disgrace to the service. Their camp is only a quarter of a mile from us and I see some of them nearly every day. Norn and Ogden raced here to see me only two or three days ago. Ogden is fat & tough as a bear but Norn looks quite thin and is not well. I have never regretted that I got out of the Regt when I did. It is almost a disgrace to belong to such a Regt. I know men there who say that they would willingly serve the remainder of their time in my Co, if they could get out of the 75".

In a November 1863 letter he told his family the story of one officer who tried to get rich.

> Capt. Corning has got himself into a pretty tight fix, according to all accts. One day last week some of the Rebel cavalry made a dash at some of our baggage trains and the 75" were ordered out in a great hurry to catch the Rebels. When they came back Corning left one of his men at a plantation to guard some cotton which he had bought. On an inquiry as to where the man was he said he was sick and left behind. Fearing that there might be some trouble he went out and sent one of their picket guard to tell the man to tell the same story about sickness, but he lost his way and ran among the enemys picket and had his horse shot and was wounded. At the same time an Officer of the Reg't went out with a squad of men and arrested the man who was guarding the cotton and he (fearing that he should get into trouble) told the whole story. Corning is now

5. 3rd Engineers, Corps d'Afrique

Figure 6. John Chamberlin's photo album. Courtesy Lelia and Paul Klear.

under arrest by order of Gen. Weitzel and it is likely that some of his former cotton and sugar speculation will be investigated and he may get out of the service in a way he may not be very much pleased with. There are a great many circumstances connected with the affair that I have no means of finding out, but from all that I can gather I think his position is not at all an enviable one.

Captain of Black Soldiers

Chamberlin's commission as a white captain of a black company conformed to a pattern that was seen throughout the Union Army by 1863. When General Butler called the Louisiana black militia units into Union service, he appointed a mixed lot of officers, some white and others black. This plan to use black officers did not last long, for several reasons. Joseph Glatthaar reports, "In late 1862 and throughout most of 1863, the employment of black soldiers was still in the experimental stage.... Many believed it was best to give them the finest officers available—who happened to be white veterans." Hopefully the leadership of these white veteran officers would instill "excellent performance on the battlefield [which] would offset the losses to the black races caused by the limitations on the growth and development of black leadership in the military." Racial prejudice may have been another reason for not using black officers. Glatthaar writes, "The Lincoln administration was struggling to convince the military and public to accept black units. Having black officers was a step beyond that." Brig. Gen. Lorenzo Thomas (1804–1875), who spent much of the Civil War recruiting and organizing black troops, made another argument for having white officers. According to Aaron Sheehan-Dean, Thomas noted that negro slaves were brought up to obey white men. "Now, when organized into troops, ... the negro promptly obeys his [white officer's] orders."[5]

White officers were interested in leading black troops for at least two reasons. Abolitionists saw the potential of the former slaves, and ideally wanted to lead them to fight for their own freedom. The careerists wanted to take advantage of the opportunity to be promoted for leading black soldiers. John David Smith believes that, whatever their reasons, some white officers were "stained by the white racism of their age." But many changed their negative views when they saw the

5. 3rd Engineers, Corps d'Afrique

success of the black soldiers in battle. Fortunately, especially due to the actions of the examining boards set up by the Bureau of Colored Troops, the U. S. Colored Troops (U.S.C.T) received "a generally strong leadership base." This bureau, established by the federal government in May 1863, examined officer candidates and supervised the recruitment of black men in both the North and the South. The examining boards "determined who qualified for an officer's commission and for what rank the individual had demonstrated competence." The boards wanted, in Glatthaar's words, "intelligent white men with high morals who were willing to make a commitment to uplifting the black race." Thus, the boards looked for men "who genuinely wanted to work with black soldiers."[6]

According to the Bureau of Colored Troops, over 9,000 soldiers applied to be officers. Approximately sixty percent of the 4,000 who took the examinations passed. "Only one in every four [of the 9,000] applicants received a commission in the U.S.C.T., because of the effective screening process.... For the first time, the federal government screened candidates for officers' rank in volunteer units during wartime. It was a positive development both for blacks who served under these officers and for the American military establishment in general." According to Glatthaar, "the quality of the officers was definitely superior to those in white volunteer units."[7]

Black Troops at War

Chamberlin's new engineering company had a variety of responsibilities, such as deploying pontoon bridges, clearing waterways, and digging roads. As a leader in these activities, Chamberlin also had opportunities to recruit new black troops. One of his first leadership roles took him to Texas. He told his brother, in a letter dated September 11, 1863, about his first foray with his new regiment.

> On board the Steamer Laurel Hill—
> near the mouth of the Miss., Sept. 11, 1863
>
> Dear Brother:
>
> For fear you might borrow much trouble about me I will write a few lines so that you may hear from me as soon as possible, although the

Captaining the Corps d'Afrique

motion of the boat renders it almost impossible for me to write intelligibly. The 75" left N.O. on the 4th of Sept. together with quite a large force for Sabine pass. I was detached for special service in the 3" Regt. La. Engineers Corps d'Afrique on the 1" of Sept. so I was not with the 75".

The 3" Engr's left N.O. on the eve of the 6" of Sept on board the Gulf Steamer Nassau,[8] having in tow the fine Schooner Okolonce with the Pontoon bridge.[9] We—that is the Officers of the Regt.—had first rate accommodations on the Steamer and had a very pleasant voyage and arrived off the mouth of Sabine Pass at midnight on the 8". Here we anchored until morn when we learned that we had been repulsed with the loss of two Gunboats. We immediately turned around and arrived at the mouth of the Miss. this morn. at 10 o'clock. Here we have learned some of the particulars of the disaster. On the P.M. of the 8th the Gunboats Clifton and Sachem ran up to the mouth of the Sabine Pass and opened fire upon the rebel Batteries there, which it seems were mashed and did not reply. About 90 volunteers from the 75th were on board the Clifton. After firing for ½ an hour they attempted to run by the Batteries into the River, but got aground on a sand bar. The Rebel Batteries now opened up on them with very heavy guns at such a short range that they soon put some balls through the Boilers of the Sachem and blew her up, and so completely riddled the Clifton that her commander turned one of his heaviest guns upon the machinery of his own boat and tore that all to pieces so that it could not possibly be of any service to the enemy, spiked all his guns and each one took his chances. Three of the 75th men escaped—the others are either killed, wounded, drowned or captured.

According to historical accounts of this battle, the troops of Maj. Gen. William B. Franklin and Gen. Godfrey Weitzel "set off September 5 on an abortive, disorganized Texas expedition into Sabine Pass." They wanted to take Fort Griffin (the Confederate fort that guarded the pass) and begin an occupation of Texas. When the Union gunboats approached the fort, the Rebel cannons fired on them with great accuracy. The Union expedition ended in retreat, after the loss of two gunboats and several hundred men. Reports varied on the number captured (from more than 200 to as many as 400) and killed (42 to 50), with no losses to the Confederates.[10]

Chamberlin continued in his September 11 letter to his brother:

On the last day of the voyage back to the Miss. we had quite a gale. The Laurel Hill had some 300 mules on board belonging to our pontoon train and the Brigade to which our Reg't belongs. The Laurel Hill is a river boat

5. 3rd Engineers, Corps d'Afrique

and was in tow of the Beloidere,[11] but the sea became so rough that the Officers of the boat threw all the mules over excepting 5 to save the boat.

In a **September 12** diary entry, Chamberlin recorded that "the Officers and crew of the Boat are all under arrest for throwing the mules overboard."

After the disastrous Sabine Pass engagement, Chamberlin described in early October 1863 diary entries the black soldiers' work of removing sunken boats in the Vermillion Bayou, Louisiana (fig. 4, chap. 4):

October 5: Started at 7 A.M. and followed up the army (the 19" Army Corps) and halted at 2 P.M. near a sunken Steamer in the Bayou. Put up our tents and prepared to get the Steamer out of the stream.

October 6: Worked all day on the sunken Boat; removed the engines and everything movable and lighted the Boat so that she floated. Quite an extensive job.

October 7: Pulled the old wreck around out of the channel early in the morning. Four companies marched up 2 miles to where the Rebel Steamer Hart blockades the Stream. This is our next job and is likely to prove a very formidable one.

October 8: Went to work with considerable vim. Removed all that we could from the deck. Cut away the guards and raised one end of the Boilers up above the deck. Three powerful Boilers below the deck. If the boat had been finished it would have been a very formidable antagonist.

October 9: Put a big blast of Powder under the farther end of the boilers and ended them completely over and dragged them off of the boat. I went across the Bayou and back into the country and got some eggs, honey, ducks and 10 recruits for the Regt. Gen Banks came up at night.

October 10: Made out Enlistment Papers for 12 Recruits and mustered them into the service in the A.M. Went down 2 miles in the P.M. and unloaded a load of Commisary Stores from the Steamer Red Chief. Work progresses slowly on the Hart. We shall have to blow her to pieces.

October 11: 4 Companies worked upon the wreck and the other two unloaded 100000 Rations from a barge at the landing below. A very busy day. Enlisted 6 men. Gen. Banks came down at midnight on his way to New Orleans.

October 12: The Steamer Brown came up in the P.M. and succeeded in pulling a part of the wreck from the stream and passed through to New Iberia—the first boat for nearly a year.

Captaining the Corps d'Afrique

Two days later, Chamberlin wrote his mother: "Of course there was a considerable excitement among the citizens of the village [New Iberia] as they saw the smoke stacks of the Yankee Steamer approaching. I hope that they duly appreciate the benefit of the resumption of navigation to their village."

A few days later, he told a brother:

> We have completed a good bridge across the stream and a part of one company with 72 feet of the pontoon bridge have gone back to N.O. and we shall probably remain here untill the wagons come back from New Iberia. We had a Regimental Inspection by Col. Dudley the Inspector General of the Dept. of the Gulf,[12] and the men made a very creditable appearance.

Working in the countryside offered a particular benefit: the recruitment of black soldiers for the Union Army. Chamberlin mentioned his recruiting activities above, and described them after the stream was cleared to New Iberia.

> I remained behind with a squad of men to pick up any stray darkies who might wish to enlist and having a good pony and saddle, I got along very easy. During the last three days I have enlisted 29 good men. We take none but good ones as we need only 120 to fill up the Reg't. I have 43 men in my company and I am entitled to 8 more.[13] We have very fancy uniforms for the Engineer Corps. A Jacket and pants of gray cloth, the pants with a red cord on the seams, the jacket with red cuffs and collar and scarlet caps. You never saw children prouder of new clothes than they are of theirs.

The idea of recruiting slaves and free black men to become Union soldiers was certainly influenced by the battlefield performance of black soldiers at Jacksonville, Port Hudson, Milliken's Bend, and Fort Wagner in the first half of 1863 (chap. 3). President Lincoln wrote on March 26, 1863, "The colored population is the great available and yet unavailed-of force for restoring the Union." The recruitment of black soldiers ate away at slavery, since many recruits were escaping their masters. Glatthaar states, "Approximately 144,000 of the 178,000 blacks who served in the Union Army during the Civil War came from slave states." He also maintains that for most blacks, especially ex-slaves, service in the Union Army "was a great opportunity to prove that blacks merited full citizenship." Eric Foner declares that army service certainly was a "recognition of the Negro's manhood."[14]

5. 3rd Engineers, Corps d'Afrique

The federal government stood firmly behind the recruitment of black soldiers when it established the Bureau of Colored Troops. By the summer of 1863, this Bureau had assigned numbered U.S. regimental designations to most black soldiers in the newly organized U.S.C.T.

Frederick Douglass, the well-known escaped slave and abolitionist, strongly encouraged black men to enlist, for their own benefit, and that of the race. Philip Foner quotes him as saying:

> Never since the world began was a better chance offered to a long enslaved and oppressed people. The opportunity is given us to be men. With one courageous resolution we may blot out the hand-writing of the ages against us. Once let the black man get upon his person the brass letters U.S.; let him get an eagle on his button, and a musket on his shoulder, and bullets in his pocket, and there is no power on the earth or under the earth which can deny that he has earned the right of citizenship in the United States. I say again, this is our chance, and woe betide us if we fail to embrace it.[15]

In mid–December, the 3rd Engineers started work on fortifications in Berwick City, Louisiana (east of Vermillion Bay, fig. 4, chap. 4). They set up camp and Chamberlin noted in diary entries from **December 18** to **December 31**: "Made comfortable quarters for myself in an unoccupied house. We are to remain here some time. We are to fortify this place with earthworks and a fort inside." The troops spent Christmas week (except the 25th) working on the fortifications, and Chamberlin moved into a tent. He closed the year with a "Farewell to 1863. It is leaving us in a storm—fit emblem of the condition of the country during the past year. God grant that the end of the next year may find us a free and united and happy people."

CHAPTER 6

Loneliness of War

Although Chamberlin seemed fairly content and found his work stimulating, he felt invariably lonely. Thus, he was excited about a visit from his brother Charles early in March 1864. One has to wonder how his brother could come all the way from New York to southern Louisiana in the midst of a war. This is a letter Chamberlin wrote to his mother after Charles left:

My Dear Mother:

Charles will sail for home to-day on the steamer Creole. He left here yesterday morning on his way to New Orleans. Charles made a short visit, but it did me all sorts of good. He seemed to think he was well paid for his trip down here before he went home. His experiences of men and the ways of life away from home will be a great advantage to him—something that he will always remember. It was difficult for us to talk enough with each other about old times and the people in the neighborhood. Sometimes we talked nearly all night. His visit was so short that we had to visit as fast as we could while he was here.

It made me feel almost homesick when he went away. "Good bye & good luck to you" was all that either of us could say. The tears would start but I smothered them back, jumped into the boat, waved a parting farewell pulled my hat down over my eyes and in another moment was out of sight in the dense fog that shrouded the Bay. Every stroke of the oars seemed to echo with fearful distinctness "Alone" "Alone" and I must own I never felt so lonely before. Enshrouded in the fog the whole animate world seemed dead and I alone with the stable oarsmen, gliding on toward the boundless Ocean of the great unknown future. Would I reach a quiet haven at last or be tossed forever on the rough tempestuous sea. Would the future bring me good or evil, joy or sorrow, and then the lines of Longfellow occurred to me[1]:

6. Loneliness of War

> Trust no future how'ere pleasant,
> Let the dead past bury its dead:
> Act! act in the living present
> Heart within and God o'er head:

and I sprang on shore with the determination to do my duty manfully from day to day and leave the disposal of the future with Higher Power than mans.

It is impossible for me to shake off entirely the depression of the morning, but at noon came an order for 100 men to unload our Pontoon Bridge from the cars on the Brashear side & I was detailed to superintend the work, and was soon lost in the great roaring sea of life. How miserable a man must be without any aim or object in life—without any care or responsibility. Without it life would be a great blank to me and it must be to any one who has an intellect above the beasts that perish.

This letter shows a Chamberlin not seen very often in his letters. Usually he is an analytical man of duty and high moral principles, often looking to the future. But he clearly had his moments of loneliness, as all soldiers must. However, in the end, he relied on his faith in God. Chamberlin closed this March 9 letter to his mother:

> I wished very much to send something home to all of you but could send very little but love which, if you receive a tithe of what was packed up for you, you will be well provided for in that essential article. I would enjoy taking you all by the hand again as well as all my Friends in Sennett, but in place of that I have sent my regards, and in some instances my love, by the mouth of a living witness.
>
> > With hope and courage your affectionate Son
> > John N. Chamberlain

Another way he dealt with his loneliness was by reaching out to Anna Bullock, a special "old school mate" from Sennett, New York. She had moved with her family to Waterloo, Iowa, in about 1855.[2] When she left New York, Bullock was fifteen and Chamberlin was eighteen.

> Berwick City La., Feb 22 1864
>
> Dear Friend Anna:
>
> Many long years have passed since your fathers family found a home among the people of the far West. Since that time there have been many changes among individuals and changes in the National History. Years of political strife and animosity have ripened into the great civil war which

Captaining the Corps d'Afrique

now shakes the very continent. From the bashful boy of ten years ago I have grown to be a man and have tried to serve my country faithfully in this great struggle for national life. In the Autumn of 1861 I enlisted in the 75" N.Y. Vols. and at about the same time I heard that Howard had enlisted in an Iowa Regt. & got his P.O. address and wrote several letters to him and recd several from him, but never rec'd your P.O. address or I should have written to you also. Harriet [Chamberlin's sister] wrote me a letter not long ago giving me your address. I can think of you as no one else but the same girl as you left your native place, but I know you are now a woman and have (no doubt) seen no small share of care and trouble and sorrow.

I have outgrown my bashfulness very much or I should not have the courage to commence a letter to you at this time. But I have considered the matter well and know that even if you are a married lady my ignorance of the fact will be a very good excuse and that I am so far away that I may consider myself safe enough at any rate and so I write as I would talk with you were I to see you in your northern home.[3] I often think of the happy days when we all were at school together, of the practice in the Grammar class and the tough problems in Algebra and Arithmatic and about all the glorious times we had at spelling school—you know that I always considered myself a great speller. Oh! there are a thousand incidents that recall those days as vividly as though it were only yesterday.

And then the evening visits in the neighborhood and the games of "Blindfold" and "Button, who's got the button" and to make the young blood tingle a good "spell" of sliding down hill and all those winter enjoyments that are unknown among the children of the sunny south—happy days that have passed away forever. All of us who now live are facing the stern realities of life.

I am all alone in this Dept. of all the boys that went to the old schoolhouse. No doubt your brothers are doing their duty nobly if they [have not] ere this fallen in the terrible storm of war. Howard and I were always brothers together and I must know where he is if possible. I had hoped that we might meet sometime but I have given up that long ago as he must be very far from the Dept. of the Gulf. I have been a Private, corporal, sergeant, and 2" Lt. in the 75" N.Y. Vols. and am now a captain of a company in the Corps d'Afrique. You may think that this is not an honorable position, but I am doing my duty as well as I can wherever I am.

I believe the war will leave us a free nation. Equal and exact justice will be meted out to all men and the spirit and letter of the Immortal Declaration of Independence will be carried out as it was meant to be by the framers of the constitution. I am no negro-worshiper, but give them a chance to assert their manhood and in this terrible war that threatens the

6. Loneliness of War

life of the nation if they can help to work out their own freedom, in Gods name let them do it. The whole Nation is guilty of the crime and curse of American Slavery and I look upon this war sometimes as a punishment for tolerating so great a stain upon the National character. [Once again Chamberlin foreshadowed Lincoln's words in his Second Inaugural Address; see chap. 2.] A nation that has boasted of so much freedom and all the time held three millions of human beings in the most abject and hopeless servitude, was looked upon with derision by the nations of Europe and it is not a matter of surprise that this great calamity has come upon us.

But though we now sow in tears and blood, we shall yet reap an abundant harvest of national peace and prosperity, when arising from the smoke and carnage of this terrible conflict and purified and invigorated by this terrible baptism of fire and blood the nation may go onward in a career of glory and greatness the admiration of the nations and wonder of the world. If we should fail to carry this war through to a successful end we should be untrue to the great and solemn trust imposed on us by an all-wise and overruling Providence. God grant that we may soon see peace like a dove spreading her wings over the land and the Union once more joined together in Freedom and Truth.

I wish you to write and let me know how you are all getting along in the western country and let me know where the boys are. My regards to your Father. Please write soon and believe me, as ever, your true friend.

>John N. Chamberlain
>Direct to Capt. John N. Chamberlain 3d Engineers
>Corps d'Afrique New Orleans La

Presumably, this first letter reached Bullock in mid to late March. Apparently she wrote a reply soon after, which unfortunately has not been preserved. Here is his response to the missing letter:

>Alexandria, La., on May 2"/64.

Friend Anna:

I recd your welcome letter of March 31st on the 28th of April, and although there are so many miles of sin and secession stretching between us, and although so many years have passed since we have met, yet the letter, to me seemed a mirror of your former self as in the days of "Auld lang syne" we recited our lessons in the same class in the old "stone school house" in "Freeman Street." Then no shadows darkened our paths and we looked forward to the future, little knowing or dreaming of the Stern realities of life that were in store for each of us. I lived at home until the breaking out of the war and had no particular trials or hardships to

Captaining the Corps d'Afrique

endure. When the terrible storm of war broke over the land I enlisted as a private in the 75th N.Y. Vols. in September of 1861. Our folks thought that it was a great sacrifice when I left home for the "wars" and I don't know what they would have done if Charley had gone too. Charley made me a short visit this spring while I was at Berwick city which did me all sorts of good.

Since my enlistment, I have been a soldier in the service of my country and I trust I have always done my duty faithfully. As you say, I also regret the cause that has brought sorrow and desolation to so many hearts and homes all over our fair land, and is making a ruin of the beautiful South, but still I have never regretted that I entered the service. It is a war in which all the friends of Freedom, Humanity and Christianity are on our side, and we cannot, we must not fail, every one of us, to do our full duty to our country in this time of her trial.

"For Right is Right since God is God,
And Right the day must win
To doubt would be impiety
To falter would be Sin."[4]

But, after all, I think it is a good thing for young men to be away from home for a few years. It teaches a fellow self-dependence at any rate, but is a bad school in the army I assure you. Leaving the restraints of home, and more especially of female society render many of our young men reckless in regard to their conduct and habits. Human life and property are not the only sacrifices of war. The characters of many of our bravest soldiers are in more danger than their lives.

A soldiers duty is to obey orders & we have very little time to speculate on the probable chances of a speedy restoration of Peace, but we long for the time when the war will be over just as much as any one.

You ask me if I have reenlisted. I have not, but it amounts to about the same thing. I am sworn into the service for three years from the 12" of last Sept. [1863] but an Officer has more opportunities to get out of the service than an enlisted man does, but I shall probably remain in the service while my health continues so good as it now is. I sometimes have longings for home and friends that no tongue can tell, but they are only momentary & I suppose it is better to be so.

But I have not told you anything about the country I have been living, or rather soldiering in for nearly three years. It is beautiful country and under the invigorating hand of free labor it might be made a perfect paradise. The climate is so mild that roses bloom 9 months in the year. I have seen more that is beautiful in Nature in this country than I supposed possible. The ground and gardens of many of the planters are magnificent beyond description. There is only one hindrance to this country in

6. Loneliness of War

comfort and health and that is the scarcity of good water. The best water that can be had is rain-water, which is caught in large wooden cisterns above ground. The streams are all very dirty and in the lower part of the State, almost stagnant during a great part of the year. I have sometimes thought that I would live in this country after the war rather than return to such a cold climate as the North. If I could persuade half a dozen good families to emigrate here I think a very pleasant township might be established. But there is no use of building air castles.

I would very much like to hear what kind of a place your home is in and all about it. Write and tell me in your next. I will accept your invitation to attend your Good-Templors [sic] Lodge some Friday night, but the particular Friday I am unable to specify. I never belonged to the organization as I never lived where one existed, and there are no Temperance Societies in the army so far as I have seen. I will say for the benefit of the cause generally that I am still a temperance man, although in the army. Whatever sins I may be guilty of I hope I may never be intemperate.

Throughout his letters Chamberlin commented on drinking and temperance—an interest he shared with Bullock in particular. The Temperance Movement was first founded in Saratoga, New York, in 1808, and was dedicated to promoting moderation, and, more often, complete abstinence from the use of intoxicating liquor. The Good Templars organization was established in early 1851 as the Independent Order of Good Templars (IOGT). It originated in Utica, New York, as the first international temperance organization, then spread gradually throughout the United States and Europe. Its structure was modeled on Freemasonry, with lodges and similar ritual and regalia. Unlike many organizations, however, it admitted men and women equally, and made no distinction by race.[5]

Apparently in Anna Bullock, Chamberlin had found someone to whom he could describe his activities and surroundings, and with whom he could share his rambling thoughts. A few months later he wrote:

> Your kind and very welcome letter of Sept. 30th was recd about a week ago. When I first came into the service as a private in the 75th N.Y.V. I had no lack of correspondents, all of whose letters I answered promptly, but year after year, as the war has absorbed the whole energies of the people and has come to be a real matter of fact business, many of my friends have almost ceased to write to me. Some have gone to the war & others are very busy in making snug fortunes not out of the misfortunes of the

Captaining the Corps d'Afrique

country (I hope). Some of the girls are dead and some are married, only a few I am happy to say to save some anxious young chap from the chances of a draft. [This is a reference to the Draft Act of 1863.][6]

Others I think have pretty much forgotten me. One or two rather elevate their nasal protuberance on account of my being in a colored Regt. as Capt. Toward the latter class I entertain the most serene indifference. What wonder then that when I receive a letter from an old school mate and friend I am not totaly indifferent to it. This is a very matter-of-fact kind of a world, but after all there are a great many things that cannot be reckoned in dollars & cents. Such are these letters, coming to me in all honesty and sincerity from one whom I always trusted and loved in childhood, they are as rays of golden sunshine upon the restless, uncertain sea of life.

Right from the beginning, the importance of Chamberlin's correspondence with Bullock is shown by the fact that he responded so promptly to her first letter, even though he was engaged in the Red River Campaign, as the next chapter shows.

CHAPTER 7

The Red River Campaign

The Red River Campaign consisted of a series of battles fought along the Red River in Louisiana between March 10 and May 22, 1864. According to several historians, including Dobak and Ludwell Johnson, some of the goals for this Union campaign were to capture Shreveport, Louisiana (seat of Louisiana's Confederate government); to control the Red River to the north; to occupy east Texas, which was the source of much-needed guns, food, and supplies for Confederate troops; and to confiscate tons of cotton desperately needed by Northern mills. In addition, Gen. Nathaniel Banks, commander of the Union soldiers, thought a successful military campaign would help him to win the 1864 presidential nomination. According to William Winter in a letter quoted by Sheehan-Dean, although General Grant "considered the campaign a needless diversion from the goal of seizing Mobile, the Red River expedition was strongly supported by President Lincoln," partly "to restrain French actions in Mexico." Unfortunately for the Union, this campaign was a failure.[1]

On March 10 the 3rd Engineers (including Chamberlin's Co. E) left Berwick City, Louisiana, to join General Banks' Army of the Gulf (fig. 4, chap. 4). They marched for 250 miles in all kinds of conditions, typically for about fifteen miles a day. Occasionally they spent a day in camp or they repaired roads or bridges that had been destroyed by the Rebels. Chamberlin's diary provides details about their trip.

March 18: We caught quite a number of sheep, pigs & poultry on the march and arrived in camp so late that our wagons were not inspected by the Provost Marshall. Very strict orders against foraging but we must live and I, for one have no compunctions about confiscating what I need from the Rebels.

Captaining the Corps d'Afrique

March 19: Since we left this area last Spring the Rebels have built a very fine bridge across the Bayou from Washington which they had just finished as our cavalry came into town. Two companies of their cavalry who were guarding the bridge were gobbled by our men. We are not at all sorry about the bridge as it saves us the trouble of building a new one.

March 23: The regiment crossed the Bayou and marched two miles and encamped on Brig. Gen. Staffords (Rebel) Plantation.[2]

March 24: We camped on Mr. Chambers Plantation 11 miles from Alexandria. Staid in a very fine negro cabin but there were more bed-bugs than were allowed by army Regulations. Slept very well however.

After 15 days of marching the 3rd Engineers reached Alexandria, Louisiana, where 32,000 Union troops were gathered.[3] The next day, **March 26**, Chamberlin's company had to "march 7 miles up the River and build a bridge across a Bayou that the Rebels had burned." For the next twelve days, the 3rd Engineers worked with a pontoon bridge to help the Union make river crossings on the Red and the Cane (fig. 4). These troops found themselves more and more in the middle of the battle, and more often in danger. From the village of Pleasant Hill, Chamberlin described the **April 8** confrontation with the Rebels at Mansfield.

> The battle of the 8" was in an open field in the midst of the pine woods. Our [Banks'] army was in very small space & the road blocked up with wagons. The Rebs lay in ambush until our forces had advanced to the trap when they sprang upon them and caught them perfectly. A continual roar of artillery at the front nearly all the P.M. Our cavalry were driven back and our infantry not coming up as promptly as they should have done. Our wagons became blockaded in the woods and 25 pieces of Artillery was captured by the Enemy. Many of our wounded and ammunition and supply trains and even Regt. baggage fell into the hands of the enemy. A big haul for the enemy, a regular ambuscade.

According to Chamberlin's diary, the news the next morning (**April 9**) was no more encouraging:

> General Ransom of the 13" Army Corps mortally wounded. The whole town [Pleasant Hill] is filled with our wounded and the whole field around the town is filled with trains and troops of all arms. Formed line of battle at 8 A.M. and awaited orders. General Smith with 10,000 moved up to the front and handled the Rebs. very severely to-day.[4] Captured considerable of our artillery from the Rebs. [After this fight Banks' army retreated

7. The Red River Campaign

to Grand Ecore (fig. 4). Chamberlin reported very heavy and rapid artillery firing toward night.] Made 22 miles at midnight and bivoucked in the woods. Teams nearly tired out.

As Chamberlin described, the large Union Army was forced to retreat to Alexandria, a movement that took fifteen days and resulted in the capture of many wounded (who had been left in houses at Pleasant Hill) and of a great many wagons. Heavy skirmishing occurred in front of and behind the retreating army. Chamberlin reported:

April 23: Heavy firing at Cane River in the morning; the enemy were disputing the Ford.[5] Union Brigades were attempting to gain the Heights on the other side of the Ford. Our rear was attacked at noon so that we are now between two fires. After Union forces attacked the Rebel flanks and after General Smith's victory in the rear, Co. E moved forward to the Cane River & laid the bridge.

April 24: We worked all night crossing the trains of the army. The last of Smith's army crossed the bridge at 2 O'clock and we took up the pontoon bridge and loaded it in just 25 minutes. The enemy appeared on the other side but we had 2 Batteries in position on the heights and two Regts of Infantry so that it would have been very dangerous to try to drive us away. Marched 15 miles through the pine woods and encamped within 16 miles of Alexandria. Some skirmishing in front and rear.

Finally they reached Alexandria on **April 25**; Chamberlin wrote: "We are all pretty well tired out. The days of marching and fighting has given the army a terrible trial. Men dropped from the ranks and died by the road-Side all along the line of march. It has been one continual battle every day since we commenced the retreat." When they arrived at Alexandria, they discovered that the river was so low at the rapids above the city that it was impossible for the heavy gunboats to navigate.

Conflicting reports attempt to explain the reason for the low water levels necessitating the building of a dam at Alexandria. According to Richard H. Holloway, the water was falling because of an annual spring tradition of drainage. Although some authors have speculated the Confederates had blasted the levees upstream to release the river water, and some documentation exists that the aforementioned plan was discussed, no actual evidence has surfaced of any water diversion by human hands. The *New York Times* reported that the boats had a great deal of difficulty going upstream, and were hoping for the usual spring run-off to get them back downstream. Another article in the *New York Times* reported the Confederates had built a canal north of Grand Ecore to divert some of the river water to Grand Lake. However, the writer stated that the water would be returned to the Red River downstream, still above the falls at Alexandria, so it wouldn't present a problem.[6]

Chamberlin's diary **April 28**, 1864, stated: "We are to construct a dam across the river and raise the water 6 feet at the rapids to allow the fleet to pass down. It is a gigantic enterprise but I have confidence that we shall be successful."

In his official report Col. George D. Robinson stated that Lt. Col. Joseph Bailey, acting military engineer, 19th Army Corps, approved the idea of building a dam to raise the level of water in the river.[7] "The 3rd Engineers were employed in collecting and hauling the necessary material, and the Fifth Engineers in constructing the dam. The regiments were divided into two reliefs, which relieved each other every six hours, working day and night."[8]

Chamberlin reported that when the 3rd Engineers built the dam between April 30 and May 11, 1864, he had charge of four companies which seized vast amounts of lumber and brick from people in the city. On **April 30** he wrote in his diary: "Rather a disagreeable job as many of the owners of lumber claimed to be union citizens, but my orders were from Gen. Banks and I took whatever I could find Even to fences quite reluctantly. Gen. Grover sent his Provost Marshall after me but he couldn't do anything."

Chamberlin wrote the following extensive account of the campaign in the following letter to Bullock.

Morganza, LA, May 24, 1864

Dear Friend Anna:

I recd your kind letter while at Alexandria and was glad to hear from you and also to hear that the boys were still in the land of the living.

When we reached Alexandria, we immediately commenced building a dam across the river at the rapids and after two weeks of incessant labor, night and day, we succeeded in raising the water sufficiently to let every boat pass through in safety. It was quite a triumph for us, as quite a number of good Engineers thought the enterprise could not be successfully carried with the materiel at hand in the limited time allowed.

7. The Red River Campaign

In the mean time, the Rebel Gen. Dick Taylor had moved his army below us on the river and captured several of our smaller Gun-boats and transports and succeeded in completely blockading the river by batteries placed behind the levee. Our forage was all gone and the army was reduced to half rations. The last boat passed down through the dam on the morning of the 13th and the whole army and Navy commenced moving down the river the same day.

Early in the morning some thoughtless or malicious person set fire to a large hotel in the business part of the city and all attempts to subdue the fire were unavailing. [Johnson states that it was Union troops who set the fires that burned Alexandria.[9]] When my Regt. passed through at noon it was apparent that nearly the whole city would be consumed. Alexandria was the finest city I have seen in the South, about as big as Elbridge—containing in prosperous times a population of 3,000 but not more than half that number were living there when we occupied the city. It was the saddest picture of war that I have ever seen and I have seen some sad ones I assure you. Women and children were hurrying through the streets with what little they could carry to places of safety in the open fields. Two little girls that I noticed were carrying a mattress and seemed so pleased to think that they had saved that, that they seemed to forget that everything else was perishing in the flames. It was the wildest scene of agony and distress among the defenceless that can be imagined. God pity them and deliver me from another such scene. It was more painful than the carnage of a battle field. Hundreds who were nurtured in luxury and refinement had nothing but the blue canopy above them at night.

After this terrible fire the whole Union Army and Navy moved south from Alexandria to the Mississippi River. The seven-day retreat was marked by periodic skirmishing with the Rebels, long marches, and contested river crossings. At one of those crossings, Chamberlin wrote in his **May 15** diary:

> We cut a road 3 miles through the woods to Choctaw Bayou [fig. 4] and laid the Pontoon bridge. The army commenced crossing at 10 A.M. Sharp fighting in rear all day. I was left behind with my company to take charge of the bridge and take it up or burn it according to circumstances. The army finished crossing at midnight and we took up the bridge in just 15 minutes and moved forward without having a shot fired. Marched 8 miles through the woods in Egyptian darkness and overtook the Regt. at daylight the next morning.[10]

Col. George D. Robinson, commander of the 97th U.S.C.T. (formerly 3rd Engineers), confirmed what Chamberlin described in his

Captaining the Corps d'Afrique

diary on **May 15, 1864**. Robinson was near Scraggy Point [Snaggy Point][11] on the Red River, about 24 miles below Alexandria, where he was ordered to repair the road to Bayou Choctaw (four miles distant).

> This stream is narrow but deep, with very high banks. The bridge was laid and the approaches completed at 10 a.m., though the train did not arrive until 12 m. I left one company of the 3rd Engineers under Captain Chamberlain, with orders to remain at the bridge until all the troops and trains had crossed, and then to take up the bridge and join me as soon as possible, which he did on the following morning at 4 a.m., having marched all night.[12]

Chamberlin reported on another crossing in his diary entries of **May 19** and **20**, 1864.

> The army is crossing the Atchafalaya on a bridge of Transports. A part of the army is embarking to go up the Mississippi to the Dept. of the Cumberland, I suppose. Expect to take up the bridge some time tonight. Shall probably get a few shells from the Rebels. The remainder of the army commenced crossing the Pontoon bridge at midnight and were all across at 3 ½ O'clock the morning of the 4th day. Took up the bridge immediately. The Enemy didn't trouble us. Moved forward and reached Simmesport [fig. 4] at Sunrise.

Anna Bullock's brother Bert was also at the Atchafalaya crossing on May 20, 1864. His Iowa regiment was in a severe fight there, and he commented later that "the whole expedition has proved a fizzle."[13] Another of her brothers, Howard, was also involved in the Red River Campaign, although he did not specify where. He described his experience in his letter to Anna.[14]

Modern historians are even more critical than Bullock's brothers were. Dobak says Banks' "expedition had been a failure, expensive in casualties, time, and opportunities lost in other theaters of operations." Sheehan-Dean states that the campaign "cost the Union about 5,500 men killed, wounded, or missing, the Confederates about 4,300." Ludwell Johnson argues that this unnecessary campaign delayed the end of the war by at least a short period of time, perhaps two months, and that Banks' mistakes on the Red River tied up as many as 20,000 men who could have been used to reinforce Sherman's army operating against Atlanta or who might have started a campaign against Mobile, Alabama. In non-military terms, the campaign was also a failure. Most

7. The Red River Campaign

of the cotton Banks had hoped to glean was burned on the approach of the Federals or lost in the hasty retreat from Grand Ecore. Based on the failure of the Red River Campaign and other engagements, General Banks was removed from field operations.[15] Dobak quotes a soldier's parody of William Cowper's hymn, "Banks moves in mysterious ways, His blunders to perform."[16]

Without the benefit of our historical perspective, Chamberlin too described the Red River Campaign in his May 24, 1864, letter to Bullock as "very unsuccessful." He concluded that letter with a grim view of the whole war:

> War has been truly said the greatest curse that can befall a nation. It levels the cottage and the palace alike. Nothing is so sacred but is desecrated by its fiery hand. In an enemy's country the torch and cannon are applied indiscriminately to the dwellings of friend and foe alike. God grant that the North may never be made the theater of such a fierce desolating war as this. The North suffers to be sure in loss of her noble sons, and there is scarcely a fireside but has its vacant chair, and sorrow and anguish is brought from the battle fields of the South everyday to many a family circle, but the graves of such are hallowed as martyrs to the great and holy cause of Freedom, and the memory of those who are daily passing from the bloody fields of this terrible war, to the last great "Review" will ever be held sacred by a grateful posterity. Not so with the South. In her mad attempt upon the National life her sons die as "the fool dieth" traitors to their country.[17] The country is swept as it were by the besom of destruction.[18] Everything beautiful and lovely and holy in Nature and in Art is laid waste, and in place of the lordly mansion decorated with all the most wonderful fertility, all is a ruin overgrown with rank weeds. It always makes me feel sad to contemplate the terrible havoc that this war is working throughout one of the most magnificent countries in the world.
>
> J. N. Chamberlain

Chapter 8

Coping with the Misery of War

Empathy with the South

As can be seen in the previous letters, as the war progressed Chamberlin became increasingly distressed about its brutal nature and violence, thus asking many questions about the meaning of life in general and his life in particular, also about the need to look for joy in one's surroundings. He described the destruction of the countryside and the desperation of the people in the South, including soldiers, in an early 1864 letter to a sister.

> The Rebels are now fighting through sheer desperation & they fight well. If the prisoners that we took in the late scrimmage are a fair specimen of the soldiers of the Confederacy, they must have a plenty of faith in the justice of their cause or else they have very slight hopes of getting out of the service. They were the most poorly clad that you can imagine any men to be. Some of them had not enough rags to cover his nakedness. One poor fellow in particular had nothing except an old pair of pants & an old tattered blanket over his shoulders, tied around his shoulder with strings. Thus they fight on, but many of them could do no better out of the army in the present state of affairs. It is a time of the year when they can raise nothing & some enter the army to get a living & many because they are forced to. They are the poor whites & are just such a class of people as Mrs. Stowe & other writers describe them to be—lower than the negroes.[1]

The Rebel shortages that Chamberlin described—food, clothing, medicine, and shoes—increased as the war continued. The Confederacy's inability to provide for the soldiers' basic needs was largely caused by

8. Coping with the Misery of War

bad logistics. According to David Ulbrich, the movement of supplies from storage to battlefield was hampered by poor administration, miscommunication, and lack of transportation. In addition Union forces seized Confederate food and isolated Confederate armies from agricultural production areas. On the other hand, because of the Union's efficient logistics, "Union soldiers rarely suffered in the long term from shortages of food, clothing, shelter, or ammunition."[2]

In an August 4, 1863, letter to Bullock, Chamberlin looked at the war from the perspective of the Southerners.

> The people of the South who fight desperately for what many of them have come to think is the most sacred cause on earth, although they are fighting against principles as eternal and unchanging as the throne of the Most High, yet they are entitled to some respect for trying to maintain their principles no matter how detestable they may be.

While riding through the countryside to recruit black soldiers, Chamberlin saw the difficult situation the Southern plantation owners faced. In late October 1863, he described it in a letter to his mother.

> I find splendid houses entirely deserted with all the furniture (frequently of the most magnificent kind) left in the rooms just as if the occupants were there. In one house I found a beautiful Piano in perfect order that the negroes said cost 1000 dollars. All the moveable small articles of value have been taken away by the owners. In one house I found quite a Library consisting mostly of Law Books. I took two Volumes of a Book Entitled "Democracy in America" by M. D. Toqueville,[3] A Political Encyclopedia (a very interesting work), a good feather pillow and a fine picture of "Shakespeare and his friends" which I have rolled and in my chest. The owner had gone to Texas. Hundreds of families in this section have left their homes in this way. They wish the war to close and many are anxious to return to their allegiance, but for them to show any symptoms of loyalty when the Rebs. are in possession of the country, it is worse than ruin. It would be death. So rather than abandon everything to a merciless mob of Jay-Hawkers (as they call the Texans)[4] they take what they can and flee the country.
>
> I know there is little enough Union sentiment in this part of the State, but I tell you it is a very trying position for a man to be placed in here if he is a Union man. Having all his worldly possessions here, we may come and occupy the country and he will take the oath of allegiance, then as soon as we abandon the country, as we did last Spring, the rebels immediately take possession and then who will protect his property? He will be

Captaining the Corps d'Afrique

ruined by them at once. On the other hand if he refuses to take the oath, why then he is rebel and forfeits his property to us.

The people of this country begin to think that if "the Lord be God" they will serve him, but if "Baal be God" they will serve him,[5] and it is rather difficult for them to say which is to be in possession of the country the longest.

Chamberlin relied on his strong religious faith to guide him through the difficult times in the war. However, he noted in a June 24, 1862, letter to his mother:

Not many soldiers of the army of Freedom have such an opportunity to attend religious services as the 75th & yet very few improve it. The spirit of war & carnage & the Spirit of Christianity are altogether incompatible. In fact there are so many brutalizing & demoralizing influences about war that most men cease to think of better things or if they do they heed them not & they are soon forgotten. Many things are done in the army which the same men would not think of at home.

Danger of Drink

Rather than religion, many soldiers found another form of relief, as Chamberlin wrote to a sister on February 21, 1864:

Tens of thousands of noble, generous souls who are now in the grand army of Freedom will go down to their graves with bitterest curses on their lips against the more than infernal demon of strong drink. The clarion voices of those who fought under the Banner of Temperance, are drowned with the din of arms. And seldom it is that we hear the echos of their voices through the pauses of the strife. The Nation is in a terrible contest for its very life and all minor interest are aside and while the young men of the North are sacrificing the comforts of life and security of dear friends at home to maintain the honor of the "Starry flag" an enemy more fatal and insiduous is taking possession of them which will require a most desperate and determined struggle to escape from.

In whatever way I may be brought into disgrace—it will never be the terrible disgrace of the drunkard. The more I see of the effects of the use—even moderately as some say, of intoxicating drink, the more terrible it is in my eyes.

8. Coping with the Misery of War

Chamberlin worried about whether the influence of the army would affect future citizens' views about the use of alcohol. In a September 20, 1864, letter to Anna Bullock's brother Howard, he wrote:

> I often think that if I ever do get to be a citizen again, I shall have such a spirit of recklessness & restlessness that I shall never be contented to settle down anywhere and call it home. Three years of life as a soldier, and all the rough characters with which a fellow is of necessity associated with together with the absence of all female society has not the most refining tendency, and although I have not fallen into the too common habit of swearing & drinking, yet I often think that I would be noticed by every one for my awkwardness and oddities, were I once more in civil life. But I won't borrow my trouble about that until there is a reasonable prospect of getting out of the service.

Chamberlin had first discussed temperance with Bullock in May 1864. He commented further on temperance organizations in this October 23, 1864, letter to her.

> I am somewhat surprised to hear that you still keep up your temperance organizations in the West. A Temperance Lecture is something I have not heard of from home for more than a year. It has sometimes seemed to me that the whole Nation is drifting into one terrible Gulf of Intemperance. When I left home we had a temperance Society in Sennett of which I was Secretary, and we numbered more than 300 members.
> But it is now among the things that were. If we had organized some such Lodge as you have it might have been in existence now, no doubt. I am glad that there are some in the North, who amid the terrible trials of this great conflict do not altogether lose sight of the great cause of temperance. God grant that we may not come out of this war a nation of drunkards.

Bullock agreed with Chamberlin; she told him in an August 5, 1866, letter:

> Am afraid I shall have to give somebody a lecture on Temperance. I am a Good Templar no longer, but vindicate the cause of Temperance none the less. Did I tell you that Gib [her brother] formed the habit of drinking while he was in the army. I thought that I stood up for the principles of Temperance, as much as one could before that, but found it to be altogether different afterward.

Captaining the Corps d'Afrique

Focus on the Future

Chamberlin's ideas about whether to live in the South or the North after the war kept changing as events of the war swirled around him. He told Bullock in his May 24, 1864, letter:

> I would give something if you poor frozen people of the North could see some of the beautiful gardens of flowers in the South, that I have seen literally trampled into the dust. I believe my love for flowers has increased every year since I was a boy and used to admire the pinks and peonys along the walk in front of your fathers house in Sennett. I believe I should like to live in the South if for no other reason. I could have such magnificent roses nearly all the year.

By August 4, 1864, he told Bullock of some objections to living in the South.

> I have an idea that there is more timbered land in Iowa than on the Plains of La. & then the great heart of Freedom and enterprise beats firmly there and the soil has never been cursed by the feet of slaves. The great objection to this state is that apples will not grow here and on that account, if for no other reason, I would not make up my mind to settle down here for life.
> My admiration of the country while campaigning sometimes has been such that I have almost made up my mind to marry some "widder" with a plantation, but they are all so cross looking here in the south & their daughters are frequently not much better and more than likely if you see a real good looking one, she will call you a "damned Yankee" as soon as your back is turned if she does not to your face, for it is a solemn fact that many of these southern ladies do swear most horribly when they get excited. So I have thought I might better let the fine plantation go than to fall into the clutches of such a one.
> You say in your letter that you think that Uncle Samuel cannot find husbands for all his fair daughters and that there are very few that would consent to have any other but a soldier, this is highly flattering and gratifying to me for I had an idea, by the cold reception that some of the old Regts. had when they went home as veterans that a soldier was looked upon at the north as a sort of nescessary evil—to be tolerated because of nescessity, but if things are really in such a state as you represent, up in Iowa, why, I shall come up there when my time is out in preference to going to New York.[6]

8. Coping with the Misery of War

A few weeks later Chamberlin told his father: "I think more and more that I will never settle down in the cold, frozen North to live. It is never too hot here for me and it is very pleasant to have warm weather all the year."

He wrote his parents in late September 1864: "I have made up my mind after mature deliberation that I choose to live <u>at home</u> however <u>uncongenial</u> the <u>climate</u> than to <u>exist</u> as <u>these</u> people do on this desolate island [Dauphine Island, Florida]."

In this October 23, 1864, letter to Bullock he provided the greatest details about his goal of avoiding the cold North:

> A farmer's life is the most independent, happy life of any under the sun, and I shall be a farmer if I ever get out of the army, which I sometimes almost despair of ever doing. I like the sunny south and were it not for the class of society that will be in the south after the war I should certainly live here. I have an idea in my mind which I have the vanity to think is a very good one. After the war there will be vast quantities of land in the South, that under a proper system of enlightened cultivation, might be made to blossom like the rose that might in fact be made a perfect paradise. This will be held as confiscated rebel property by the Government, which if not given as bounty lands to soldiers, will at least be sold at a cheap rate.
>
> I hope to help carry that [above plan] into execution before I am many years older. The great fear of sickness at the South is considerable of a humbug in my opinion. To be sure it is a change of climate to a person coming from the North, but the great amount of sickness in most localities is more oweing to a general disregard of the common laws of health and a lack of a liberal application of soap than any particular desease that is common to the climate. It is a glorious country and will yet be the home of prosperous & happy people. A country uncursed by the feet of slaves. All this upon the consideration that the cause of Justice and Freedom is to triumph in this great conflict, of which I never allow myself to entertain the least doubt. We are fighting in behalf of truths as eternal as the throne of the Most High and we cannot fail.

Although uncertain about his future, Chamberlin seemed content in his day-to-day comfort. On July 23, 1864, he wrote his brother from Carrolton, Louisiana:

> We are living very well here in camp and have things very comfortable. We are luxuriating in melons, peaches, figs &c. I have Lieut. Thompson on duty with my company & we have two Wall-tents,[7] one of which we

Captaining the Corps d'Afrique

use as a bed room and the other as a dining room &c. We each have a good bunk and musketeer bar. I have some nice cotton sheets that I captured at Cane-River crossing and I sleep between as clean clothes as you do.

 I have Fate for a housekeeper,[8] Oliver for cook & a lady of African descent for Laundress so that every thing goes on as in any well regulated household. A nice little girl comes twice a day and brings us fresh milk & I don't know but I am just as well off as if I was at home (in some respects). After all if a fellow is contented it don't make so much difference where he is.

CHAPTER 9

Changes for the Black Soldiers

Consolidation of the Black Regiments

While Chamberlin struggled with his future plans, his troops were facing some big changes, the first being a modification in organization. On July 23, 1864, Chamberlin wrote his brother from the Camp of the 97th U.S.C.I., Carrolton, Louisiana, to tell him about some major revisions in the black regiments.

> Quite an important order has been issued in this Dept. in regard to the consolidation of the colored Regts. in the Dept. There are some 23 colored Regts organized and they are to be consolidated into 10 Regts. There are to be three of the new Regts. constituted Engineer troops. Ours will be the third. A board of examination is to be appointed to examine all Officers for the positions in the new Regts. and all the supernumerary Officers are to be mustered out of the service. If the examination is carried out to the letter there will be very few Officers remaining in the service.

Apparently the changes caused some confusion. General Orders No. 88, dated July 11, 1864, ordered by Maj. Gen. E. R. S. Canby, stated: "The colored regiments of the Corps d'Afrique in the Department of the Gulf will be consolidated and reorganized as follows: ... the Eighty-second to be formed by consolidation of the Ninety-seventh and Ninety-ninth. The 82nd is constituted engineer troops." However, Chamberlin referred to the 97th U.S.C.I. as his regiment throughout the rest of his service, including when he mustered out on April 1, 1866. OR records from April 1864 to April 1866 refer to the 97th U.S.C.I.;

Captaining the Corps d'Afrique

in December 1864, both the 82nd and the 97th U.S.C.I. are listed in a battle at Pine Barren Creek.[1]

Officer standards were high. Official army records state:

> The boards of officers ordered to be convened from headquarters Department of the Gulf, for the examination of officers in regiments of black troops, will be governed by the following rules: ... All candidates for positions in the engineers below the rank of major, in addition to what is required for same rank in infantry, must be proficient in algebra, geometry, trigonometry, &c, surveying, linear and topographical drawing, the elements of civil engineering, especially those which relate to building materials and strength of materials such as appertain to bridges, locks, dams. &c., the elements of field fortifications, and manner of making reconnaissance and keeping journal of march, &c., the different styles of pontoon bridges, their equipment, &c, and the manner of laying them down and taking them up, the different styles of raft, flying bridges, &c.[2]

Chamberlin's July 23 letter continues the explanation:

> Officers who pass the examination for Officers of Inf'ty, but fail to pass as Engineers will be recommended for positions in Infantry Regts. but you may depend on it, I shall either stay in this Regt. as Engineers or leave the service.
>
> I don't propose to go into any colored Infantry Reg't. The Government does not have the moral vim (or if it has it does not exercise it) to protect the Officers of colored troops from all the ferocity of Southern Devils & I for one, don't propose to risk my valuable life in any such position.[3] In these new Regts. of Engineers, they will be used as sappers and miners during sieges and in building fortifications.[4] It is very difficult to tell at present when the consolidation will take place, but we are all anxious to have it as soon as possible so we can go home before winter if we go. Certain It is, I don't lose any sleep or flesh in view of the coming change. I think I have been in the Service quite long enough at any rate, and should not feel bad to go home.
>
> Write Soon. Love to all & all the neighbor's children & girls.
> John N. Chamberlin

Pay Equalization for Black Troops

A second major change during the summer of 1864 was a long-overdue pay equalization for the black troops. Chamberlin's Co. E, 97th

9. Changes for the Black Soldiers

U.S.C.I., was sent from New Orleans to Bayou St. John on August 1. Two days later in his diary he described a long-awaited change:

> An order recd at Hd. Qrs. giving colored troops the same pay, rations, clothing, medical attendance and every-thing excepting Bounty that is allowed to white soldiers. When our men get their next 4 months pay they will receive 88 dollars apiece. They have been encouraged to think that they were to have the same pay and allowances as other soldiers so long that I am glad that the order has been Recd.

Unequal pay for black soldiers was a complicated issue, as Smith describes. In August 1862, Secretary of War Stanton had promised equal pay for black and white recruits ($13 per month, $3 of which constituted a clothing allowance). However, in 1863, the War Department ruled that under the Militia Act of July 1862, all blacks were to be paid $10 per month with $3 withheld by the government for clothing. Writers of the Militia Act had assumed that blacks would serve as laborers, not as soldiers, and thus should be paid less than whites. Abolitionists and the black soldiers themselves protested the inequality of pay, arguing that not only had blacks performed courageously in combat, but because of their race they were also exposed to greater risks than white troops.[5]

President Lincoln and Frederick Douglass disagreed over the issue of pay for black soldiers. According to Smith, Lincoln urged the blacks to be patient. In August 1863 the President reminded Douglass that many whites still considered the idea of black soldiers offensive, and that paying them less would make their enlistment more acceptable. Nevertheless, the black leader remained dismayed at the government's unequal compensation for black and white soldiers, even when at the time of their enlistment the black soldiers had been promised the same pay as the whites.[6]

As Chamberlin reported above, Congress finally acted on this issue on June 15, 1864. Smith reports that pay for black and white troops was finally equalized, but with a major qualification. Soldiers who had been enslaved at the start of the war would receive retroactive pay only to January 1, 1864. Men who were free at the beginning of hostilities would receive back pay to the date of their enlistment, as well as bounty payments. On March 3, 1865, Congress finally granted full retroactive pay to all black soldiers who had been promised equal pay upon mustering into the service. Two months later the War Department authorized bounties for all black recruits who enlisted after July 18, 1864, no matter when they had been freed. Slaves who enlisted before that date, however, were denied bounties. The War Department considered the slaves' freedom to be adequate bounty.[7]

In spite of terrible living and fighting conditions, black troops were amazingly resilient and performed valiantly. In Smith's words:

> In exchange for the hardships and indignities they endured—half wages, inferior medical care, inadequate weapons, inappropriate rations, insufficient training, the prospect of being enslaved or executed if captured, repeated insults from white troops, brutal punishments that smacked of slave discipline, and much more—the U.S. Colored Troops carried out various military duties, and in the process surprised a doubting Northern public and their severest and most racist critics.[8]

New Duties for the Engineering Regiments

The third change for Chamberlin's black troops was the assignment of new duties. Formerly they had worked around waterways—clearing channels and building dams and bridges. In May 1864 they helped build a fort in Morganza; this work included digging rifle pits, leveling hills of dirt, and cutting trees, as well as more skilled jobs like making hurdles and facines (described in Appendix C). By the fall of 1864, using Chamberlin's training as an engineer, his company built traverses, bastions, parapets and embrasures.[9] He described his training in a July 8, 1864, letter to his sister.

> I will now take a few moments to write a short letter to you. We are still in Camp at Carrolton. We have been quite busy of late, making out Returns of Property for which I am responsible, such as Ordnance & Camp Equipage, 1½ hours drill in the morning and a long lesson in Duane's Manuel for Engineers, having a Recitation by all the Commissioned Officers at 3 O'clock P.M. every day and practice in constructing facines, Hurdles, Gabions & in the Practical Operations of a siege. I like the exercises very much.

Chamberlin was referring to the important training manual, *Manual for Engineer Troops*, by Capt. J. C. Duane,[10] published in 1860. Chamberlin was studying Parts II and III, sections of which are reprinted in

9. Changes for the Black Soldiers

Appendix C. This reprint illustrates—especially in section 34, "OF HURDLES"—the complexity of his engineering work and the detailed instructions available to him.

On August 20, 1864, Chamberlin and his regiment were ordered to go to Mobile Bay, where they put their new engineering skills to work by repairing Fort Gaines on Dauphine Island. Chamberlin wrote to his father on August 23 in the letter excerpted below.

Fort Gaines, Mobile Harbor, Aug. 23d 1864

Dear Father:

We left New Orleans Sunday night the 21st Inst.[11] at 9 O'clock P.M. We embarked on a river steamer without any chart of the Gulf, and at Pilottown took a pilot on board who proved to be very ignorant of the where abouts of things in general in the Gulf. We went straight ahead about in the direction of the Island of Cuba, as near as I could judge untill we came upon a low Island and came near being stuck in the sand, but the boat was stopped and turned about and by the aid of a pocket map of Louisiana we searched around till night when we arrived at Ship Island, and at midnight anchored inside a little Island about 25 miles from Mobile. At daylight this morning we moved up and arrived at the wharf at Fort Gaines at 9 O'clock A.M.

We are now on shore and have gone into camp near Fort Gaines. Fort Gaines is situated on the East end of Dauphin [sic] Island and is quite a formidable work, although far inferior in strength to Fort Morgan. The Island very-much resembles Santa Rosa being low and narrow and formed of white sand. The upper part of the Island is wooded with Norway pine, and this end is covered with low shrubs and bushes. It is difficult to say how long we shall remain here, but I presume a movement will soon be made upon the city [Mobile] & then I hope to be there myself. I suppose the Rebels have some Gunboats yet in the harbor but it strikes me that the surrender of these two forts [Gaines and Morgan] must sound like the trumpet of doom to frightened people of Mobile.

We had a very pleasant voyage here & I think this is a much more healthy place than New Orleans, as we have a fine place for sea-bathing.

I am in good health & hope this will find you all enjoying the same blessing.

From your affectionate son,
John N. Chamberlin

On September 21, 1864, "Captain Chamberlain" was ordered to "act as Asst. Engineer and general Superintendent" in the repairs on

Captaining the Corps d'Afrique

Fort Gaines, reporting for orders to Lieut. C. J. Allen (see Appendix D). Allen wrote:

> I propose to recommence work to-morrow, by dividing the force, so as to put half upon the body of the place, and the other half upon the works in the covered way. The carpenters to be kept, distinct, from the rest. The work upon the body of the place consists in raising the parapet upon the curtain in rear of the Demi-lune,[12] three feet and placing the guns in embrasure, finishing the bastion, & traverses, and erecting a bomb-proof in rear of bastion no 4. In the correct way, there are traverses and platforms to be erected. The best workmen will be required upon the body of the place. We will also want a small squad of men to tar bags for the embrasures. By dividing the force in this way, or an approximation to it, I think that the work will proceed more systematically. A few sharp spades will be required, for skimming the turf from the parapet. The teams will report, as usual, to haul lumber, or earth, as may be required.[13]

In a late September 1864 letter to his parents, Chamberlin described the work.

> Our Regt is now detailed on Special duty in repairing Fort Gaines under the direction of an Officer of the Regular U.S. Engrs. We are to work exclusively on the Fort and are to furnish no other details. We work from 6 to 9 in the A.M. and from 3 to 6 in the P.M. and have no drill. Only a part of the Officers work daily so we do not anticipate a very severe time of it while we remain here. I am sure I like to be here as in New Orleans and it is much better for the Regt for obvious reasons.

Educating Black Soldiers

The fourth change for the black solders was the possibility of learning to read and write. Chamberlin had been a teacher prior to the war and considered education essential to the nation, as he described in this letter to Bullock on August 4, 1864.

> You are training intellects that may yet sway the destinies of Nations & mark their names upon the age in which they live. Your task is one involving more of responsibility than we are apt to realize. The influence of the schoolroom has more to do with moulding the character of a Nation than all other influences combined. This is a sweeping assertion, I know but from all that I have seen I believe it is true. The influence of home is

9. Changes for the Black Soldiers

considered stronger than all others, but I take into consideration the multitudes of the young who have no good home influence thrown around them. The position of the teacher is an important one, for the bulwark of our free institutions is the proper education of the children of the nation. Why! I don't believe that these fellows down here would have kicked up this infernal war if they had had plenty of Free-schools, with good faithful School-ma'ams. They are the most ignorant people as a class that I ever beheld.

In a letter written to Bullock May 2, 1864, Chamberlin wrote:

You wished to know all about my company. Well, I will give you a little information on that point. I have 54 black men under my charge in the uniforms of "Uncle Sam's children" armed and equipped and ready to fight or work for the downfall of the Slaveholders rebellion and their own freedom at the same time. My appointment as Captain came from Maj. Gen. Banks and I feel it to be a position of considerable responsibility and trust.

My company has been in two slight skirmishes and were exposed to fire at Port Hudson almost as much as any of the troops there and they have always behaved well.[14] When I first came among them they all looked alike to me, and I didn't like to get too near them but this repugnance has worn away and I can now see as much difference among them as among white men and I have many a man in my company that I should feel more honored in taking by the hand than some of my old copperhead friends in Sennett, and elsewhere.[15] On the whole I like my position in the Regt. very much, and although I sometimes get almost discouraged and homesick, yet I always try to make the best of the circumstances by which I am surrounded and hope for brighter skies in the morrow.

When I first took command of the company not a man knew B. from a broomstick, but I bought some primary reading books and with a little assistance quite a number of them can read considerable now. An Officer in one of these Regts, if he does his duty by the men under his charge has very much more to do than an Officer in a white Regt. There is so much thinking and planning to do for them and so many letters to be written to wives and sweethearts for them and then many of them are anxious to learn to read (and I can-not refuse to show them when I have time). On the whole I am generally pretty busy. I think any company would make a pretty good school for you if you wish to preside over a small congregation of "wooly-heads." But it would be very discouraging business to try to instruct them after they are grown up, for although they are only grown up children in intellect, it is difficult for many of them to retain much in their memory.

Captaining the Corps d'Afrique

In these last lines, Chamberlin would have been influenced by the racist views of his times. He may also have been reflecting the challenges of trying to teach adults who had no previous schooling and only haphazard education in the army.

Chamberlin wrote his brother in mid–October, "We are busy drilling our men and had the first Batillion drill this P.M. The men are all anxious to learn and in many things improve faster than white soldiers. Most of them express an ardent wish to learn to read and if we ever get into camp I shall try to teach some of them." According to Eric Foner, many former slaves learned to read and write in the army. They were taught by northern aid societies or by literary clubs organized among themselves. Keith Wilson gives extensive information on literacy among the black troops. He describes how reading became a revolutionary expression of liberation from slavery. Chaplains encouraged reading as a way to improve the spiritual welfare of the troops. Some officers saw literacy as a way to prepare men for citizenship after the war, while others realized that teaching troops to read improved military efficiency and created a pool of non-commissioned officers to help with routine administration. Reading and letter-writing became popular recreational activities. Educational opportunities were varied and haphazard, and often the soldiers taught themselves, aided by a few who were slightly literate. Many officers and chaplains supplied basic materials and helped when possible.[16]

A white officer was bound to establish a strong connection with his black troops through the teacher/student relationship, also through the very personal actions of writing and reading their letters for them. Smith gives other reasons that some white officers bonded with their black troops. He describes the troops as cleaner, more sober, and more respectful of white women than the white soldiers whom these officers used to command. Glatthaar states that some white officers and their black soldiers developed a degree of dependence on each other because the Confederates threatened to execute captured white officers and enslave captured black troops. The black troops realized that the white officers "were voluntarily placing their lives in grave jeopardy. And the white officers, recognizing the perils of surrender, had to depend even more on the performance of their troops in battle."[17]

Chamberlin described another way that his soldiers depended on

9. Changes for the Black Soldiers

and also trusted him in an **October 11**, 1864, diary entry, "Received 4 months pay from Paymaster Maj. Geo. Truesdale. The men recd from 64 to 125 Dollars each. My men have brought me about half a bushel of Green-Backs for me to keep. Shall have to invest it somewhere in New Orleans."

Some black troops were grateful for the extra time the officers spent helping them. Chamberlin's troops were very thankful to him, as he told Bullock in this letter:

Camp of the 97th U.S.C.I., Fort Gaines Ala, Oct 23d/64

My Dear Friend:

To-day is my birth-day. To-day I am 27 years old. Whew! how time has sped. I am really getting to be an old "feller." It occurs to me that the caution I once voluntarily gave you, (to not laugh at such fellows as Bill Tanner, or you would wake up some fine morning and find yourself an old maid,) might better be taken home to myself, for in the natural course of time I may wake up some fine morning, or some morning that is not so fine and find myself an old bachelor—well never mind I won't think any more about that. I have been in the war more than three years. Been three years without any home, not knowing where I might lay my head from one night to another. I didn't have much idea of what a blessing a good home was untill after I came into the army. When I had been in the army about three months, how I used to think of home & I thought then that if I ever did get back, there might be a great many little vexations that I should never find fault about again. Then, I was a little home-sick (I suppose) but I have got over that, however I sometimes have a good many thoughts about getting through this wild roaming life in the army and living again in some place that I may call my home. I believe I could appreciate it now.

Have just recd a present of 75 Dollars from my Company. I intend to send north and get an American Lever silver watch with a suitable inscription upon it. I don't know but I feel just as proud of it as I should if it came from a company of white men. It is a birth-day present that I shall always remember with great pleasure.

At that point the net monthly pay for black soldiers was $7. According to Chamberlin's October 17, 1864, official report of "Receipt-Roll of Clothing Issued in the Month of October, 1864," there were forty-seven non-commissioned officers, musicians & privates in E Company (see Appendix E). An equal share from each soldier for

Captaining the Corps d'Afrique

Chamberlin's gift would have been $1.60 out of their $7 monthly income.[18] That was a very generous birthday gift!

With new organization, better pay, training in news skills, and the beginnings of literacy, military service was preparing the blacks for a hopeful future. Would the 1864 presidential election set them back?

CHAPTER 10

The Presidential Election and the War

Chamberlin's black soldiers were very concerned about the outcome of the 1864 election. The Democratic platform called for peace, with many supporters saying, "peace at any cost." A compromise with the South would leave the blacks in submission. The possible influence of the election results on the outcome of the war weighed heavily on the minds of the soldiers, black and white. Were their sacrifices in vain? Chamberlin concluded his October 23, 1864, letter to Bullock with some strong comments.

> There must be the most intense excitement at the North in regard to the Presidential Election. It is more momentous in its results than any that have preceded it since this has been a nation. I have often wondered that such a meeting as the Chicago Convention could have been allowed anywhere at the North.[1] But after all perhaps it was better to allow them to unfold their treasonable schemes. What an unenviable position McClellan now occupies. A man who has been so long a Maj. Gen in the army of the Union accepting the nomination for the presidency from the foulest most infernal conclave of traitors that have ever held session on earth. That convention has said about as plainly as words can say, "We will have peace on any terms." That means Submission to the demands of the Rebels and a peace on their own terms, which can only be ruin and dishonor to the North. It would take a chapter to enumerate the evils that would inevitably befall the people of the North. No wonder when our pickets hurrah for Lincoln, the Reb hurrahs for McClellan. It almost makes my blood boil to think that there are so many in the North who would thus sell their great birth-right of Freedom & security of life and property for less than a "mess of pottage."[2] Some of those old scoundrels will suffer, as you say when "we all come home from the war." I have a sort

Captaining the Corps d'Afrique

of itching in my finger ends to get hold of some of the home traitors. I tell you they will have to keep just as still as mice to be at all safe.

The election of Lincoln, which is almost a foregone conclusion in my mind, will be a greater blow to the Rebels than two Atlanta's,[3] but we have a desperate enemy to contend with, and nothing but grim terrible war can be relied upon to bring them to submission. The end must be near.

> My kind regards to all, Write sooner and believe
> me as ever your true friend,
> John N. Chamberlin

Chamberlin amplified his thoughts on the upcoming election in an October 30, 1864, letter to his sister-in-law Sarah (George Chamberlin's wife). He concludes this letter with a personal touch.

Every day, as the election approaches, all see that this Presidential Election is of the most immense importance as regards to future glory or shame of the Nation. The election of Lincoln will be the death knell of the hopes of the Rebel leaders in a divided North. It will be worth more to our cause than any one victory in the field.

It is their only hope. Let such a weak minded vacillating man be placed in the Presidential chair, who would certainly gather around him such men as Seymour, Wood, Valandigham [sic], Vourhies [sic][4] & Co. as his political advisers, and the South could see through their troubles pretty clearly. In the first place the war would stop. That is one of the cardinal principles in their policy. Peace on any terms. That simply means to let the rebels alone to have there own way. Withdraw all our armies from the territory claimed by the Rebels, give up all the Ports & the Mississippi River, and begin to build forts on the frontier (I suppose) to keep the Rebs. out of the North, for that must be a natural consequence. Then the whole North go down on their knees to the south chanting the 51st psalm,[5] and then if they in the abundance of their brotherly love saw fit to come back into the Union, with what vile, dirty old sins they have left clinging to them. Receive them with open arms, like the prodigal son, shoulder their debt and in every way treat them like good decent fellows who only kicked up this little riot just for the amusement of the thing. But if they won't consent to come back with all these inducements and all others that we, in our very "umble" condition, see fit to grant, why, as "the war has been a failure" we will let them go, and recognize their concern as an Aristocracy on the broad domain of what was once the United States of America.

But I believe the people of this country are not ready for any such kind of a peace as that would be. Peace is a boon to be desired. Oh! how gladly

10. The Presidential Election and the War

Figure 7. Johnny R. Chamberlin, born in 1864, son of Sarah Higgins Chamberlin and George Chamberlin. He was the nephew of John Chamberlin, to whom the photograph was sent in October 1864. From John Chamberlin's photo album, see figure 6. Courtesy Lelia and Paul Klear.

it would be welcomed by the soldier in the field, in the Hospitals, and in the camps, but never a peace with the angel of Liberty dropping her tears over the grave of American Freedom. Better a whole eternity of war than any such humiliating submission to the demands of the infernal traitors North & South. I don't know whether I shall live to see the end of this war, or not, although I expect to if I don't die pretty soon, but if ever such a man as McClellan is elected President by the free people of the North, and the plans of the Northern peace sneaks are carried out, I mean to leave the country and never come back. I shouldn't fear that I could get into a worse place any where this side of Pandemonium.[6] But I won't indulge in any gloomy apprehensions for the future, for McClellan ain't going to be elected, and the glorious old Republic ain't going to the Devil half as fast as some of our friends at the North try to persuade themselves, and every body else.

Captaining the Corps d'Afrique

Much obliged for the Photograph of your 2nd edition [Johnny, apparently named after his Uncle John]. Someone said he resembled me [fig. 7], but I don't have a very distinct recollection how I did look at that tender age. However he is a fine looking chap & will (no doubt) make some noise in the world, if nothing more. God bless the little fellow whether he ever amounts to any more in the world than his name-sake or not.

On November 8, 1864, Chamberlin's mind was back on the election held that day. He wrote the following to his father from Fort Gaines, Alabama:

The waves break in monotonous music on the beach, and the balmy South wind sweeps across the Inland in fitful gusts, but there is nothing peculiarly unusual in Nature to indicate that this morning's sun ushers in a day more important in its results upon the future than any that ever yet dawned upon the American people. It will be a day all through the North of intense excitement.

In the army, not so much of excitement, but of some anxiety for the soldiers want to know just about who are their friends at the North and who are their enemies, for disguise it as they may, the people are either for us, or most decidedly against us. I say there is very little excitement here for although we frequently talk about the approaching election, it is with no doubtful fore-bodings of the result, for that is a forgone conclusion in the minds of most of the soldiers, and it is now only a question of majorities with us. We have now and then a man who says he is for McClellan, not so much that he has any preference for him as to have an argument with some one upon the subject.

The day will pass off quietly enough here, and there will be no black eyes or bloody noses in consequence thereof I dare venture. But it strikes me if I were in Sennett to-day, which there's no great danger of, I should feel some like disturbing the equanimity if not the equilibrium of some of those old hoary rebels who, under the specious plea of peace, are trying, however unsuccessfully it may be, to vote upon us an eternal war or, what would be worse still, an ignominious and dishonorable peace. What effect this election will have upon the rebels remains to be seen, but it is very evident to every one that the guiding star of their hope has been in a divided North and the election of a peace candidate. The army has been knocking the pegs from under them some of late, but it seems to me that this election must be quite suggestive of an elevated position with a strong smell of hemp & sulphur, and nothing to stand on, to the leaders of this foul revolt, and anything but encouraging to the great unwashed, uncombed, and shirtless that compose the rank and file of their armies.

10. The Presidential Election and the War

> I have come to look upon this struggle for Right and Freedom, as one that however long the dark clouds may lower over us, that there is a tranquil and serene sky beyond, and that the old ship of state is sailing, through the midst of the breakers and sand bars of this terrible rebellion, and the ice-bergs and chilling breath of foreign scorn & contumely and manifold protestations of sympathy with our enemy, to a haven of lasting quietness and peace, where the breezes of heaven may never fan the cheek of a slave, but where "justice and Freedom may flourish out of the earth and righteousness look down from heaven."[7] It takes the most fiery trials to bring forth the sterling qualities of Nations as well as individuals, and after the smoke of this tremendous conflict has rolled away, if we are not a freer, a more just and merciful people, we may at least have learned the great lesson that national crimes against justice and humanity, although perpetrated upon the most degraded of all the great Brotherhood of men, must sooner or later be visited by the just judgments which they deserve.

In his Second Inaugural Address on March 4, 1865, as Goodwin notes, President Lincoln "suggested that God had given 'to both North and South, this terrible war' as punishment for their shared sin of slavery."[8] This issue will be discussed in more detail in chap. 14. Chamberlin closed his election-day letter to his father with a critical view of the North's responsibility for the Civil War.

> But I was going to add that when you come to simmer the whole thing down, you will see that we at the North are in a measure to blame for the present state of things. It was all along very convenient for us to get cheap sugars & cotton, and for all we were so loud in our protestations of sympathy with the poor, abused, manacled "nigger" why we didn't see what we could do—the Institution would ruin itself after a while—and we must leave it to other generations to settle this thing, and have almost said mentally, with a confused notion that we had nothing to do with the matter: "Well, God is over all, and there are souls that must be saved" and the time will come when this thing will be shaken from our skirts, but the good Lord only knows when, but it must be in the future and although I have fearful and bloody apprehensions for the future, of battle fields and midnight conflagrations and all the grim untold horrors of war yet it won't do to trouble these southern fellows too much in our day, at least.

In a letter written approximately November 17, 1864, to one of his brothers, Chamberlin talked more about the reelection of Lincoln and the war.

Captaining the Corps d'Afrique

Next Thursday is Thanksgiving (I believe). Three years since I was at home at a thanksgiving dinner or any other kind of dinner. To look back to that time it don't seem long, but events that might make the history of a lifetime have been crowded into those three years.

What effect the reelection of Lincoln will have upon the duration of the war remains to be seen. Whether the people of the south, seeing their cause is hopeless, will attempt to make some arrangements with the federal Government to come back into the union, or stung by the tremendous losses and desolations of the war, their leaders will control them to fight to the bitter end, remains to be seen.

One thing, however, is now certain. The whole energies of the nation will still be steadily exerted with terrible crushing effect upon the sinking energies of the rebellion. It is a terrible—an inexorable, a resisters power which has been called into existence by the madness of the slaveholders rebellions. The prophesy of A. H. Stephens has been more than verified in the untold suffering, devastation and loss that the South have endured.[9] Could all the people of these deluded states [have] looked through the vista of these three years of fire & blood and have seen the dire panorama of woe that has been presented, how would they have shrunk in horror from the contemplation of it! If they conclude to continue the war till the bitter end, it cannot protract the contest many months more, for I believe they have reached an extremity that is very bitter to them already and the election of Lincoln will be a pill that will have very little of sweetness in it for them.

The future of the Republic is yet sublime, and many of us will live to see the Nation redeemed, clothed and in her right mind. In full faith of the good time coming, when we shall be a nation of Justice and universal freedom, I remain, as ever your Brother
                John N. Chamberlin

Chapter 11

Return to Florida

The End Is in Sight

Chamberlin may have assumed the future of the nation was secured, but there was still work to be done. His regiment was ordered to return to Florida and to repair Fort Barrancas. The soldiers arrived near Fort Pickens and the Fort McRee lighthouse[1] on the steamer *Clyde*[2] on November 14, 1864, and spent the next few days cleaning up their camp and fixing up their tents, necessitating a steamer trip to Pensacola to get lumber. Chamberlin commented in his diary on **November 17** that "the greater share of the city [Pensacola] has been burned. The streets and gardens are all overgrown with rank weeds and bushes and wild animals frequent the streets. It is a sad picture of ruin and desolation. Secured a good supply of lumber and got back to camp at 9 O'clock P.M." After a second trip to Pensacola, he related, "The people of the city say that they can't stand it there this winter they have nothing to eat but sweet potatoes and the supply is very limited. They have all their earthly possessions in Pensacola and if they come within the lines they will have to leave almost everything behind."

According to diary entries of late November, shortly after his arrival at Fort Barrancas Chamberlin had made his tent comfortable with a good floor and frame. He had also gotten a load of bricks and had a chimney built. After he had made himself comfortable in his new setting, his thoughts turned homeward. He wrote to his brother:

> It is quite chilly tonight and is raining fast. It reminds me of an old October rain at home, when we used to sit around the fire and read the news and eat apples &c or go upstairs and braid up seed corn, or in utter desperation for something better to do, go hunting and come back wetter,

Captaining the Corps d'Afrique

but better men, for the exercise. Well those were in our young day, but now it strikes me, we are pretty old "fellers." I expected that before this you would be chased up so close by some of those nice, disinterested young "femuales" that you would have to surrender from sheer exhaustion. Bully for you: old boy. You have held your ground well. Don't give up the ship untill you see the proper moment at any rate. You may have to go to the wars yet and how "drefful" it would be to leave a poor childless widow and fatherless "orphings" to lament your untimely "draft." If you ain't gobbled up by some of "em" when I get home I will probably get you started on some Utopian scheme in some direction or settle down quietly with you and keep bachelors Hall, but if you are gone the way of all flesh, when I get home, I shall have no resource left but to look around for some one else, for after very mature deliberation for several years, I have come to the unanimous conclusion in my own mind that it is wholly incompatible with any man's health, comfort, happiness, good temper and even his religion, to sleep alone, especially in cold weather. Acting upon these considerations I have taken a bedfellow, (nothing improper do not suppose) one Lt. Peter Thomson of our Reg't who is also alone. I think that I forgot to mention that I am again alone with my company. My 1st Lt. [Charles P.] Haseltine, is detached from the Reg't and has gone to Texas to take charge of some earthworks on Brazas [sic] Island.[3]

On Thanksgiving Day (**November 24**) he noted in his diary:

No work done to-day. Just three years ago today that I was at home to Thanksgiving dinner. During those three years of war, I have seen very much of the world and of the unspeakable horrors of war. It has carried mourning and desolation into every neighborhood and almost every family in the land, and still the strife goes on with a steadily increasing magnitude and bitterness. The south is not yet subdued but they tremble with weakness and the end can-not be far off. Didn't do much but sit by the fire. Had a very good dinner and a good appetite.

He expanded more on his thoughts about the long war in a Thanksgiving letter to his mother.

Camp of the 97th U.S. Col. Infty., Fort Barrancas Fla., Nov. 24"/64
Dear Mother:

To-day completes three years since I was at home to thanksgiving. How little any one then anticipated what these three years had in store for us, and it is but natural for me at the end of these three years to take a retrospective view of the past. It has been a long time to me and were it not for the continual changes and excitements of a soldier's life, I am sure it

11. Return to Florida

would have seemed much longer. During the first year of my service although I was never homesick, yet I was continually thinking of home and hoping and expecting the war to close, but gradually as the desperate character of our enemy became developed I came to the settled conviction that at the end of my three years we should not see peace, and therefore I made up my mind to it accordingly.

My intercourse with all kinds of men in the army has given me a good opportunity to study character, which is of some advantage to me. I find that although the maxim "to treat every man as if he was a rascal untill you find him to be an honest man" may be the best policy, yet it is a very disagreeable way to associate with ones fellows. Better to have a little faith and trust in our common humanity and consider every man honest until you find him a rogue. I suppose you may think that after three years of this wild roving life—exposed to all manner of dangers and hardships from the Elements of Nature and the more vicious Elements of Secession, that I have become a wild, heartless, aimless adventurer, or on the other hand a sour, gloomy Misanthrope. Well! this is not exactly the case, for although I often have a great many roving Devil-may-care thoughts, still when I come home from the war, I believe I shall appreciate the comfort and quiet of home quite as much as if I had never been away. I tell you that for all I have mixed so little of home with my correspondence, there have been times out of number when I have kept up a terrible thinking about that particular locality. But I generally don't accept it as my fate to stay in the service until the war is over if the rebels don't get me out of it first.

Three years ago to-night I left home with a determination to do my duty wherever I was placed. Since then to the present time the most terrible war that ever desolated any nation has made the old Republic tremble, and to-day the most formidable and effective armies of modern times are confronting each other. During those three years what an untold sea of woe and crime has rolled over the nation.

The Slaveholders in their mad lust for power let loose upon themselves the most terrible scourge that ever befalls a people. There is nothing too holy for war to lay its hands upon. On every campaign, no matter how strictly orders are carried out, one sees enough of desolation and ruin, of misery and wretchedness, of homeless and helpless humanity, of faces in which hopelessness and despair are depicted, enough to make angels weep and devils jubilant, enough of everything unholy and unclean, to make a man curse a thousand times the authors of this foul revolt. From the time that the old 75th left Santa Rosa [in May 1862] until this day, the wildest tales of romance would scarcely equal the horrors of this war. I have seen very little of what has transpired and yet I hope never to see so much of suffering and woe hereafter. This once happy and peaceful nation has been made one vast boiling seething hell and devils incarnate have seemed to walk the earth. What are the leading men of this unholy rebellion if not embodiments of old Satan. They know what they are attempting. It is no excuse that they are sincere and persistent in their designs, they know that they are rebelling against the most free and liberal government on earth, and they know that there schemes are devilish. But what shall be said of that other class of men at the north who would sell out now at this late hour of the conflict, not only all the material triumphs of the war, but also the sublime moral victory we have achieved, to the base scoundrels who have so long trailed the national banner in the dust. To sell out all this for the transcient dream of an ignominious peace which can never be realized.

When the future historian of this great conflict records the names of those who stood by the country in her hour of peril, where will the names of these men appear? Their names will be with the long black list who sought to overthrow the constitution and dethrone the Goddess of Liberty on the American Continent. For the enemy who take up arms and fight for what they claim we can have some respect, but language can frame no epithet that will sufficiently express the baseness and treachery of the Northern Copperheads.

Around Thanksgiving, having set up camp, Chamberlin and his men went back to work on their first assignment: to raise the parapets of Fort Barrancus and Redoubt three feet higher and make embrasures for the guns. Chamberlin was in charge of the revetting.[4]

The day after Thanksgiving, **November 25**, the soldiers "worked on the Fort. Only two teams to draw sods, so the work progresses very slowly. The revetting is all done with sods and it takes a great quantity of them."[5] On Saturday, **November 26,** they worked on the fort in the morning and drilled from 4:00 p.m. until long after dark. On Sunday, **November 27,** Chamberlin said, "Had Brigade drill from 10 A.M. to 1 P.M. We the line Officers prepare to enter a protest against this way of doing things while we work five days and a half in each week. We don't care to drill nights and Sundays to make some one think he is Brig. General." On the next Sunday, **December 4,** Chamberlin noted, "Had a Brigade drill 2 hours in the A.M." He wrote in his diary that work on the fortifications and some drilling continued during the week. However, they did not drill on the following Sunday, either because it was very cold or because of their earlier protest.

11. Return to Florida

Battle of Pine Barren Creek

In mid-December 1864 Chamberlin described in his diary the fight in which his regiment (the 97th U.S.C.I.) and the 82nd U.S.C.I. participated at Pine Barren Creek.[6]

December 13: Recd orders in the morning to be in readiness for a march at 12 O'clock M. Left Barrancas at 3 o'clock P.M. and marched 13 miles and encamped 6 miles North of Pensacola. Three Rebs came in and gave themselves up. Slept very nicely in the pine woods. No enemy to be seen. The cavalry 15 miles ahead.

December 14: Were up at 3 O'clock and started at 4½ O'c/A. Very good road through the woods. Marched till 5 O'clock P.M. and made about 25 miles.

December 15: Reveille at 2 O'clock A.M. and after Breakfast they started at 3 A.M. Our reg't guards the train. We have 45 wagons. Cavalry overtook the Enemy at 11 A.M. Posted at the farther end of bridge which they tried to burn, had several men wounded, put out the fire before the bridge was ruined. 10 prisoners captured. Marched 27 miles and encamped within two miles of Pollard [fig. 1, chap. 1].[7] Expect to have a fight there tomorrow.

December 16: All quiet during the night. Reveille at 5 A.M. Cavalry started at day-light. Marched into Pollard without opposition. A small village of 30 or 40 houses & a large rail-road Depot. Destroyed the R .R. toward Mobile & Montgomery.[8] Quite a large amount of tents and other Q. M. stores in town which were all burned. Nearly the whole town destroyed. A locomotive came down from Montgomery in the P.M. but upon seeing what was up went back immediately. A courier arrived from Barrancas with orders for us to return at once. Marched back 12 miles at night and encamped about 3 miles from Escambia creek. Were obliged to ford one stream as the bridge was burnt. The Rebs are after us.

December 17: No fires allowed last night. Started forward at 4 O'clock A.M. Found a small force of the enemy posted across Escambia creek at the bridge which was partially torn up. Gave them one round from our two howitzers and then our Reg't. charged across the bridge. Col. Robinson badly wounded in the thigh. Lt. Boughten killed, Lt. Burnham wounded and several enlisted men killed and wounded,[9] <u>no prisoners taken</u>. Found a whole Brigade of the enemy in front, but they dare not stand against us. Marched through the woods in line of battle all the A.M. skirmishing all the time. Stopped half an hour at noon to repair a bridge. The enemy appeared at dusk in our rear in full force. Had a sharp fight

Captaining the Corps d'Afrique

with them. One of my men killed. Enemy repulsed, continued the march, the Enemy still harassing our rear. Reached Pine Barren creek at 11 o'clock P.M. Bridge gone, had to ford the stream. 4 of our wagons were stuck in the mud. The Rebs. came as expected. Our Reg't. and the 82nd all lay down on the crest of a hill and on came the Rebs. with the most devilish yells. When within ten rods we gave them a most terrific volley and followed them. No prisoners were taken.

Gen. St. John Liddell, a slaveholder and a commander of the Confederate cavalry on December 17th, gave the black Union soldiers a compliment. According to Sean O'Brien, Liddell admitted, "The Negroes fought well, obstinately, and pressed us back steadily."[10]

December 18: As soon as our train had crossed the creek we continued the march untill 2 O'clock P.M. making 36 hours of continual marching & fighting. Halted 2 hours for dinner. The rebs. thought to gobble us all in the night. This midnight fight in the pine-woods was the most thrilling and beautiful scene that I ever saw. The rebs. were commanded by a Brig. Gen. and he was killed in the night. We found Gray-backs all through the woods where the enemy retreated but none of them will ever cost the U.S. anything for rations. Marched untill 8 O'clock at night and encamped in the woods. I went out on picket with 50 men. All quiet during the night. Beautiful night we have had fine weather ever since we started.

December 19: Reveille at 3 O'clock A.M. Resumed the march immediately and arrived opposite Gun-boat Point at 10 O'clock A.M. Here we had to ford an arm of the sea about ½ mile, but not deep. Reached camp at noon pretty well worn out. The whole distance traveled must have been 150 miles and I didn't blister my feet at all. We were gone just six days. To much praise cannot be bestowed upon Lt. Col. Spurling of the 2" Maine Cavalry who took command of the Expedition after Robinson was wounded.[11] He is a strictly temperant man and to his clear unmuddled brain we owe very much. He seemed almost omnipotent and decided the course to be taken under all circumstance without the least hesitation. He deserves promotion if ever a man did.

In an official report dated December 31, 1864 (Appendix F), Chamberlin described the losses at Pine Barren Creek.

I certify, on honor, that on the 18th day of Dec, 1864, at Pine Barren Creek Fla, the Stores enumerated below were lost under the following circumstances.

The Regt. to which my Company belongs was engaged with the enemy, and one Private was killed and one Private wounded in my Company. The

11. Return to Florida

arms and accoutrements of these men were left on the field, as the Regt. fell back immediately after the engagement, and they could not be recovered.

Several other reports on Pine Barren Creek illustrate the difficulty of accurate reporting. Brig. Gen. Thomas J. McKean's brief official report generally agreed with Chamberlin's description and noted that "our loss is 1 officer and 16 men killed and 3 officers and 61 men wounded. Colonel Robinson, commanding the expedition, severely, though not dangerously wounded." Confederate Gen. G. T. Beauregard officially reported that after the Union soldiers left Pollard, "they were pursued thirty miles, losing a portion of their transportation, baggage, and supplies, leaving many dead negro troops on the road."[12] Arthur Bergeron adds this account: "The Rebels [under General Liddell, commander at Blakely] pursued the Federals for about 30 miles, skirmishing all along the way, then finally gave up the chase because the Confederates' horses became too exhausted to go farther." The Confederates had the railroad at Pollard repaired by Christmas. Enoch Miller, a chaplain for the 25th U.S.C.I., reported after the skirmishes.

> Our men [the 97th and the 82nd U.S.C.I.] returned, having accomplished a march of one hundred and twenty-five miles, fought with men who were perfectly acquainted with the country, whipped them, brought off our wounded, and captured about thirty prisoners, beside bringing in about two hundred colored people. With one exception, our troops behaved splendidly. The exception consisted of the killing of prisoners. Some of those men, who have been slaves, remember old grievances, and seek to avenge them on such occasions.[13]

By the end of December 1864, the tide was turning for the North. In the fall the Union armies had some remarkable successes. Bruce Levine highlights some of them—the capture of Atlanta, the closing of the port of Mobile, and the rout of the Rebels in the Shenandoah Valley. President Lincoln had been reelected, and slavery was doomed. According to Levine, Confederate soldiers were deserting "in greater numbers than ever.... By the end of 1864, the Confederacy had only a quarter as many soldiers in the field as the Union."[14] O'Brien states that General Liddell, the Rebel leader whom Chamberlin had fought at Pollard, expressed the pessimism of the South when he said in late December that "he was convinced the war was lost unless the South could either secure foreign military support or free the slaves and enlist black troops." In fact, according to Sheehan-Dean, in late February 1865, the Confederate Congress narrowly voted to authorize "the Confederate army to enlist slaves with the permission of their masters." The result was that only a few hundred black soldiers enlisted. Ironically, according to Levine, as early as 1863, after being driven out of Chattanooga, Gen. Patrick Cleburne had proposed training slaves to shore up the faltering Confederate Army, but Jefferson Davis and his cabinet rejected the idea. Gallager, et al. state, "Critical in the adoption of the policy [when it was proposed in 1865, for the second time] was a statement from General Robert E. Lee." Sheehan-Dean quotes a letter Lee wrote to Andrew Hunter, a Virginia state senator, on January 11, 1865:

> I think, therefore, we must decide whether slavery shall be extinguished by our enemies and the slaves be used against us, or use them ourselves at the risk of the effects which may be produced upon our social institutions. My own opinion is that we should employ them without delay. I believe that with proper regulations they can be made efficient soldiers.[15]

The Rebels were facing inevitable defeat.

Chapter 12

Camp Life

Before the final battles of the war, Chamberlin's regiment experienced a period of relative calm. He used this time to read and reflect as he dealt with the everyday activities and problems at the camp. The year 1865 began with celebrations and news of Union successes. His company E continued working on the fortifications around Fort Barrancas.

January 1: Great meeting of the colored troops, and the colored population generally as a celebration of the anniversary of the Emancipation Proclamation. The Chaplain of the 2nd Maine Cavalry and a Chaplain from the Navy made some very appropriate and able remarks. Also Col. [Andrew J.] Woodman of the 2nd Maine Vet. Cavalry Commandant of the Post.

January 2: The Garrison of Fort Barrancas 25th U.S. Colored Infantry had a great celebration this P.M. Among the performances were—A Wheelbarrow race, men blind-folded, Running in sacks, Jumping, Dancing, hunting in a half bbl. of meal for a half dollar with the mouth—hands tied behind the back, Climbing a greased pole, and finally a burlesque dress-parade by the enlisted men. Every thing went off well without any quarreling and afforded a good deal of fun for all.

January 3: Received news from Sherman at Savannah. He had captured Fort McAllister and had cut off all communication with the city and had Hardee with 30,000 men cooped there with the assurance that he would capture the whole crew.[1] The prediction of Gen. Grant, that Sherman would prove that the Confederacy is a shell is verified by Sherman's unimpaired march through the heart of the enemy's country. Sherman is yet to do some great things.

January 7: Sherman presented to the President as a Christmas gift the city of Savannah, 150 pieces of Artillery and 25000 bales of cotton. He is reported as chasing Hardee in the direction of Charleston. Thomas had achieved the most complete and decisive victory of the war.[2]

Captaining the Corps d'Afrique

January 11: Capt. Palfrey Adj. Chief Engr. Dept. of the Gulf, visited the works today. Seemed highly pleased with the appearance of the work we had done.[3]

January 12: Quite anxious to get a mail as we have had none in 4 weeks.

January 13: A large mail arrived. Hallelujah! I had 9 letters from home and elsewhere. Everything looks brighter. Had a fine time in the evening reading my letters. Recd. blanks from the chief of Ordnance for making out my Returns, so made them out instead of answering my letters. <u>Business</u> before <u>Pleasure</u> although somewhat against my inclinations. On the whole we have <u>reason</u> for being <u>jolly</u>.

Barrancas Fla., Jan. 15th 1865

Dear Friend Anna:

Your kind letter of Nov. 20th reached its destination on the 10th of Jan. not quite two months on the way. I might expect to get a letter from you about as soon if you lived in the Sandwich Islands instead of the United States. The long-hoped-for letter has been recd however at last, and it is a pleasure to me to know that I am still remembered by you.

Ever since I enlisted as a soldier, my correspondence with my friends has always been my greatest enjoyment, and the letters that I have recd from friends in the north, almost always filled with words of hope, have done more than all else to make me contented and to guard me against temptation which without them could not have been so easily avoided.

Since I wrote you last we have changed our camp from Fort Gaines, Ala. to Fort Barrancas Fla. so that I am now within a mile of Fort Pickens where I first saw many of the realities of war. Our Regt. is at work repairing and strengthening the Fort and building quite an extensive line of earthworks for the better protection of the Navy-Yard of Pensacola Bay. I have been at Pensacola once after lumber, but it is not the pleasant thriving city that we left two years ago, but has become almost a waste, howling wilderness. It is one of the saddest pictures of war and desolation that I have ever seen. This terrible and devastating war which the deceived people of the south have brought upon themselves, has not only filled the land with mourning, but has covered the whole fair south with ruins.

You, at the North, can have no idea of the frightful desolation at the South especially in the regions where our great armies have moved. The very face of Nature has been changed, great forests cut down, beautiful groves and orchards destroyed, rivers turned from their courses, hills leveled, and all the improvements of man swept away—the very sepulchers of the dead have not been sacred enough to prevent the rude hand of war from disturbing the quiet of the sleepers. The people of the South have

12. Camp Life

clung to their cause with a pertinacity and courage worthy of a better cause.

But courage and persistance are of no avail when contending against the eternal principles of Right and Justice. The hosts of freemen who rally around the standard of the Union are yet to sweep the last vestige of this accursed rebellion from the country, and I live in hope that the time is not very far distant.

I am afraid I shall be a queer sort of a fellow if I ever get out of the army. I'll bet there wouldn't be any three good looking girls quite neglected even if they were school ma'ams if your humble servant ever does become a citizen again. Do you propose to be a school-maam all your natural life? It is a very honorable position, but not always a very pleasant one. I would like to look into your school-room and see how you do preside over the young ideas. Wonder how you would entertain me any how. Made application to go home a few weeks ago, but it was disapproved, as I was not sick. It is very difficult for an Officer to get a leave of absence from this Dept. for more than 20 days unless the Officer is sick.

It has been more than three years since I was at home. That was the 27th day of Nov 1861 Thanksgiving Day. The last three thanksgivings I have spent in the army, and I think I could appreciate a thanksgiving day in N.Y. Oh! how much I would have given to have been at home last Nov. and to have seen you there and all my friends.

Excuse this rambling letter as I was interupted to write a love letter for one of my men, (lucky if I hain't got some of it mixed with this). My regards to all the school-marms and to all the family. Write soon, As Ever,

   John N. Chamberlin

January 18: The weather to-day is as warm and the skies as soft and beautiful as June.

> "A dead calm rests upon the bay
> The winds to sleep have gone."

Were it not for the barren desolate appearance of every-thing excepting the old swaying, singing, pine-woods one might easily imagine it was summer. But we shall soon enough wake up to find that this is only a prelude to some cold storm and boisterous weather of some kind. But this is a beautiful world whether in storm or calm to any one who has half an eye for the beautiful and sublime any where.

"The clouds, floating on high like islands of the blue. The winter sunsets glowing like the gates of some far off paradise or ocean with pure heart-rendering Heavens purified image or writhing and tossing like the stormy beast of a chained giant in his agony."[4]

Captaining the Corps d'Afrique

January 20: All women are moving out of camp today and their husbands are fixing them gardens out-side the limits of the camp. Some of these women are useful as seamstresses but otherwise they are neither <u>useful</u> nor <u>ornamental</u>.

January 30: There was some trouble in the <u>women's</u> camp. A fight was extemporised between a man and his better half. Put the man in the Guard-House and gave the woman a moral lecture on the duties of wives. Don't know as I told her much truth but I am sure I did some <u>common sense</u>.

Wilson gives a good analysis of the "women's camps," which varied over time throughout the army, raising many complicated issues.[5] If women remained with their original owners, they were often punished because their men had joined the Union Army. Then, too, as male slaves left their masters, many women escaped with them, flocking to the Union Army camps, as they had no other means of protection and support. Their presence left the army with the huge problem of feeding them all. Some of the soldiers stole army rations to feed their families. Some army units attempted to make the women self-sufficient by putting them to work on neighboring plantations raising food, as well as employing some of them to cook, sew, and wash clothes.

Obviously having families gathered around the army camps was a hindrance, if not a real danger, in times of battle. Between battles, the presence of the women and children was a distraction to the soldiers, who often left their duties to spend time with their families. Some officers solved the problem by sending the families to distant camps, but that caused another problem: men deserted to join them or to check on their safety, which was definitely in jeopardy. The women had nobody to protect them from Rebel soldiers or former owners, and in many cases they were beaten and sexually abused. Many women were also sexually abused in the camps close to the army, often by white officers. A number of women became prostitutes, not all by choice.

Many of the families had been living together on the plantations without the parents being officially married. Army chaplains performed many weddings, particularly for couples who had been living together for an extended period. Before performing a marriage ceremony, the chaplains often attempted to educate the couples about religion and family values. Many younger couples who had just met were also interested

12. Camp Life

in marriage. In many cases the chaplains discouraged them for fear they were marrying just for convenience without long-term plans for building a life together.

> **February 5:** It's getting to be an awfully dull time in camp. Suppose however, that a fellow is just as contented here as he would be anywhere else.
> **February 6:** Rained most of the day as usual. Nothing done on the fortifications to-day. Things are getting desperate. If this state of things continues much longer we shall be obliged to extemporize a <u>row</u> amongst ourselves just for to disturb the monotony of this kind of life.

One way Chamberlin passed the time was by reading. In his diaries and letters he quoted or referred to a wide-ranging variety of works by many authors including Herman Melville, Harriet Beecher Stowe, M.D. Tocqueville, John Milton, and William Shakespeare, as well as poems by Geoffrey Saxe and George Prentice and essays by Samuel Taylor Coleridge. Over the course of about three weeks in January and February 1865, he recorded in his diary that he had read Tom Moore's poetical works, *Love's Labor Won*,[6] and *Martin Chuggleruit*.[7] He

> finished reading the first Vol. of Barun Jominis life of the Emperor Napoleon.[8] Quite a ably work but not as comprehensive as one could wish. It is written more as a military work than a history of the terrible struggles that shook Europe during the rein of the great Napoleon. However it seems written in palliation of his accursed ambitions and covers him with a false glory as a philanthropist and patriot. Perhaps altogether he caused oceans of blood to flow and he did much to forward the cause of liberty.

By early February, stories of peace negotiations were emerging.

> **February 6:** The latest sensation rumor from outside the lines is to the effect that Jeff Davis has sent 5 Commissioners to Washington to negotiate <u>peace</u> on <u>any</u> terms. The day passed in the usual routine of eating, reading, writing, talking and raising the <u>Devil</u> generally as much as circumstances would admit.
> **February 11:** Rec'd New Orleans papers of the 9th Inst. but nothing new in the regard to the Peace rumors. It is only a visit of Blair [see below] to the Confederate Authorities so as to show the people of the north that no <u>honorable</u> means is left untried to close the war. I have no faith in any rumors of an adjustment of our differences but by the strong arm of the military power. But about one more pressure by our armies may bring them to "<u>time</u>."

Captaining the Corps d'Afrique

According to Goodwin, Frances Preston Blair (1791–1876) was a "powerful player in Democratic politics," an editor, and an advisor to Pres. Andrew Jackson. Blair was convinced that Lincoln's reelection in 1864 might make another attempt at peace successful. Lincoln gave Blair a pass for Richmond, where his discussion with Jefferson Davis on January 11, 1865, led to Davis' appointment of three "peace commissioners," who conferred with General Grant and then with Lincoln in early February. With the notice that Congress had just passed a constitutional amendment banning slavery, and with Lincoln's determination that the only way to restore the Union was for the South to cease their resistance, the "peace conference" ended.[9]

On February 16 the regiment received orders to pack up their camp equipage and stores and board the Steamer *Alabama*.[10] In the evening they headed toward Fort Gaines and Mobile, where the Rebels had been gathering since the end of 1864 for one last major effort.

CHAPTER 13

The Defeat of the Rebels

By the end of 1864, troops in the Department of the Gulf were gathering for a final campaign; they concentrated on central and southern Alabama (fig. 1, chap. 1), especially Mobile.[1] As a part of this effort Chamberlin and his troops left the Pensacola area in mid–February 1865 and headed toward Fort Morgan in Alabama. On **February 17** they were "ordered to Pilot Town four miles above Fort Morgan. The iron-clad monitors were there preparing themselves with apparatus for fishing up torpedoes preparatory to a move up the Bay."

According to Chamberlin's **February 18** diary entry, they received orders from Gen. Gordon Granger to assemble the pontoon bridge at Fort Morgan.[2] They got ten boats from Fort Morgan and enough equipage to make two hundred feet of bridge. For the next few days they practiced unloading the pontoon bridge, laying sections of it, and taking it up. Heavy gales made the water in the bay very rough. General Granger inspected and seemed to be well-satisfied with the work they had done. Chamberlin drew forty-four pairs of shoes for his company, so each of his soldiers would have an extra pair. He guessed that they might "take quite a tramp before they get into civilized country again."

March 7–12 Chamberlin recorded in his diary that Capt. John J. Smith, who formerly belonged to the 97th Regiment U.S.C.I., arrived with his company of pontoniers.[3] Brigades of infantry and artillery moved up the peninsula, and monitors and tinclads started going up the bay.[4] The boats drove the Rebels from two batteries that were about five miles from Mobile.

Captaining the Corps d'Afrique

March 17: A large part of the Army moved up to-day, and the U.S. Military Telegraph is following the army this P.M. so that telegraph line communication will be open to Fish River about as soon as the army arrives there.

March 18: Capt. Smith's company made the bridge into rafts of four boats each. The rafts were towed up the Fish River, some twenty-five miles up the Bay.

March 20: All the monitors, all the tinclads, and sixteen transports loaded with troops also moved up.

March 22: Because of wind, the Steamer Jenny Rogers was driven ashore, with two Companies of our Reg't on board.[5]

March 29: The Monitors moved up but were obliged to retire on account of torpedoes. Soon after the turreted Monitors O'sage and Milwaukee[6] were blown up and sunk by the torpedoes floating down against them. They lay in shallow water with their flags still flying.

April 1: Went over to the front and saw the 30 lb. parrots[7] work on the fort [Spanish Fort, see fig. 1], although the enemy did not reply. Our rifle pits were within 100 yards of the Fort. Capt. [James Gilbert] Hill and myself commenced a mortar battery within 300 yds. of the enemy line.

After working day and night, Chamberlin's men finished the battery on April 3. Meanwhile General Steele experienced sharp fighting and commenced a siege at Blakely.[8] Chamberlin amplified his description of events near Mobile in a letter to Bullock.

Hd. Qrs 16th A.C., In the field Before Mobile, April 4th 1865

My Dear Friend Anna:

My last letter to you was written Jan. 17th since which time I have heard nothing from you. We don't get mails very often here, but when we do I feel a great disappointment in receiving no token of remembrance from you. I believe if Uncle Samuel would be a little more careful with a soldier's correspondence it would add to their happiness as much as anything that could be done. My last letter contained a similitude of Capt. John N. so if you didn't receive that you haven't got the letter. And if you did get it and didn't write, why: here is another letter out of spite.

I am now detached from my Regt. and am at the Hd. Qrs. of Maj. Gen. A. J. Smith. Was ordered to report to his chief Engr. for duty and have been building Batteries for the past week. Our Army has advanced upon Mobile and here within 8 miles of the City and in plain sight we are brought to a stand-still and shall be compelled to await the slow process

13. The Defeat of the Rebels

of a siege to take the Rebel forts that confront us. The Navy cannot cooperate with the army on account of torpedoes [mines] in the Bay. In an attempted advance 10 days ago, 2 of our iron clads were blown up and sunk. They are very liberal with these infernal engines of war for they not only fill the Bay with them, but bury them on land in our paths and in every probable place for us to advance.

Torpedoes refer to naval and land mines employed mainly by the Confederates. The naval ones consisted of large barrels just below the surface of the water, or boilers on a riverbed, both loaded with powder. They came in many configurations, and were deployed in three ways: (1) drifting on the river current, causing random collisions; (2) anchored to floats just below the surface of the water; (3) attached to small semi-submersible ships or open canoes below the waterline. Land mines, known as *subterranean torpedoes*, were made from various artillery projectiles with a sensitive friction primer. Any disturbance of the primer caused immediate detonation.[9]

The letter continues:

> Our army is pressing the enemy vigorously however and is within 200 yds of their line already. We had 70 pieces of Artillery in position yesterday, and at 5 O'clock P.M. opened fire and continued until dark. They have good guns in the forts, but did not reply. They evidently expected an assault and were mustering their forces to repel it. I was within 800 yds. of the enemy's line where I could plainly see the whole scene, and it was magnificent and sublime.
>
> The music of bird and bee, the soft sighing of the summerlike breeze through the pines, the gentle murmur of the Bay, and all the soothing—all the sublime, soul-inspiring harmonies by which Nature moves, were drowned in the tremendous roar of artillery and, Pandemonium seemed to be let loose upon earth. If there are any righteous or wicked left in Mobile, they had better get out of it for we intend to take the city if it takes us all summer to do it. We hear of the capture of Charleston, Columbia & of Sherman's triumphant march and we are anxious to accomplish something here. The army is in good spirits. All hope that the war is nearly over. Charleston was burned. I think that was right and I am glad it was burned by the enemy. A monument should now be erected there of the ruins and the site be sown with salt. If any city in the South merited a purification by fire, it was that same city of Charleston.[10] Discord to its ashes.
>
> You may think that I like a soldiers life better than any other, or I would

Captaining the Corps d'Afrique

not remain a soldier so long. I do not like life as a soldier. On the contrary I detest it. I should prefer almost any other. I am tired and sick of the sights and sounds of war, and many times had I the power I should have left the army forever. At other times I could see no pressing reason why I should leave the army more than thousands of others, but I don't propose to stay in the army after my present term expires at any rate. I long for the quiet, the comfort and independence of life on a farm, there is no other life with half the enjoyment, no other home with a tithe of the comfort the genuine happiness and independence of a home among the green fields and leafy woods where Nature is an open Book, which I can never tire of studying.

>Then give me back my cottage roof: I ask no palace dome,
>For I can lead a happy life with those I love at Home.[11]

Tell me how you get along with your school. I suppose you have quite a mixed population to contend with. All nations I suppose are represented in your school. No doubt you have about as good facilities for the study of Entomology (especially that part that we have no account of in the Ark) as a soldier has. I have seen none but two legged gray-backs on this campaign, however. Write soon. I am not dying to hear from you.

There is no mortal man or woman that will ever bring me to that, but don't fail to write and send the photograph. My regards to the whole family and the school-ma'ams, tell Howard he has not answered my last letter, & accept the best wishes of your sincere friend:

John N. Chamberlin

Additional diary entries give an ongoing record of the battle at Blakely.

April 8: Rumors among the men in the rifle pits that the enemy are leaving the place. Very few casualties in our Army each day.

April 9: We have struck 'ile'. Our whole line advanced at midnight with a rush and occupied the whole of the Rebel works [apparently Spanish Fort]. One thousand prisoners were captured. A large part of the [Rebel] Garrison escaped up the Bay on their boats. There is a great amount of enthusiasm among our men. The enemy had no stores, but left all their Artillery behind, among which are 7 seven inch Brooks rifles.[12] One very fine 30 pound parrot made by the rebels at Selma and marked March 1865. As many as forty guns in all, I think. Went through all the Rebs works in the A.M. Some torpedoes buried in front of their works, but marked by a little stake and a piece of white cloth to warn their own men. News at 8 o'clock P.M. that the works at Blakely have just been charged and taken with 5000 prisoners [later estimates were 2,600].

13. *The Defeat of the Rebels*

April 10: The Hd. Qrs. of the 16th Corps moved up to Blakely.... Fort Huger [fig. 1], which is on an Island, had not yet surrendered. Until that is taken our base of supplies must still be at Starks Landing, as they can shell our Transports when they come up.... Mobile is in sight at Blakely, but there are two rivers to cross, and the <u>lord</u> only knows how many Forts to take before we get there.

April 12: Fort Huger was evacuated by the Rebs last night and taken possession of by the Navy and Battery Tracy was blown up.... The latest and most startling news from the north, is the surrender [of General Robert E.] Lee with his army to Gen. Grant [on April 9].... The Navy are moving up cautiously fishing up the torpedoes. They have already learned from dear-bought xperience that they are dangerous things to travel amongst.... Gen. Granger occupied the city [Mobile] this p.m. with a part of his Army.[13]

April 14: Started for Blakely by land with my Company as an escort for the wagon at 2 P.M.

April 15: Rec'd Official confirmation of the surrender of Gen. Lee with the whole of the Army of Virginia [officially on April 12]. So the war is, in our opinion, virtually closed. No more great battles are to be fought, and if Jeff. Davis still persists in fighting he cannot by any possibility get another effective army together. The best thing he can do is to now make the best terms he can with the Federal Government. Great rejoicing everywhere North and South.

April 17: We all feel that the days of the Confederacy are numbered but just how long the Rebs intend to make any resistance to the Cause, it is quite difficult to tell.

Apparently the Union Army was not sure that all fighting was indeed over. On April 20, Chamberlin's company was put to work. He wrote his sister in late April.

I am still at Blakely. All but two companies of the Reg't have gone down the Bay six miles to repair one of the rebel Forts. I am left here in charge of the construction of a small Fort for a Garrison of 300 men with 6 guns [Appendix G]. I have a detail of 150 men daily from the 20th Wisconsin & the 28th Iowa Reg't. Have been at work just a week and shall get done in a week more, I think.

This small fort or "redoubt," as it is labeled on the map used by Chamberlin (fig. 8), was apparently located less than a mile northwest of the town of Blakely. It was built on slight rise near the Tensaw River

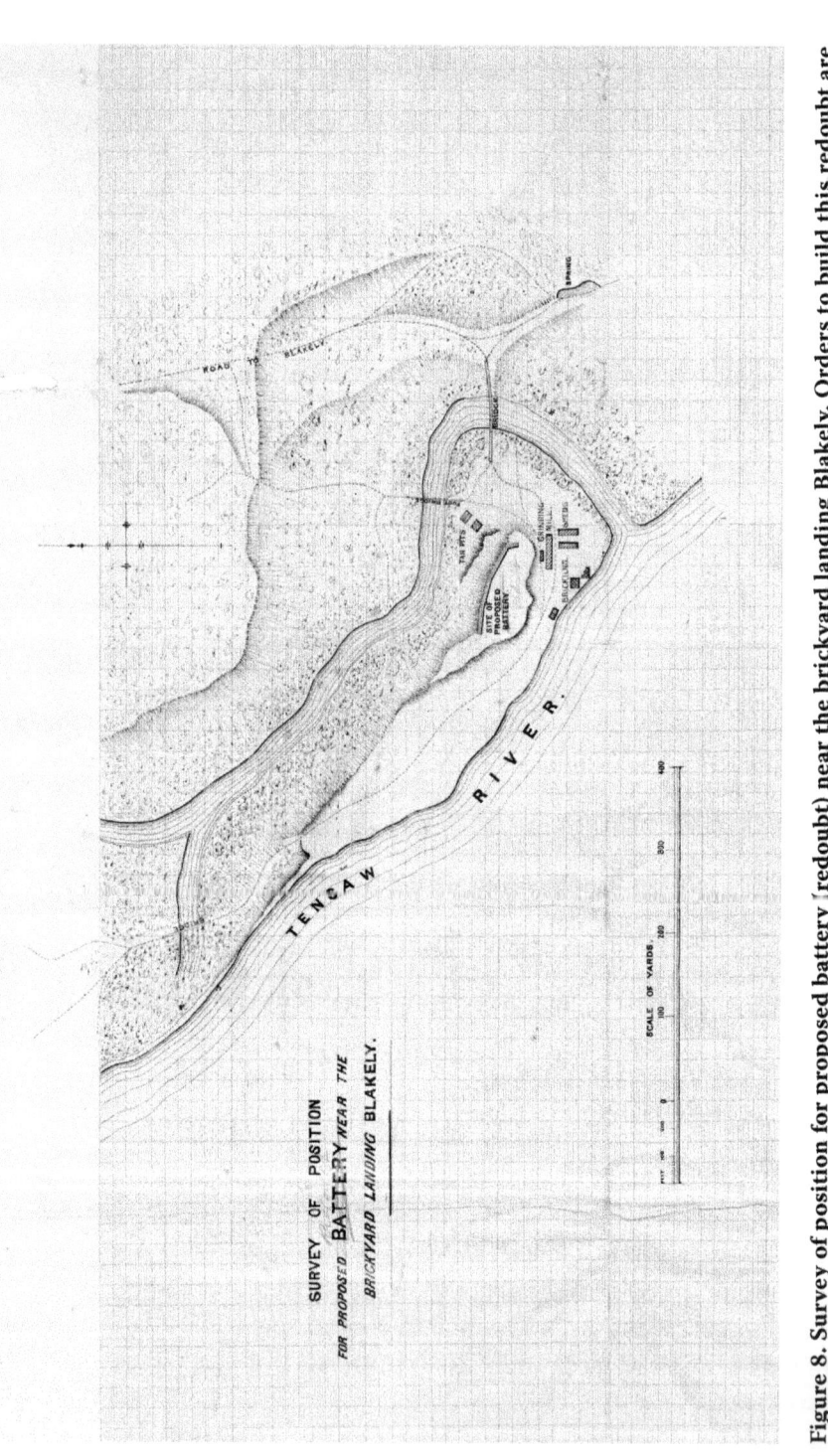

Figure 8. Survey of position for proposed battery (redoubt) near the brickyard landing Blakely. Orders to build this redoubt are shown in Appendix G. Original in possession of John Bisbee.

13. The Defeat of the Rebels

and was surrounded on two sides by the Baptizing Branch which flows into Bayou Salome; this stream was not labeled on Chamberlin's map.[14] The redoubt, made of earthworks, extended approximately 120 yards. While Chamberlin's company was busy with this project, momentous events were happening in Washington.

CHAPTER 14

Victory at What Price?

Assassination of the President

On the day Chamberlin's company began building the redoubt at Blakely, a telegraph message arrived. He recorded in his diary that day:

April 20: A telegraphic dispatch has been going the rounds this evening, to the effect that [the] President has been murdered and that Secretary Seward and two children mortally wounded by J. Wilkes Booth—Actor.[1] This dispatch was dated Washington April 15. We will not believe until we have strong confirmation. We all hold our breath and say—What next. I feel more anxiety about this report than I did the surrender of Lee. What are we coming to?

Excerpted sections of two letters Chamberlin wrote to his sisters offered further reaction to the assassination of the President:

Camp of the 97th U.S.C.I., Blakely Ala., Apr. 20th/65

Dear Sister,

Morning 21st. It has just been announced in Gen'l Field Orders from the Hd. Qrs. of Gen. Canby that The President was assasinated by J. Wilkes Booth—Actor, at the theater in Washington & that Seward was murdered in his bed at the same time.[2] God save the Nation now for I fear that the Vice-President is not the man for the occasion. Guns are now being fired each half hour. We can scarcely credit anything about it. It seems as if it must be some horrible fantasy, but the grim terrible truth is before us and I greatly fear that there can be no mistake about it. Every man in the army will shut his teeth tight together and cry Vengence! There is a feeling among all to extirpate every one of the infernal devils and not let a single traitor live. I believe that our armies in the field cannot be restrained from slaughter and they ought not to be. We have very few particulars, but enough to show that the act was authorized by the

14. Victory at What Price?

Rebel chiefs. This is indeed the most startling scene in the whole dire drama of blood. I cannot see how it will help the rebel cause but it is cause for the deepest regret that we could not have been spared this great blow. We wait with anxiety further particulars, and hope that it may all prove a canard.

   Yours ever,
   John N. Chamberlin

James McPherson states that Jefferson Davis was falsely accused of complicity in Lincoln's assassination. Many rumors circulated about a possibly conspiracy behind the killing; most were based on wild speculation, rather than facts or eye-witness accounts. Certainly it couldn't have been mere coincidence that so many of the people who helped Booth escape were either strongly pro–Confederates or actual Confederate agents. The federal government attempted to blame the leaders of the Rebel government, but could never find proof. William Tidwell poses a possible scenario that involved the C.S.A. He alleges that in 1864 plans were made to take Lincoln hostage, as well as to take direct action against other Union officials to disrupt Union command and cause confusion. Tidwell suggests that Booth was following plans made two weeks before the assassination for a "wartime attack" on Lincoln. After Lee's surrender on April 9, the murder on April 15 was seen not as an act of war, but a "last-gasp."[3]

No matter who planned the assassination, Chamberlin, like many other soldiers, was thinking about vengeance. O'Brien says, "The news of President Abraham Lincoln's assassination filled the Yankee soldiers with shock and anger. Many of the men were predictably outraged and vengeful toward the South." He quoted Captain Thomas Stevens: "'[L]et the army destroy everything from the face of the land they claim. [L]et them reap the whirlwind of destruction & shame, desolation & sorrow.'"[4]

   Blakely Ala., Apr. 27th/65

Dear Sister:

We have rec'd full confirmation of all the startling and horrible events up to 18th of the month. The fearful indignation of the army that was everywhere apparent upon receiving the first report of the murder of the President, although not as apparent to a stranger, has settled down into the firm resolve in the heart of every one, that if the south in their madness, continue the war still longer, it must be altogether a different war than has been heretofore waged by the Union army. A war of extermination has never been talked of in our army until now.

I doubt not that the people of the North feel as much sorrow at this hideous crime as our soldiers do and the cry for vengeance may be quite as fierce and bitter, but an army of half a million with all the terrible appliances of war, is an organization in which threats of vengeance and retaliation are not always empty boasts. We have the power in our hands to extirpate the whole traitor brood, and it speaks well for the intelligence, the humanity and the discipline of our army, that so few scenes of violence and blood have been enacted in the moments of fury and rage on hearing the dreadful announcement of the cowardly assassination of the head of the Nation.

The people of the North cannot realize a tithe of the terrible realities of war, and God grant that they never may. These brave men, who in the strength of their manhood fall upon the field of blood are not the only, nor are they most harrowing, scenes of war. The aged, the women and children of the south, have suffered and are suffering more than tongue can tell. We all look upon the contest as virtually ended. Many think that there will not be another battle and I think so too. A guerrilla warfare may be kept up for a time in some remote sections of the south, but the people will take it into their own hands to quell all such disturbers of the peace, for they are a terror to friend and foe alike. The "last ditch" has been reached and they have been hammered out of that, and nothing remains. The great bubble has collapsed, and it is very difficult to see the fragments. Jeff. Davis and his Cabinet and Congress, must be a jolly set of fellows now!

I suppose they will have a snug little sum laid by somewhere, and if possible get out of the country with it. But there is no place on this round world where such men can escape the pangs of remorse. The worst punishment they can have inflicted is to let them live, execrated and despised by all, and it's a consolation to know that there is a warm locality fitted up for them in the great hereafter. The army are willing to accept such men as Lee as men and soldiers, but there is no term bitter enough to express the deep detestation in which Davis and political confederates are held.

I am well. Write soon. As Ever
John N. Chamberlin

Celebrating the End of War

While Lincoln's death dampened the enthusiasm over the Northern victory, feelings of joy could not be squelched. One large celebration

14. Victory at What Price?

took place in Washington, D.C., on May 23 and 24. According to Sheehan-Dean, "Over the course of two days about 150,000 men from the Army of the Potomac and Armies of the Tennessee and Georgia marched along Pennsylvania Avenue from the Capitol to the White House." The *New York Herald* wrote:

> It is not mere numbers, however, which make this display at Washington so grand. This review is a review of triumph. The gallant conquerors ... are going home to share the blessings they won for the nation. They have been battling for that great principle of democracy, ... and they have secured the perpetuity of that Union upon which the hopes of all oppressed of climes and countries depend. They are the champions of free governments throughout the world. From one end of the world to the other the people thank our soldiers for having conquered in the people's cause.

In the *Detroit Advertiser and Tribune,* Lois Bryan Adams wrote, "These are all citizens who know the value of their country and their Government. They saw the danger and averted it, and are now quietly disbanding to go home and be citizens again." Ironically, according to Adams, no black regiments marched in the parade to celebrate the end of the war and the freeing of the slaves. The only blacks in the review were a few attached to Sherman's army, who were armed with picks and shovels.[5]

Most of the blacks were still in the field. At this point Chamberlin and his men were probably unaware of the festivities in Washington. However, the news of the review reached Bullock almost immediately.

After a long silence, Bullock finally writes to Chamberlin.

Waterloo, Iowa, May 25th/65

My Dear Friend,

> I have no doubt but that before this time I am put down on your list of delinquents. My last to you was written Feb 22nd which it seems you have not yet rec'd. Yours written the 4th of April reached New Orleans the 11th & here the 19th & why letters going South should require so much more time, is something I cannot understand. But then women folks are not generally expected to know much about war.
>
> I am anticipating a nice visit at Mr. Pratts when Mollie goes home. They are the most thorough farmers I know of. When you come to Waterloo we will go out there, and you can see for yourself. Mollie has

Captaining the Corps d'Afrique

given you a standing invitation already.[6] Our Lodge is prospering finely. We have some substantial evidences of good that has been done, but there is abundant need of hearty earnest work yet. Had I told you that our Grand Lodge meets here next Sept. We are expecting a good time.—You see I send my phiz [*face*, presumably meaning a photo] this time. It is called good & I guess it is. I imagine it has changed considerably in the last nine years. I can hardly realize that it has been so long since I left my early home. I am almost afraid it will be as long again before I can visit it & then the changes would be so great that I should experience as much of pain as pleasure I fear.

Do you begin to feel as though you could almost see home? The review of the Eastern troops took place last Tues. the 23rd. The paper stated that there was 21 miles of soldiery, 60 abreast.[7] It must have been a grand night.

We have commenced to Hurrah over the return of our "boys in blue" already. Some that were in hospital got home last week. You must have been right with some of our Waterloo boys during the siege of Mobile, but if you did not get my last letter, you probably knew nothing of it. They belong to Co C. 82nd Iowa.

How little we thought at the first call that we should have to pass through such a four years struggle. At what a sacrifice have Right & Justice been established, & how dearly have we paid for our National sins. "Let my people go" had rung in our ears, until we became deaf to the sound, & were aroused from our lethargic slumber by the hand of an avenging God. How do you like our President. It seems impossible that we should ever love & reverence any man as we did Lincoln. But that was another stroke, to show us that our trust & dependence rested not alone upon man. The negroes must have felt it keenly. They had come to look upon him as their deliverer & protector, which in truth he was. The rebs too have lost their best friend. [Bullock had amazing insight for 1865.]

What a coming down for the Chivalric South to have their President try to evade our troops by donning a woman's apparel.[8] I don't know how it is in other parts of the country, but you cannot find a copperhead around here. They have all shed their skin as any other snake does. They know that if they live within the limits of civilization they have got to even forget what they were. A woman from South Carolina was about 25 miles from here on her way to this place to deliver a course of Medical Lectures when they rec'd the news of Lincoln's death. She said she was glad of it. The conductor immediately telegraphed to W [Waterloo]—letting the people know who was coming so they were prepared for her arrival. She could not find a place to stop either at a Hotel or private house, but they finally let her stay at one of the Hotels until the next train went East. The

14. Victory at What Price?

last we heard of her she was in Illinois & had not come to a convenient stopping place yet. She probably concluded that her efforts were not appreciated.

I think it an excellent place for you to vent your spite in writing letters, especially if they are directed to me. I am fully aware that I get more than I deserve now, but Uncle Sam will have to bear part of the blame for your not hearing from me more often. Please write again soon for I am always waiting to hear from you.

     As ever your true friend
     Anna Bullock

Looking Back on the War

Obviously Chamberlin had not received the above letter before writing to Bullock again. Apparently by this time he had special feelings for her because he was persistent in continuing the correspondence. In the following letter he described his personal war experiences and those of his troops.

     Mobile, Ala., June 2" 1865

Dear Friend Anna:

With the dawn of Peace came thoughts of home and friends, and I am naturally anxious to know why I get no letters from you. The last letter you wrote I recd Jan. 13th since which time I have heard nothing from you, or Howard although I have written to both of you. Whether the fault lies with you or with "Uncle Samuels" mail agents I am unable to say, but as I wish to find out the party on whom the blame rests, I can see no better way than to write another letter to you.

From the terrible storm of four years of war I have come out unscathed and in looking back upon the past it seems more like some horrible dream, than a stern reality.

34 of the 100 men who entered the service when I did in old Co. "D" of 75th N.Y. sleep in honored graves on the battle fields of the Union. Their graves are wide apart from Virginia to Texas. Many others are maimed for life, but of those who remain unharmed there are very few. While with the Reg't for two years I was always exposed to the same dangers and hardships as others, but since that time, have been in only two battles of any consequence.

Why I have been spared more than others I cannot tell, but he who has

Captaining the Corps d'Afrique

lived through the last four years, whether as a soldier or citizen must be blind indeed not to recognize in all the momentous events that have transpired the hand of a more Omnipotent power than man's. The campaign against Mobile was short and decisive, but there was one element of warfare introduced into the strife here by the Rebels that was attended with more of horror and dread by the army than any of the common appliances of war. They not only filled the waters of the Bay with torpedoes, but planted them in every foot path around their works, around springs and water courses, and in every imaginable place men were killed by this infernal means. But the Union army has triumphed over all and now we see an end to armed rebellion. I believe the people of the South, as a mass are heartily glad that the old flag floats once more all over the land never more to be torn down by traitors. There is much destitution here among all classes of people and were it not for the humanity and generosity of the Government, many would suffer for want of the nescessaries of life.

Now that the dark clouds of war have passed away, and we can calmly look upon the ruins it has wrought all over this fair land, who can fail to thank God that out of so much of suffering and sorrow the Nation is to reap an abundant harvest of peace, prosperity and universal Freedom.

There is mourning all over the land for there is scarcely a household that has not an empty chair. In every community some Rachel weeping for her children and will not be comforted because they are not.[9] I know it must be so at the North, and the fact is apparent to the most casual observer here.

It is a terrible lesson to the people of the North and South alike, for were not all to blame for the war? Who shall say that the whole fault is with the misguided people of the South or even with their educated, unprincipled leaders. Did not northern lust for gold help to remit the fetters upon the limbs of the slave.[10] Ah! Those who rebelled against a good government were not the only guilty. The whole machinery of government was corroded by the baleful influence of Slavery—the whole body politic was corrupted to the core, and nothing short of the tremendous hurricane of war could clear the political atmosphere again. It teaches us that no nation can persistently follow in a course of sin and crime against any class of our common humanity but sooner or later it will receive its just retribution.

A number of scholars give perspective on Chamberlin's views. McPherson notes that an unparalleled rate of growth, considered progress by most people, took place in the United States in the first half of the nineteenth century. Blacks, one-seventh of the population, bore most of the burden of this progress but reaped few of its benefits.

14. Victory at What Price?

Slavery proved enormously profitable. Crops grown by slaves aided the era's economic growth and its territorial expansion. "The cascade of cotton from the American South dominated the world market, paced the industrial revolution in England and New England, and fastened the shackles of slavery more securely than ever on Afro-Americans."[11]

Robert Fogel and Stanley Engerman agree. Many segments of society profited from cotton produced by Southern slaves. Cotton accounted for the majority of the nation's total exports, helping pay for imports from abroad. It also fed the early industrialization in New England's textile mills. As Howard Dodson explains, cotton was shipped from the South, through New York, on its way to American and European manufacturers, giving employment to many people along the way. Banks and financial houses in New York benefited when they financed the purchase of land and slaves. Eric Foner summarized the situation in New York.

> Even after slavery ended in New York, the South's peculiar institution remained central to the city's economic prosperity. New York's dominant Democratic party maintained close ties to the South, and some local officials were more than happy to cooperate in apprehending and returning fugitive slaves.[12]

Chamberlin concluded that not only Northern economic complicity but also national political forces supported slavery. Slavery was built into the U.S. Constitution and reinforced by subsequent laws. Article IV of the 1787 Constitution required the federal government to pursue runaway slaves. The 1793 Fugitive Slave Act provided for the return of slaves who escaped from one state into another state or territory. According to Gallagher et al., the 1820 Missouri Compromise, which admitted Missouri to the United States as a slave state and Maine as a free state, permitted slavery in future western states that were south of an extension of Missouri's southern border. The Fugitive Slave Act of 1850 stopped state governments from interfering if a slaveowner recaptured an escaped slave. The act also authorized federal officers as well as appointed commissions to facilitate arrest and removal of suspected fugitives. In 1857 the U.S. Supreme Court ruled in the Dred Scott case that Congress could not prohibit slavery in territories not yet divided into states. In the words of Gallagher et al., "The Court

Captaining the Corps d'Afrique

endorsed what Southerners had believed all along—slavery was protected by the Constitution." However, influenced by their preference for free labor, by the 1852 publication of *Uncle Tom's Cabin*, and by Lincoln's 1858 "House Divided" speech, many Northerners believed that slavery was incompatible with democracy and should be contained if not prohibited.[13]

Charles Francis Adams, grandson of John Adams and son of John Quincy Adams, commented on the protection of slavery. He wrote to his son in the Union Army from his post as U.S. minister to Great Britain on June 17, 1864.

> The consequences [of slavery] we now see and feel in the events that are passing in front of Richmond. As I read the sad accounts of the losses experienced by both sides in the strife, the warning words of Jefferson will ring in my ears—"I tremble for my country, when I reflect that God is just." The moral evil which we consented to tolerate for a season has become a terrific scourge, ... Only one thing is clear to me, and that is the paramount duty to future generations of not neglecting again to remove the source of that evil.... Yet I cannot conceal from myself the nature of the penalty which all of us are equally to pay for our offence before God. If the great trial has the effect of purifying and exalting us in futurity, we as a nation may yet be saved.[14]

Slavery was gone, but the scars of the war could not be forgotten, as Chamberlin told Bullock in the continuation of his June 2 letter.

> The nation has been tried in the fiery crucible of war, and has come forth with enlarged and purified ideas of civil Liberty and national greatness.
> The old hatred of the North, engendered by 4 years of war, still burns fiercely in the bosoms of multitudes of the Southern people, and whole generations cannot efface it. The South has not submitted only by dint of hard knocks and because she could continue the war no longer, and many recognize the old flag only as a conquered people. Northern institutions must supplant those of the South. The school house and the church must take the place of the slave-pen and auction block. These have passed away forever and it now remains for us to bind up the nations wounds,[15] and in what way can we do this so successfully as by the education of the masses at the South. The brutish ignorance of white and black is beyond all belief to one who has not seen the people.
> Already many schools have been opened and within the coming year there will be a great call upon the intelligence and philanthropy of the North to supply teachers for the people of the South. I suppose if you are

14. Victory at What Price?

not a ministers wife or are not in danger of capitulating to some other fortunate youth, your natural goodness of heart will prompt you to do something for the elevation of this people, & I shall see your name as a teacher in some part of the South. It is a work in which the Great Father will liberally reward every earnest worker, but I very much doubt that I have sufficient courage and philanthropy to engage in it myself.

It is difficult for me to say when I shall get out of the service, but they can't keep me much more than another year at any rate. No resignations are recd here only "for the good of the service" and I don't care to get out in that way now. No leaves of absence are granted only for physical disability and I am so well that there is not much prospect for me to go home yet. My Regt. is encamped in a very fine place near the city [Mobile].

I wish you to write at once and at least let me know the cause of your long silence. If, for any reason our correspondence must cease it would be a relief to me to know it, and if you are wholly excusable for seeming neglect, and there is yet any regard for me, write soon, and with the hope of seeing you again, I will remain ever your debtor.

> My regards to all, and believe me, as ever,
> John N. Chamberlin

While waiting and hoping to hear from Bullock, Chamberlin wrote to a sister. In this letter he penned a moving tribute to the "Private soldiers," who bore the burden of the four-year conflict.

> Mobile, June 11th/65

Dear Sister,

After four years of the most terrible and bloody strife it seems strange enough for me to settle down with no accounts of campaigns and battles to break the monotony of every day life. Still it is a great relief to me to know that we have no more fighting to do. I was not of the number who went into the war without any thought of the terrible chances of war. I thought probably as much as any one of the perils and hardships of the war that was to desolate the land. And I have seen and endured enough of campaigning. In some campaigns I have been in very little individual danger apparently, while in others it has seemed indeed to me that a soldiers grave must mark all that remains of me. But still such is the attraction of war and manifold changes and excitements of active service in the field. I have always enjoyed myself better when in the field than when in camp.

The dull routine of camp duty soon becomes monotonous and it is the same as with us everywhere, we desire some change, and don't stop to consider whether it is to be for our benefit or not.

Captaining the Corps d'Afrique

It seems that most of our army is to be disbanded to beat their swords into plowshares,[16] & their rifles into implements of peaceful industry. What history would the lives of thousands of these men for the last four years make. The Private soldiers of this great Union army—those who have borne the old banner in a thousand fields, who in prosperity and adversity, on many a noble plain in the Gulf States, have bared their breasts to the storms of treason, and have been a wall of fire and steel around the glorious old constitution of our fathers! What historian shall ever do justice to all the rank and file. Honor to whom honor is due,[17] and while I am willing to give all due honor and praise to all good and true leaders, I cannot forget the men, who, with the bayonets point have crushed out this foul rebellion. I have carried a musket too long myself ever to forget them. Men, whom I loved and respected as brothers have fallen right by my side and Oh! how I have cursed the plotters of this war and when I have thought of the infernal cruelties to which union prisioners have been subjected, such an unconquerable hate of the whole devilish crew has took possession of me that I have often vowed I would fight to all eternity rather than see this foul plot succeed.

The Civil War took a terrible toll—suffering and death, injury of body and mind, and destruction of homes, crops, and a way of life. At last it was over and people all across the nation were beginning to rebuild.

CHAPTER 15

Post-War Nation

What Will Peace Look Like?

As Chamberlin contemplated what his life would be like after the war, he was encouraged when he finally received the May 25 letter and picture from Bullock. Apparently he was hoping they could be more than old friends.

Mobile, June 14th 1865

My Dear Friend:

You guess that your picture is a "good one" but there need be no doubt on that subject. I know it is a good one. You have changed less than I have in your looks in the last nine years. The only wonder to me is that anyone who has been a teacher for nine terms should retain the same frank genial expression of countenance that I remember of Anna Bullock—the school-girl. I believe women make the best teachers any-where. There are very few men who can make themselves a place in the hearts of the young so soon and so firmly as a woman. I tell you it did me a heap of good to see your likeness for I sometimes think I am never to see the original. Accept my sincere thanks for this token of your confidence and regard.

As to your needing sympathy, why, I can't see as you need sympathy from me for I am an old codger by the side of you. The sympathy, if there is any, should all be on the other side. I'm about 28 and I can't say that I am ashamed of it, for I don't consider myself to blame. As you say—there is no place that seems so truly home as the home of our childhood. I tell you, if I ever get out of this army (and I have good reason to think that I will sometime) I am going to visit all my old schoolmates that I can find, and I assure you that I am coming to see you about the first one after I go to Sennett.

The change from a state of war to one of peace—from the terrible clamor of battle, of trampling hosts and charging squadrons, and all the

Captaining the Corps d'Afrique

din and discord and the horrible sights and sounds of the great strife, to this glorious peace, seems so sudden and complete, that it is difficult for a soldier, at least, to realize that our great war is really over. I sometimes almost involuntarily look into a newspaper for accounts of battles & sieges, and the long, black lists of our honored dead.

But the war is over. The great slaveholders rebellion is crushed out, and all sympathisers with the accursed system are buried beneath the ruins of the vile fabric which they sought to erect over the spot once occupied by the proud temple of Liberty. The Queen of May that has been crowned, is no imaginary form, but the ever radiant, star-eyed Queen of Peace.[1]

Annihilation was not desired by the Southern people, more than by others, and when they avowed they would accept that sooner than give over the contest it was only a sample of their chief staple—impudence and bravado and meant plainly enough that they would give up as soon as anyone else when they had got a sound thrashing. There's plenty of Secession in the hearts of the people still, and a century can hardly obliterate the deadly feeling against the North and her institutions. It will be handed down from father to son as a sort of heir-loom of intense bitterness and hate. How do you like the new amnesty Proclamation by President Johnson, up in Iowa. It suits me to a t. Whoever got up that proclamation had a pretty sound idea of the causes of the Rebellion. The educated, rich class of the South are alone responsible and they are the ones who should suffer. That $20,000 clause is what will bring them down to their marrow bones sooner than anything else.[2]

You wished for a sample of the letters I write for my men, but it would be unsafe for me to attempt any such thing. I should soon make myself, if no one else, believe that I was writing a love letter.

    Regards to all,
    As ever your true friend.
    John N. Chamberlin

The May 25 and June 14 letters were significant markers in the development of the relationship between Chamberlin and Bullock. About a year later, he described the closing of Bullock's letter of May 25, 1865, as

> about the most hopeful letter that I had from you. Oh! It was such a good letter and you closed with "Please write again soon for I am always waiting to hear from you." I read over that last line a good many times, and thought that there might be a little hope in it, but then I thought this may only be the kindly feelings of an old school-mate, and I can never blame her if her love is given to someone who she can see occasionally, rather

15. Post-War Nation

than me, who have been seperated from her by ten long years and thousands of miles. However much I tried to make myself believe that there was no more than a feeling of friendship existing between us, still there was always a feeling that there was something higher and deeper than any mere friendship connected with it.

About the same time (in 1866), Bullock made the following comment concerning the same letter: "I wondered if that last line would disclose more than I cared to have it." In another 1866 letter she stated:

> How eagerly I used to look for those letters. Through their influence I believe I was wholly yours. I tried hard not to acknowledge it, even to myself, for it is rather of an humbling fact to a woman, to know that she has given her love unasked. But in spite of all I could do, I could not resist it, & someway I used to think that your letter gave me some encouragement.

Looking back, both Chamberlin and Bullock realized that June 1865 had been a turning point in their relationship. The end of the war left Chamberlin optimistic. As he saw a ray of hope for his personal future, he was also cheered by the jubilation of the blacks, about whom he cared, and the possible promise of brighter days ahead for them.

Celebration of Freedom

By July 4, 1865, the former slaves had realized that they were truly free, and they joyfully took center stage in the Independence Day celebration in Mobile. However, the white citizens of that Southern city did not celebrate. Chamberlin wrote to his mother on July 5, 1865, describing the celebration in Mobile.

Mobile, July 5th/65

Dear Mother:

The anniversary of the National birthday has come and gone again, and every true, loyal pulse has beaten quicker in remembrance of the past and with hope for the future. In Mobile, the great feature of the day was the celebration by the colored people. The different trades were represented carrying flags and the different implements of their industry. The Masonic and religious Societies were also a part of the procession, which was comprised on the whole of something like 5000 people. Nearly all

Captaining the Corps d'Afrique

> were very neatly dressed and looked well. They were of all ages and all shades, from fair, dark eyed octoroon to the darkest shade of ebony. The 96th and 97th Regts. of Colored Troops acted as escort, and the procession marched through the principal street to the public Square, where the Declaration of Independence was read and an oration delivered by a colored man. I tell you, whatever prejudice I may have toward the blacks, (and I don't think they will ever be the equals of the white race in intelligence and enterprise) still I was glad to be there and see so many happy free men and women. They all seemed as Joyous for this great day of Jubilee as the same number of white children would at the North, and in a much more expressive manner. Then there were many sound citizens among them, Men of some property in the city.

The *Mobile Tribune*'s July 6, 1865, editorial description of this celebration in Mobile was similar to Chamberlin's.

> There is no denying that, as a mere pageant—without moral at the bottom—it was very interesting.... Four thousand of our own black townsmen and townswomen, it is estimated, were in this extraordinary procession, and all of them, as far as we saw, conducted themselves with perfect African propriety. They insulted none of the white men, and seemed to be perfectly satisfied with the honor which they received in being escorted front and rear by two regiments of negro soldiers.[3]

Chamberlin closed his letter to his mother with a description of the public reaction to the 4th of July celebration.

> Oh! It is worth something to a fellow, who has been fighting these southern hounds for four years to see the citizens scowling upon a celebration, such as took place here on the 4th. They looked daggers, and no doubt would have been glad to use daggers against every one of us had they dared. The most perfect order and decorum prevailed throughout the entire proceedings, but today the city press teems with the most scurrilous articles in regard to the procession stating that the troops turned out with loaded muskets to prevent disturbance—a most dastardly outrage upon the people of the city. Misrepresentation and downright falsehood are freely used to show the celebration in a bad light. And one of these editors is a man from Boston, Mass.
> Oh! Shame, where is thy blush![4]

According to the *Boston Liberator*, "A special correspondent of the *New Orleans Tribune*, writing from Mobile under the date of July 5th, says: 'The ever-memorable Fourth was celebrated here by the

15. Post-War Nation

colored population in fine style.'" He described the procession of two regiments of colored troops, as well as organizations representing businesses, fraternal groups, and churches, then went on to say:

> A large number of enfranchised citizens turned out to witness the demonstration. Many "looked daggers" but could not prevent it.... Upon the very spot where, a few years ago, the apostle of human slavery (W. L. Yancey), stood up and declared that slavery was a divine institution, stood Capt. J. H. Ingraham and others,[5] and declared that slavery was dead.... Everything passed off quietly and with satisfaction. One thing I noticed— most all the insults and injuries that our people received were from the hands of men wearing the garb of the army and navy of the United States! ... I never saw a meaner or a more negro-hating class of people than the men who are now on provost duty here. They are all Western troops, from Illinois and Indiana.[6]

Peace-Time Duties

According to newspaper reports, the white citizens of Mobile and the Northern troops were hateful. Chamberlin found a different attitude when he was given a new assignment. Still in the Mobile area, he worked to reunite the people of the Alabama pine woods with the Union. Apparently for a while he was provost marshal of Conecuh County, as noted on September 4, 1865, when the *Jennie Rogers* was ordered upriver to report to him so that he could use the boat for transporting men, animals and wagons to Mobile (Appendix I). He described some of his activities and impressions in a September 10 letter to Bullock.

> I have just returned from the wilds of Ala. where I have been for the last three weeks administering the Amnesty Oath to the sovereign people. My Office was at Sparta the County seat of Conecuh Co.[7] And such a country—such people, such cattle & such everything in fact I never saw before. The country is all one big pine woods, and the land is so poor that it wont raise white beans. The only redeeming feature in the country is the abundance of beautiful springs of pure, cool water and plenty of game in the woods.
>
> The country is terribly used up by the war. Out of 1200 voters who lived in the country [probably "county"] when the war began nearly one half have perished in the Army. There are more widders and marriageable

Captaining the Corps d'Afrique

girls in proportion to the men than I ever saw in a country before. Quite a right smart chance for a fellow to get a wife you will perceive.

The people generally were eager to take the Oath and come back into the Union on almost any terms.

I was treated with a great deal of respect much more than I had anticipated. They had scarcely seen a Yankee in that section of the country before and there was naturally, a great curiosity to know what I said and did, and what I thought of the country and the people. I found some young ladies who were as well educated and refined as I would find at home, and had some very sensible notions in regard to the existing state of affairs in the Nation, but they were exceptions to the general rule. The young men, on the contrary are generally disposed to sit down and bewail the loss of the slave property and say that the country is ruined past praying for and don't even think that they can do anything to bring about prosperity again. The idea of their ever having to work for a living themselves is the most galling thing of all. But I tell you they have got to come to it. And before three more years roll around many of them will be forced into it by hunger, and I believe there are many who would about as soon starve as earn an honest living by their own labor.

I never realized so fully the ruinous effects of slavery upon a country both Morally and Materially, as I did during my stay in Sparta and I felt to thank God that the great shame and disgrace had passed away forever, from our land. Some of the people are still so foolish as to think that when Congress meets, that all the late rebellious States will be fully represented and that immediate Emancipation will be reconsidered and some plan of Gradual Emancipation with compensation will be substituted in its place.

Eric Foner summarizes the two options: Immediate emancipation would end slavery at once and incorporate the freed slaves as equal members of society. Gradual emancipation would provide compensation to slave owners when their slaves were freed, and could possibly include "the colonization of the freed people outside the United States." These two approaches represented the extremes of the abolitionist views. "At various times, President Lincoln occupied different places on this spectrum. Even after issuing the Emancipation Proclamation, he continued to declare his preference for gradual abolition."[8] One result of the Civil War was the freeing of the slaves, which created new problems. Where were they to go and what were they to do?

The letter continues:

15. Post-War Nation

The question of labor in the South is a difficult one, but if the planters, who formerly owned the slaves will not take the matter in hand and hire them to cultivate the soil, there are plenty of enterprising men from the North who will do it and make money by the operation.

I found your letter of Aug 20th awaiting me on my return to Mobile, and was in the thought that I was not utterly forgotten, although I had begun to fear that such was the case.

I am almost discouraged about ever going home, or to Waterloo or any other place outside the Gulf States. If I don't get a leave of absence to go home this month I shall not try to go until my time is out, which will be next spring, I expect.

It really was a great relief to me to go up into the pine woods, for there the grand harmonies of nature made an eternal anthem of music, and I stayed with such a quiet, home-like family that it seemed more like home to me than anything I have experienced for four long years. I think it must be something such a country for wildness and beauty up where Howard is [Boonsboro, Iowa]. I should scarcely have known Howards photograph [fig. 9] if you had not told me who it was. We all change very much in 9 years.

I am well and as jolly as usual.

We have stopped building fortifications about Mobile and the Regt. is now doing guard duty over the Q.Ms. Pay, Commissary & Ordnance Departments.

I have very little to do. Am not on duty more than once a week, and you can judge of what a monotonous life it is in such a city as this. I sometimes get utterly disgusted with everything human and wish myself away off somewhere in the wood, so far that no one would ever find me. But enough of this. My regards to all, and remember me as ever your Friend

John N. Chamberlin

While Chamberlin was in Sparta, security of "the life and property of the peaceful and well disposed citizens" of that town was a problem, as evidenced by August 25, 1865, orders from Maj. Gen. K. Garrard, that sent a Union Army company to police the city.[9] Apparently Chamberlin found a different situation. He interacted with the people and was treated with respect. *History of Conecuh County, Alabama,* written in 1881, described this county at the end of the war:

> Nothing equalled the wild chaos which prevailed in the South, just subsequent to the close of the war. No shield of legal defense existed, and for once, society was launched upon a wild and stormy sea of disorder....

Captaining the Corps d'Afrique

Figure 9. Howard Bullock, Anna's brother. From John Chamberlin's photo album, figure 6. Courtesy Lelia and Paul Klear.

Every man resolved to protect, as far as possible, his own interest against the invasion of lawlessness. Hence it was to be expected that there would be occasional outbreaks of disorder.... Nothing of a serious nature arose in Conecuh.[10]

    Chamberlin was making a transition from war to peace and from life as a soldier to life as a government agent promoting unity within the country. He was fairly content with his work, but on returning to Mobile he was bored and homesick. He must have been happy to receive this letter from Bullock.

                                             Waterloo, Iowa, Oct 1st 1865.

My Dear Friend,

   A hearty welcome greeted the appearance of that letter from Mobile, rec'd just a month from the date of my last. I think there must be a decided change in "mail arrangments" for which "Uncle Sam" receives my sincere thanks.

15. Post-War Nation

Bullock told Chamberlin about her family and then she described the homecoming of a flag. Waterloo boys, in the 82nd Iowa, had been given their flag by the ladies of Waterloo when they went to war, and

> it was presented to the ladies again, on the last day of our County Fair. Bright & beautiful was it when placed in their hands as a sacred trust. It came back, discolored & rent, but not dishonored. Many of the brave boys came not with it, but their names will never be forgotten.
>
> And so you have been out in the country, rusticating. After reading your letter, I took down my atlas, to see where you had been. There are not any railroads on the map. How did you perform your journey. Not a very desirable location for a farm, I should think, from your description. Had you not written that "you were as jolly as ever" I should not have mistrusted it, for I thought you had a most decided fit of the blues. At least your letter read so to me. Else it might have been the effects of your visit to Sparta. I believe most people are subject to them at times. They do not generally last long, with me, unless the attack is so severe that I cannot sing. I believe singing, if properly applied, to be an antidote for almost every evil. You say you found some quite sensible people while on your trip. I have thought I should like the Southern people, since hearing Aunt Anna Field,[11] who has taught among them four years, talk so much about them, were it not for the idea that they are much too good to work for a living, which they will find they will have to do now, else not live. It would do them good to come up into Iowa awhile. As ever your friend,
>
> Anna Bullock

Bullock was sensitive to Chamberlin's anxiety and restlessness. He had done his duty, in war and in peace-time. Now he was ready to go home.

Chapter 16

Visit at Home

In early October 1865 letters Chamberlin told his family of his hopes for getting a leave of absence to come home, but he was pessimistic about his chances of getting one before winter. To his great surprise, he received a leave (Appendix J) and left Mobile sometime after October 10. He wrote Bullock from New York.

Home [New York], Nov 13th 1865

Dear friend Anna:

Yours of Oct 1st reached me via Mobile on the 10th Inst and I will now hasten to reply.

I reached home on the 28th of Oct. Recd my leave of absence rather unexpectedly and took our folks quite by surprise. It is needless for me to say that it was a happy meeting for all of us.

I tell you I am Jolly, and no mistake, now.

I find great changes in four years. Changes among the people, and changes in the face of Nature. I miss many faces among the old and young, and I sometimes think there must be some mistake about it, and this is not the Sennett of "Auld lang Syne."

But everything is familiar around the dear old home. The family circle is unbroken, and every old tree and bush and even the old rails on the fence seem to greet me as old friends. Oh! it does any one good to visit the home of their childhood. What countless memories come thronging in upon me. It seems as yesterday when we were all at the old stone school-house, and what jolly times we had there. The old house still stands although in quite a dilapidated condition, but of all that happy family that once gathered within its wall, few are now left in Sennett. Some have gone down amid the smoke and carnage of battle, during the terrible four years of civil war, and there is scarcely a State where some of the old school may not be found. Even the State of Matrimony has received a host while not a few remain in the State of single blessedness.

16. Visit at Home

In thinking of this, some lines by Saxe always come into my mind:
> A few have reached the goal they sought,
> And some are dead and some are married.[1]

I am still in the service and must go back to Mobile and in a few days. My short leave nescessarily defers my visit to you until I get out of the service which I hope to be able to accomplish by the middle of the winter.

I intend to go into the lumber business in Mobile when I get out of the service. I can make $10,000 as easily there as I can make $1,000 at home, and I shall remain simply to make enough money to make myself independent. It is no place for a man to live in the South.

I like the climate, but there will be no society there to compare with the society of the North, for a whole generation. When I get back to Mobile and know what I am going to do, I will write and tell you all my plans.

It is very much against my principles to tear a sheet in two but I am going to Auburn and it is almost time for the train. Write soon. Regards to all.

   As ever
   John N. Chamberlin

Bullock responded less than 10 days after she received Chamberlin's latest letter.

   Waterloo, Iowa, Nov 26th 1865.

My Dear Friend,

We are bid to "rejoice with those that rejoice" as well as to "weep with those that weep."[2] I should have rejoiced with you & "the folks at home," over your visit had I known you were there, but do so none the less, now that I suppose your visit has ended. It must have been a pleasure too deep to express, to stand once more beneath the home roof, & receive the heart-felt greetings of loved ones after a four years absence, such as only those who rallied around our beautiful starry Banner & battled with wrong & oppression, until it waves triumphant "o'er land & o'er sea," can know anything of.[3] Then there is the visiting of friends & all the familiar places, even to the old school house. I hope that may stand until I shall see it again for so many of my pleasing recollections are so closely connected with it, that I should miss it sadly.

So you have decided to stay in the South, until you have made your fortune. I wish you abundant success, & all the more so, if your visit to Iowa, is to be deferred until that time.

Anna Bullock described the work that her brothers Howard and Bertie did in Boonsboro, Iowa, and mentioned that Gib (her other

Captaining the Corps d'Afrique

brother) had moved to "Col 'Ter'" near Denver to work as a carpenter for three dollars a day. She closed the letter: "As much as I love Western life, I don't think I would care to go any farther beyond the Mississippi than where we are. Remember me to all inquiring friends in Mobile."

Mobile Ala., Dec 21st 1865

My Dear Friend:

I found your kind letter of Nov 26th awaiting me on my arrival in Mobile and although you may think me rather negligent in answering it yet I assure you that this is the first letter that I have commenced since my return. My visit home was prolonged ten days more than I had anticipated, so that I did not leave home until the 4th of Dec. arriving in Mobile on the 15th Inst. I came to Cairo and then down the Miss, to New Orleans.

As you say in your letter it did give me pleasure too deep for words to express to meet the loved ones at home once more and I must say, the great tears came into my eyes, and I could hardly tell the reason why.

No one but a soldier, who has passed years away from the old home, amid scenes of peril and hardship can appreciate such a meeting of kindred and friends. Oh! it did me more good than words can express. We had some pretty cold weather while I was at home, but then I think I enjoyed that as much as pleasant weather for I sat by the fire and talked with Mother and the girls, and it was really wonderful how many questions were asked and answered and how many things there were to talk about, and then the bread and milk and baked apple and pumpkin pies that I had—Oh! there's no use talking, that's the country to live in after all. It may be rather a humiliating fact to admit, but nevertheless I believe it to be, in a measure, true, that to make a man a happy, genial, good natured being, you must give him a plenty of good, wholesome food to eat, and then with kind friends around if a man can't be happy, he is certainly a poor specimen. If any one can appreciate home fare and home comforts, it is the man who has lived as a soldier lives in this country.

As to my remaining in the South, for some years to come, my ideas have somewhat changed of late. The people in this country are getting worse and worse every day, and swear that Yankees shall not live in the country. But they can't keep the yankees out of this country if they wish to live here, but it occurs to me that I had rather live in a country where I can sleep at night, and calculate with some degree of certainty on finding things in the Morning as I left them, than to live here where every man carries a revolver about his person, and can't reckon with any degree of certainty upon anything. In a word, I have about come to the conclusion

16. Visit at Home

that I would sooner live at the North on a pittance, than at the South on a competence.

I will say this much to you: My schemes for making money have "gone up" without any loss to me, pecuniarily, and it is very likely to change all my calculations about remaining in this part of the country. Home comforts and home friends weakened my resolution and the hostile spirit manifested by the people has weakened it still more. I like a more quiet life than any one can enjoy in this country for some years to come.

My regards to all, & remember me as ever
John—

Please excuse my long delay in writing & don't copy my example in that particular, for I shall be very anxious to hear from you from time to time. Direct as usual. Ever yours,

John N. Chamberlin

Chamberlin's reversion to thoughts about living in the north may have been influenced by conditions described in an earlier letter to his sister.

The only attraction at the city now is the Theater, which opened on the 2nd. The actors are very common place, as they must of necessity be in such a one horse city as this, but Matilda Heron is announced as one of the actors for this week, and there is some anticipation of a better play.[4] It is the only place of amusement that one can attend here, with any credit to himself. There are no Lycums [Lyceums?], or Lectures and the Theater and the Billiard Rooms are the resorts of the pleasure seekers.

A large fire occurred here on the evening of the 6th of Oct. which destroyed nearly $1,000,000 worth of cotton. Fire the work of an incendiary. As cotton is nearly all that brings money into this city, this makes quite a hole in the cash capital of the business men of the city. I suppose all the cotton in this section will have been shipped through here by the 1st of January, and then I can't see what there will be to make any business here. Thousands of the destitute are now drawing rations from the U.S.

The population is nearly equally divided—black & white, but ⅛ of those drawing rations are <u>white</u>.[5] The Bureau of Refugees, Freedmen and abandoned lands, now has charge of that,[6] but the Convention of Ala. has decided to take the support of his paupers upon his own hands. This is as it should be for by the rebellion they have brought all this poverty upon the State. I suppose they think that as they have repudiated the war debt they can now afford to take care of their own poor.[7]

Love to All.
/s/ John N. Chamberlin

Captaining the Corps d'Afrique

Apparently Chamberlin's experiences at home were starting to tip the scales toward his moving back north, although he was still vacillating. He hoped to be out of the service soon and needed to decide where he would go. Even though there was a strong possibility of his moving north, he maintained his interest in the Southern political scene.

CHAPTER 17

Final Military Days

Chamberlin's visit to New York forced him into serious reflection. He wondered where he would settle, what he would do, and when he would go home. In the early part of 1866, he was disgruntled with the current state of affairs: Southern behavior and attitudes; President Johnson's policies, and continuing unfair treatment of blacks.

In their letters, Chamberlin and Bullock exchanged views on their concern for the blacks, and also their worry about what would happen when the soldiers left the South.

Mobile Ala., Jan 28th/66

My Dear Friend:

I cannot believe that I am to get no more letters from you, but it has been a month since I answered yours of Nov 26th, and still no letter from Iowa, although I have looked anxiously for one for the last two weeks.

I know that mail facilities are none of the best in this part of the country, and that may be the reason that that letter don't come. I don't propose to lay any of the blame on you, but I will say that wherever the fault lies, it is a source of pain and discomfort to me.

By request of the General Commanding the Dist. of Mobile, some National Airs were played in the Theater about the time of the Holidays. It created the greatest confusion and excitement among the Loyal people of Mobile. There was some hissing (emblematic of the venomous character of the people) and many of the so called elite of the city left the Theater. I don't wish to stay among such a people any longer than I am obliged to.

I am glad to see that Gen. Grant recommends that some troops be still retained in the South for the protection of Freedmen and Union men in general. Were the Military force removed from here today it would be unsafe for a Yankee. Even now several men who were natives of Ala. and who served in the Union army have been notified to leave this city on

Captaining the Corps d'Afrique

peril of their lives, but I regard this simply as a menace to frighten them away, but let the Federal forces be removed and such threats would be something more than idle talk.

The people had reckoned that on account of their seeming acquiescence in the Situation, that their Representatives were to be admitted into congress, and they would soon gain in the Councils of the Nation pretty much all that they lost in the arbitrament of arms on the Battle-field.[1] Their disappointment and chagrin at the failure of their pet scheme has added much to the bitterness of feeling—at least to the outward show of hatred to anything and everything Northern.

The proceedings in Congress are looked upon by all with more than common interest—in fact I believe this to be the most important congress that has ever convened in this country, and it is well for the Nation that it is composed of the proper material. The viper—Slavery is dead—but we must see that every State that has been in rebellion against us, secures to every one of her citizens equal rights. Then, and not till then, we can truly say that "all is Peace."

George [his brother] came down here with me, for his health, but intends to start for Ill. soon on his way home. We are living very quietly in camp, and have very little to do. But the winter is passing rapidly away, and we are already counting the weeks until the 1st of April when we expect to be mustered out of the service. Regiments are being mustered out every week, but we are still retained. This is now the oldest colored Regiment in the service.

When I get out of the service I am going to look about some in the West and with your permission will visit Waterloo, Iowa. I say "with your permission," because I have said so much about visiting that locality and have not, as yet fulfilled any of my promises, you may think I may as well stay away until the Millenium or some other equally remote period.

       My Regards to all, As ever
       John N. Chamberlin

Many soldiers had been mustered out. By early January 1866, Chamberlin and his men had reason to hope they would be released soon. His black soldiers had served him long and faithfully. Records show that forty-three of Chamberlin's soldiers labored under his leadership for twenty-six months, beginning even before the 3rd Corps d'Afrique became the 97th U.S.C.I. The average number of troops in his company during the war was forty-eight; after the war ended, this number increased to sixty. Thus a majority of his soldiers survived the battles and hardships of war and remained loyal. In addition, three out

17. Final Military Days

of five of his sergeants and corporals served the whole twenty-six-month period [see Appendix K].²

Waterloo, Iowa, Feb 13th 1866

My Dear Friend.

I "plead guilty" to not having answered your letter of Dec 21st yet, so the blame does rest on me. I acknowledge that I am very bad indeed. If you would only give me a good scolding, or tell me that you did not care to hear from me I perhaps should try to justify myself a little. But instead, your letters are always so kind.

It seems to me a wise conclusion for any Northern man that cares for his life, to come to, not to stay in the "Sunny South" after the military forces have been removed. Before the War, it was not safe to travel among the chivalric people of the South, unless one's mouth were as a "sealed book," & now that they have tried their all & are the losers, & the free North their victors they seem the more exasperated.

"What is to be done with the Negro" is a question that excites a great deal of interest now. And I believe that it is a question that will have to be settled equitably & justly, in the sight of God, before we again become a prosperous & happy people. An agent by the name of Chamberlin passed through here this Winter, soliciting aid for the Freedmen. The people contributed liberally as they always do.

Feb 15th. Just as I was going to commence this sheet, Mother wished me to do an errand for her down town, & like a dutiful daughter I put away my writing materials & went, & on my way met the Express Agent, who told me that there was a package in the office for me. Upon opening it, I found it contained another token of remembrance, from my friend in Mobile. It was a present I had contemplated making myself sometime, but shall prize it all the more that it comes from one whose friendship I prize so highly. Please accept my thanks.

We shall be very much pleased to see you in Waterloo, whenever it is most convenient for you, but would rather you would come some time in the Spring or Summer, because we think you would be better pleased with the country. But suit yourself. We shall be glad to see you any time.

> Father, Mother & Mollie join me in sending their best wishes.
> As ever your friend,
> Anna B.

Both Bullock and Chamberlin were following with great interest the government actions regarding equality for blacks. In February 1866 Congress tried to extend the Freedman's Bureau, but President Johnson

Captaining the Corps d'Afrique

vetoed this legislation.[3] In March 1866, Congress approved The Civil Rights Bill. This measure "offered a definition of basic civil rights that came with" citizenship (U.S. birth):

> the ability to conduct economic transactions, commence litigation, and testify in court. Each citizen was entitled to "the full and equal benefit of the laws" and should "be subject to like punishment, pains, and penalties." ... The ruling said nothing about political rights or suffrage.

President Johnson vetoed this bill as well; in early April Congress overrode his veto.[4] Chamberlin's strong negative feelings about Johnson and his policies were a thread woven through all his correspondence at this time, as illustrated in this letter to his sister.

Mobile Ala., Feb. 25"/66

Dear Sister:

Although my last letter from home was rec'd two weeks ago, that is no excuse for my delaying to write. Rec'd the Veto Message of the President of the Freedmens Bureau Bill. It creates some such feeling amongst the people here as the fall of Fort Sumpter [sic] did in 1861, although there is no such open, vociferous outburst of the popular rejoicing, it is apparrent enough to the most dull and casual observer. It is considered as much a triumph on the part of the South as Manassas was. And it is certainly a triumph for the South for it very plainly indicates what the policy of the President is.

It is not so much the vetoing of this Bill that I look at, as the idea that the President seems to entertain of putting himself in opposition to the Congress of the United States. His veto of this Bill simply indicates, that any Bill that Congress may pass for the protection and amelioration of the poor and unprotected will be treated in the same manner. I don't know how the people at the North view this matter, but I assure you that we here in the army think that either war or Peace is much preferable to this half way state of things. The President brings no sound arguments whatever to the support of his Veto. It simply says that he is on the side of the South and of injustice against liberal and just legislation. The fact of the matter is this—the President is sadly disappointing the people of the Nation.

As I have said before—better impeach the President and have Military Rule for the remainder of his term, than to lose all the fruits of the tremendous conflict. But I cannot doubt that that Power that has guided us so far through the mighty changes of the Past will not forsake us in the momentous future, but will guide us to the haven of National Peace,

17. Final Military Days

Justice and Prosperity. My health is good and although I have very little to do, still I am not wholly discontented.
Write soon, Regards to all as ever John N. Chamberlin

By the winter of 1866 Chamberlin, although interested in the future of the country and the blacks, had lost all interest in military matters, to the extent that he tried his hand at business. On January 24 he signed a co-partnership document with Peter Thompson to set up a business "for the conveyance of passengers in the city of Mobile."[5] The two men bought two barouches and five horses.[6] Thompson owned three quarters of the property, and Chamberlin owned the remaining one quarter (for an investment of $657.50). The net earnings, paid monthly, were divided in the same proportion. The partnership document was written by Chamberlin and witnessed by his brother Geo. M Chamberlin. John Chamberlin never mentioned this business again in his correspondence. However, at the end of his letter to Bullock on February 26, he discussed another business possibility.

Mobile, Feb 26th 1866

My Dear Friend:

Your kind letter postmarked Feb 16th lies before me, and I must say that great credit is due the Post Office Dept. U.S.A. for the transmission of its mail in this instance (the first indiscretion of the kind which has occurred to my knowledge, I am sorry to say) for this letter came through in five (5) days. It came through so quickly that, were it not for the warm sentiments of friendship and regard which it contained, I should almost have expected to find some of the frost of the glorious old Northland still clinging to it.

Well, your letter found me here in Mobile with very little to do and I really believe that if a man has not much to do he is almost sure to do that little badly. I have taken no interest in military matters since I came from home, and I am nearer to being homesick now than at any time during the war. If any one thinks that it is a fine thing to do nothing for $5½ a day—why let him try it—that's all. Time is not so easily killed as some folks seem to think. Why! I would sooner saw wood or break stone on the road than to have this kind of life six months longer.

What do you think of the Veto of the Freedmans Bill? I look upon it simply as a warning to congress that any and all Bills for the protection of the weak and down-trodden will meet the same fate.

I am probably no more a friend to the Negro race than the generality of people everywhere, I believe them to be an inferior race to the Anglo-

Captaining the Corps d'Afrique

Saxon, but children of the same common Father, and heirs to the same immortality as their more favored brethren, and certainly capable of much improvement. This Nation has made the race what it is among us. As a Nation we have already paid in blood for the oppression of two centuries, and it now remains to be proved whether this great sacrifice is to be heeded by us as a lesson in the future.

I wish to see Justice done by all. The Freedman is certainly entitled to protection from the Government, and it would be a breach of faith of this great nation to abandon them to the men, who for the last four years have sharpened their swords for the life-blood of the Nation. The Freedmen have fought for the Nation against the traitors who fought to overthrow it, and I am not ashamed to say that I have stood by their side in the grim conflict, when the grey Rebel line came down upon us at a charge, and seen the howling, yelping hordes of traitors scattered like chaff. They are entitled to the treatment of men and the rights of men, and woe to the nation that long withholds these rights from them. Why! The way colored men are treated here in Mobile, even with the presence of the Military is perfectly damnable. I shall soon be as radical as Wendell Philips,[7] myself.

I hear from home that Charles has bought a farm of over 200 acres that cost nearly $100 per acre. I am sorry that he bought in New-York. It is too much money for a little land. I was anxious that G & C [George & Charles] should go West but they seemed to think that it was too far from Market—in fact almost out of the world. I have been away from home so long that I should be glad to spend some time with my brothers and sisters, but it will never do for me to buy a farm in N. York, and a farmer I propose to do sometime.

My regards to all. As ever your friend
John N. Chamberlin

Like many people of his day, Chamberlin harbored some racist views about the inferiority of blacks, but felt that they were capable of improvement and that justice needed to be afforded to all. Black soldiers especially, by their long struggle, had earned their rights. As Eric Foner notes, "Racism was pervasive in mid–nineteenth-century America, and at both the regional and national levels constituted a powerful barrier to change." He quotes a North Carolina education official as saying that "nearly all white teachers, 'educated as they necessarily are in this country,' viewed black children as 'naturally inferior.'"[8] As a teacher, where did Bullock stand on the issue of black inferiority? She never stated her views directly, but she was certainly sympathetic to their plight. Although Chamberlin called the blacks inferior, his

17. *Final Military Days*

statements, "I am not ashamed to say that I have stood by their side in the grim conflict," and "woe to the nation that long withholds these rights from them," gave strong endorsement of their cause. In this, he and Bullock seemed to be of the same mind.

Waterloo, Iowa, April 12th 1866.

My Dear Friend,

I have been trying for three weeks to catch an opportunity to write to you, but have been signally defeated.

The Functionaries of the Post Office Dep't certainly deserve credit for once, I rec'd your letter just two weeks from the day that mine left Waterloo, & when I took it from the Office rather supposed that it contained one of those scoldings which you say you can administer to offenders in case of necessity, for my negligence, but upon opening it, was agreeably surprised to find myself mistaken.

I think that Charles missed it greatly, in not coming West. There is something in our being rather far from market, just now, but that will be remedied in a few years, when the several Railroads that are in contemplation are completed. But as to being away, out of the World, he is very much mistaken. We consider ourselves just about the center & when the Pacific R.R. is finished, & the National Capital removed to Chicago people away down East will begin to find out that it is so.

Have you had Johnson's message, vetoing the Civil Rights Bill. How afraid he is of doing something that will injure the feelings of the people of those states that are not allowed to be represented in Congress. Very tender hearted & conscientious he is, only the cops [Copperheads] & rebs are the only ones that seem to appreciate it. Lincoln was idolized by the people, while Johnson is looked upon with distrust & will be despised unless he changes his course of action, & that speedily.

If I have not forfeited all claims upon your time & friendship, through my dilatoriness I shall hope to hear from you again.

    As ever your friend
    Anna Bullock

P.S. By the way, you said nothing in your last letter of Uncle Sam's allowing you to go home. The papers say that cholera has made its appearance at Mobile. I should think that with the small pox & the rebs & all, ones stay must be anything but pleasant. We have heard tonight that school is to be deferred for another week. I think that I will engage a country school.

    Anna

Captaining the Corps d'Afrique

Although Chamberlin's regiment was mustered out April 6, 1866,[9] apparently Chamberlin was still in Mobile to receive Bullock's April 12 letter (above). In addition he filed a "Quarterly Return of Ordnance" from there April 12, 1866.[10] Although his whereabouts in early May 1866 are unknown, later in the month he went north on an important visit.

CHAPTER 18

Planning a Future Together

When he was mustered out, Chamberlin went directly to Waterloo; his five-day visit there changed his life forever. After years of war and politics, his thoughts moved to his future with Anna. After his visit to Waterloo, he and Bullock began a gentle, sweet correspondence. The happy couple shared some news or sometimes wrote about practical matters and specific plans. In the next paragraph, one or the other would reminisce about the time of their engagement or reiterate their feelings for the other. Selected letters from this correspondence are included here.

Chamberlin left Waterloo May 15, 1866, apparently wearing a ring Bullock had given him. On arriving home in New York, he promptly wrote to Bullock.

Elbridge Onondaga Co. N.Y., May 20th 1866

My Dear Anna:
Safe home again after my five years of wandering about the world.
I arrived here on Friday the 18th Inst. I should have been home Thursday-night, but was hindered on the D & S.C.R.R. by the breaking down of a bridge so that we failed to make connection at Dunlieth [probably Dunlieth, IL]. Stopped at rather a musty kind of a Hotel at Dunlieth, but was tired and slept well, not with-standing some of the little turtle-backs [bed bugs] that Nature is always ready to fit into the Joints of bedsteads. Left Dunlieth at 5/o'clock Wednesday morning and reached Chicago at 4 P.M.
Waited there an hour, so you see that I had very little time in the City. During the remander of the journey no incident occurred worthy of mention. I took a sleeping car on the through Express & was whirled through

Captaining the Corps d'Afrique

the country as only a rushing Railway train in this age of iron & steam can go. I went by the Southern Michigan, Northern Indiana & Lake Shore R.R.

I found the People at home usualy well, with the exception of Eleanor [one of his sisters] whose health is very poor. I told her my plans, but left the rest of the folks to conjecture. They look with a great amount of suspicion on that ring. Charley says that he never thought he should have a brother foolish enough to put a ring upon his finger. Foolish; forsooth! I'd like to have him tempted the same way that I was and see what he would do.

You will see by the heading of this that we are living in Onondaga Co., but it is only about two miles from where we formerly lived,—a little east of North. It is a magnificent place—as fine a farm as there is any where in this part of the State. The orchards are in full bloom & the woods are beautiful beyond description.

This sabbath morning seems as peaceful, quiet & holy as the first Sabbath that dawned on earth, and the heart Instinctively goes up in praise and gratitude to the great Father of all, for his mercy and love in returning me, from the perils and hardships of the last five years to the home and hearts of those I love.

There is very little to write that would be news to you from the old neighborhood where we used to live. But I intend to go to church to-day and must hasten to a close with this letter, for you know there is a certain amount of fixin to do preparatory to church-going.

I shall be looking very anxiously for a letter from you, but I have no fears concerning your faithfulness in writing now. I have a great deal more to write but must leave something for the next letter. Give my regards to your Father & Mother & the children. Also remember me to Miss Pratt.

   With much love I remain ever yours,
   Newton

Bullock also wrote to Chamberlin on May 20.

It seems a long time since the morning of the 15th. That night when school closed it seemed so lonesome, to think of going home, that I went to Aunt Katie's & stayed until most night. Stella [apparently Bullock's half-sister][1] had been home but a few minutes, before she sat down & commenced crying. Mother questioned her, & found that it was because you had gone. Don't you feel flattered! When I put her to bed she said if you would only come back, you might have me all the time. The whole family miss you, one in particular. But the waiting, & watching, is

18. Planning a Future Together

altogether different from that of the last two years, for now I am not in doubt as to your motives in visiting Iowa.

The next letter Chamberlin wrote to Bullock was dated May 26th; he reminded her of the night that he proposed in Waterloo.

> It seems a very long time to me since Friday night May 11th. Do you remember that evening? Bet you do. That night I crossed the Rubicon, and landed comparatively safe on the other side. I can almost hear the winds and waves roaring in my ears now, but then it wasn't so much a Job as I had supposed it might be, and although somewhat mixed up in my mind, what a joy to know that I was across all safe. Do you think I shall ever forget "Gentle Annie"?[2] Not "muchly."

On June 3, Chamberlin wrote:

> I don't exactly know what arrangements I can make, yet, but think we will live here this winter. How would that suit you? All are delighted with the idea of having another sister & daughter so don't have any fears on that subject. I think Charley has changed his sentiments somewhat on the subject of gold rings & don't blame me much for wearing one under the circumstances.
> By the way have you recd that package from Chicago? It is more than time. Think I will send you the Express Receipt at any rate, so that you may recover it if lost. It consisted of a dressing case & the ring was in it.

Also on June 3, Bullock wrote about the package. She told Newt, as she now addressed him:

> I was on my way "down town" in a short time after reading your letter, & was much surprised to receive so large a package, & tried in vain to conjecture what it might contain. But it took me but a few minutes to get home, & there were four pairs of eyes bent upon the mysterious package, all anxious to see it opened. All were much pleased, & decided at once that you were a sensible fellow, in choosing presents that were useful, instead of being merely ornamental. The glass, containing the small box, did not seem at all inclined to reveal its treasures, but by a few vigorous efforts it was opened, & the ring was pronounced a perfect beauty, especially by the one for whom it was intended. You could not have suited me better. I never thought that it could give me half the pleasure to wear a ring, that it does this one. By it, I am constantly reminded of one who is dearer to me by far than all others. It is a pledge too, that he will come for me. That "where he is, there I may be also."[3] What wonder then that I love to wear it. That instead of receiving it simply as a gift, it is as a bond,

drawing me nearer to the one in whom all of my hopes & joys are centered. I could not have understood all this, one month ago, but now it seems my natural element.

A week later, Bullock answered his question about living in New York.

It does not take a very long stretch of imagination, to see the Cap't metamorphosed into a citizen farmer, or even the "School mistress" into a farmer's wife, both of which it seems to me would be a desirable change. Especially if my Cap't were the farmer & I the School mistress. I should enjoy spending the Winter in N.Y. but have always thought of my home as being in the West. Have thought I would rather go to Oregon than any farther East, but have made up my mind to try & be contented & happy wherever you consider it for your best interest to make our home. It is a great comfort to me to know that your friends & mine seem pleased with the idea of having our families united.

In a June 24 letter Chamberlin seemed to agree about moving west.

The boys want me to stay here with them, and I intend to this winter, but as soon as possible, I must find me a home in the West. Tell Mrs Pratt that I thank her for her kind offers, and it is possible that I may accept them. [Bullock's family friend in Waterloo had offered him strawberry plants if he would buy a farm near her.] I was very much pleased with the country about them. The only objection seems to be the scarcity of timber.

In a June 25th letter to "Newt," Bullock reminisced.

I was just beginning to think you had forgotten me when you came, for it was the longest time that had passed without my hearing from you. But those fears were dispelled as soon as I saw you, for I felt sure you would not come here before going home, unless you cared a little more for me, than you did for the generality of womankind.

The first of Sept would not be any too soon for you to start on your Western mission, were I to consult my wishes alone, but you know there are other things to be taken into consideration. Firstly—It would make quite a difference in my wardrobe, for you know it is nearly as warm through Sept" as in Aug" & I would have to have with me a supply of Summer as well as Winter clothing, for which I do not feel quite prepared, & Secondly—the work that stares me in the face at every turn, reminds me that a little more time will be necessary in its completion. A

18. Planning a Future Together

month longer would remedy all of that I think. Are my reasons sufficient do you think? If not, & you are urgent, I will try & compromise.

A sweet "Good Night" with a kiss if you have so vivid an imagination, from your own Annie.

Sunday Morning July 1st

My Darling Annie;

One whole month gone and part of another since I left your home. I doubt not your reasons for waiting a little longer are good ones and I shall conform to your wishes in that respect, as nearly as I can. I know you must be pretty well worn out with your school, and you ought to have one month to rest up and not do anything. Then know,—from observation, that a woman needs more time than a man does to "fix up."

I don't think the wise people of Sennett have any suspicion of what my plans are. At any rate I don't bother myself to tell them. In the first place it ain't any of their business, and in the second I don't care to hear quite so much gab as some of them would be called upon to make. When any of them begin to buzz me, I tell them that I have half made up my mind to advertise for a position as Son-in-law in some respectable family and were it not that the chances were so much against me, I probably should. They certainly don't increase their stock of useful information by any onslaught upon me.

Waterloo, Iowa, July 8 1866

Dearest Newt,

I was a little anxious to get your reply in regard to putting off our marriage a little longer, yet it was what I expected, & I loved you the more if it were possible, for this conformity to my wishes. I naturally think a great deal about you & from the remembrance of our early days, & the knowledge I gained from you, through our correspondence, it seems too much happiness for me, to be your life companion. Yet I know I could never marry any one that I did not feel to be my Superior in every respect, one that I could look up to for guidance & counsel as I do to you, the chosen of my heart. All that I have, or am is thine, & I will not object if the minister does put in "obey", for when one loves, to obey is easy.

In a July 15 letter, Bullock described the day Newt left Waterloo. "I watched you as you went downtown to see if you would look back, but you did not, & I closed the door, feeling that the light & life had all gone with you. How changed everything seemed to me from what it was only the day before."

Captaining the Corps d'Afrique

Elbridge, N.Y., July 22

My Darling Annie,

I remember very distinctly the morning that I left Waterloo and the sad but joyful parting. "Don't feel bad Annie, it will be only a little while" were all I could trust myself to say, for my own tears were ready to fall, and I turned away too sad to say more or even to look back. No other parting of my life was half so sad as that, but there was more of hope and comfort in the future than in any other parting that I remember.

My visit to Waterloo was so short that I but half realized what a priceless treasure the love of woman is, and now that I am watching for the tokens of love and confidence I feel, that it is almost too good to be true that I am so truly and wholly loved by such a true noble-hearted girl. May the kind Father shower his richest blessings upon you ever, my Darling, for all these tokens of tenderness and love. I am all thine and when the minister makes me promise to love and cherish it will be only a formal declaration of that vow which is already recorded by higher authority than man's.

Home, Sunday Eve. [date unknown]

Dearest Annie:

I have written to you a good deal about coming here to live and have not consulted your wishes very much I fear, and have not written much about our surroundings.

Well! now is a good time to talk this matter over. I have no doubts about your love for me, but it is not always the most agreeable way of living in a house with another family. Geo. has three children—one an infant of two months. They are all as good as common children of their age, and I think a great deal of them—especially the oldest—Alice, who seems to love me with her whole heart. The house is a large two-story one with fine upper rooms, and no matter how much noise there may be in the kitchen, it is quiet here. Sarah and Mary Ann are like Sisters to me, as far as kindness goes, or rather Mary Ann is more like a mother.

She [Sarah, Chamberlin's sister-in-law] remembers you when you were a couple of months old and took care of you. Says you always ran out to meet her when you were large enough to run and say "Aunty have you got any cabbage?" This coincides exactly with your declaration that you are a great cabbage head. Well! the others of us are brothers and that ought to be saying enough in that respect. At any rate we don't quarrel with each other.

It is a very pleasant place here but not exactly a home of my own to be sure, but I sent my money to Geo. to invest as he chose, and I don't feel

18. Planning a Future Together

like saying to them that they must get my money at once. [Chamberlin told one of his sisters in a letter written July 8, 1864, that he had written to have his money invested in real estate.] I hope to arrange matters within a year so that I can go West with capital enough to get us a comfortable home. If I could persuade them all to go West I would like it very much. But I think it is very doubtful about my being able to do so & of course I don't feel that it would be right for me to urge the matter for as long as they are contented here I would not be instrumental in getting them in a situation where they would not be so. However I am determined to go West to make my home and the sooner I am able to go, the better, of course.

I hope you will express your mind freely in regard to these things for your happiness is the cause of my greatest solicitude.

With a good night Kiss I am, as ever your own —
Newton

Had the couple talked before about their living arrangements for the fall, or had he waited until after she had agreed to live in New York to tell her? Presumably, the recently-retired captain did not have the financial resources to obtain separate housing for them in New York. His invitation to "express her mind freely" seemed hollow, because they really did not appear to have any other alternative.

Chamberlin finished the story of Friday night, May 11, in a July 29th letter:

Darling Annie,

How vividly everything comes back to my mind now as I write. What a tell-tale your cheek was when I told you that I didn't come to Iowa to see the country half as much as to see you. And shall I ever forget the kiss that was so precious to me, and how you trembled like a frightened bird in my arms, but only for joy.

Home, Aug 17th 1866

My Own Darling [Annie]:

To-day is the 17th of Aug. and I have just been thinking that in a little more than a month I shall be on my way West. I shall be pretty certain who I am going West to see this time. I have also been thinking of some things practically. In the first place, as we are coming to N.Y. you will want a good trunk and I think it would be best for me to get one in Chicago when I come, and do you want any particular style of trunk or would you wish to leave it to my judgement. And then do you want any

Captaining the Corps d'Afrique

wedding cards? I could get them better in Chicago than elsewhere, and is there any particular article that you would wish me to get on my journey? Now tell me, Dearest, without mental reservation or evasion.

Home, Aug. 26th/66

Dearest Newton,

I shall enjoy making & wearing my silk gown so much the more that you approve of my selection. [Chamberlin had approved it in an August 12 letter.] I believe we all dress to please others more or less & who should I care to please half as much as my future Husband. Did I tell you that I was pleased with your coat? A black frock has always been my favorite style. How often I have noticed both among men & women that the dress was characteristic of the person.

About that trunk—if we stay in NY a year I will need to take all of my clothing & I would think a common packing trunk would be the best, but will leave it with you to decide, only if you get one that is too expensive I may scold you. I had thought that I would like cards enough to send to those of my friends who are so far away that they would not hear of my marriage except by writing, but there are so few of them, not more than six or eight, that unless you cared to have some, I would not get any at all. I do not like the plan of sending them around in the place where one lives, for there is always someone that feels slighted & it is sure to make hard feelings.

Home, Sept 2" 1866

My Darling Annie:

I think I will not get a very expensive trunk for you when I come, for my trunk is a large one and I shall not have it half filled and however out of place a womans apparrel might be in it now, it won't do any harm to mix things in that way then. So some of your finer clothes may go in that and whatever else you wish to bring in the other. You spoke of selling your melodeon, Don't do it, for how could you play and sing "Gentle Annie"? I wouldn't wish you to sell your watch either if it is good for any thing for I don't think there is any need of it.

Waterloo, Iowa, Sept 9th 1866

My Own Dear Newt,

I have not made any effort to sell my melodeon, for since then I think more of it than ever. I do not care to be troubled with a watch when I am not in school, & would rather dispose of mine, if I can do so advantageously. If I cannot get the money for it, I will exchange it for table silver, for I would rather have the worth of it in that way, than to keep it.

18. Planning a Future Together

Home, Sept. 16"/66

My Own Darling:

I find that a week from next Tuesday will be the 25th of the Month, and if nothing occurs to hinder me I shall start for Iowa on that day.

I am anticipating having a jolly old time this winter, in fact I am bound to be jolly for hain't I got out of the army all right, and won't I have one of the best wives that ever made a mans life happy? I assure you it does take some courage to ask the fatal question, for it is a mighty difficult thing for one to know exactly another's thoughts and feelings. Don't hardly know what I should have done if your singing "Gentle Annie" hadn't helped me along. I didn't even require a verbal yes you know, although the answer came from the lips and I felt that kiss to be warm from the heart. There certainly was very little hesitation about it and it was dearer to me than any words that you could have uttered. Oh! those were happy hours and all these long summer days seem made bright and joyous by them, and whether at work in the field or in my own quiet room, my thoughts are constantly going back to those bright blessed hours of happiness and love.

Sarah tells me that the step I am about to take is the most important one in our lives, and I believe I realize something of its importance. It is to change the whole course of our lives. It is ordained of God and witnessed by angels, and the vows then taken by each of us are more sacred and inviolable than any others that man and woman can take upon themselves. I have no fears for the future but we shall always be happy in each other's love. What though so many miles of green hills and valleys have stretched between us have not our spiritual natures communed with each other all the long summer?

It is said that "many waters cannot quench love"[4] and I have often felt that even though a whole continent seperated us and seas rolled between, you would still be as tenderly loved and just as dear to me. How strange that we should have this feeling for each other, this love which overpowers all others, and will be pure and bright through all the coming years of time. Let us always love as now and whatever the trials and cares of life that may surround us there will always be a solace to be found in each other.

I shall always look to you for counsel and guidance in the right way, for whenever I think of you it seems to me you are stronger than I for have you not been tried in the furnace of affliction? Death has come so very near to you that you have heard the rustling of his dark pinions, while I have never been called to mourn for one who was half as dear to me as a Mother. Affliction always strengthens us, and that is why I look up to you as stronger in your inmost soul than I am. Some clouds must cross the

Captaining the Corps d'Afrique

pathway of all, but I think you have had more than the ordinary share of them.

If a desire for your future comfort and happiness, and the love of so poor a heart as mine can make any amends for the long years of trial and sorrow that clouded your girl-hoods years, they are all thine, and seem to me only as a meager recompense for the great love you bear toward me.

As ever your lover,
Newton

As seen in these letters, the warrior had become a tender lover, and the soldier a farmer. The teacher was soon to become a wife, as together they ventured blissfully into marriage.

Epilogue

Chamberlin and Bullock were married on October 9, 1866, in Waterloo, Iowa. A few days later they took the train back to New York. They picked an upstairs room in George [Chamberlin's brother] and Sarah's large farm house near Elbridge, New York, and lived there temporarily, hoping they could soon buy a farm of their own.[1]

For the next ten years, limited records offer contradictory views of John Chamberlin's life. Dr. Elias Lestor, who served with Chamberlin in the war, saw him at a Soldier's Reunion in September 1868 or 1869, and wrote in an Affidavit: "He was sitting in a chair while all others were standing about. He was yellow, emaciated, and greeted me with a sickly smile and seemed very melancholy and depressed."[2] However on November 26, 1870, Chamberlin was "licensed to teach a Common School for the term of one year" in Cayuga County. Leonard F. Hardy, School Commissioner, examined Chamberlin and "ascertained his qualifications in respect to Moral Character, Learning and Ability to instruct a Common School." In May 1871 he was able to write a complex real estate agreement for the joint ownership of two farms. It was signed by George, Charles, and John Chamberlin.[3]

Another document suggests that these years were a happy time in John Chamberlin's life (fig. 10). They had five children in a ten-year period. In a letter to his wife, written in August 1873, while she was in Iowa settling her father's estate, he talked fondly about their children and happily about their family.

> Marian [their oldest child] has told me a good deal to write, but she will have to wait for some of it. She wanted me to tell you about the old cat carrying her kitties up over the kitchen & she fell down with one & we

Epilogue

Figure 10. Anna, Marian and John Chamberlin, ca. 1870. Original in possession of John Bisbee.

have baked apples & pears every day & we have such nice sweet corn & some tomatoes.

It is almost nine & the crickets chirp as they only will when one is alone & still. I love to hear them but it seems dreadful lonesome, for Howard [their second child, who was probably with his mother] used to be trotting around about this time before getting into bed.

How many still lonely hours I have passed before we were married thinking of you & the happiness in store for us in the future, & darling has not the reality been about as bright as the dream.

Unfortunately, in the late 1870's, according to family history, John was not healthy because he had contracted malaria while in the South. He fought recurring bouts of what his family doctor described as "chronic derangement of the liver followed by depression."[4] In the twenty-first century much is said and written about post-traumatic stress disorder. Nobody knows what an emotional toll the war took on Chamberlin. During one of his periods of depression, after weeks of

Epilogue

sleepless nights, he hanged himself in his barn on November 9, 1880 (fig. 11).

In 1881, Anna Chamberlin moved with her five children to Nebraska, going by train to Omaha, then by covered wagon to Wheeler County where she homesteaded. Using Chamberlin's Soldiers Right to 160 acres of land, she settled next to her brother Albert (Bertie), and spent the rest of her life in Nebraska. At the time of her death (February 6, 1892) she was living with Marian and Arba Harris, her daughter and son-in-law, in Blair, Nebraska.

Figure 11. John N. Chamberlin's gravestone in Weedsport Rural Cemetery, Weedsport, Cayuga County, New York. Drawn by John Bisbee from family photographs of the gravestone.

Appendices

A. The Chamberlin and Bullock Documents: A Brief History

During his Civil War service, John Chamberlin wrote to sixteen family members—parents, grandparents, sisters and brothers—and to his childhood friend and future wife, Anna Bullock. In 1881, after John Chamberlin's death, Anna (Bullock) Chamberlin carried a large collection of his Civil War documents, equipment, and personal items with her when she moved from New York to a homestead in the Sandhills of Nebraska. After her death in 1892, his Civil War items, including all letters and documents, were divided among the Chamberlin children. Two of those children, Marian Chamberlin Harris and Mabel Chamberlin Bisbee, eventually received all of the items known to exist.

Marian Harris' Civil War items were passed to three granddaughters, Marge Goodin, Lelia Klear, and Clarice Scheffler. Lelia Klear received the original 1865 diary and John Chamberlin's photo album, and Marge and Clarice inherited letters and documents. Marge Goodin's family prepared typescripts of the 19 original letters in her possession. Lelia and her husband Paul typed the diary entries from January to May 1865. Marilyn Young, Clarice's daughter, typed copies from 48 original letters her mother had and 55 original letters that had been passed on to Mabel's son, William. All of the originals from the latter group have since been lost.

Thanks to the kindness of family members, I now own copies of all the typescripts (103 of John's letters and 21 of Anna's, plus the diary entries from early 1865), and I believe they are accurate. From my grandmother, Mabel Bisbee, I inherited many of John's original docu-

Appendices

ments, including two letters, four diaries (of 1861–1864), 24 records of "Clothing, Camp and Garrison Equipage," and a map of a redoubt built near Mobile. I have transcribed the diaries of 1861–1864, two of John's letters, and some letters from Anna's brothers. John's jacket, musket, sword, photo album, and suitcase are held by relatives or by the Washington County Historical Museum in Fort Calhoun, Nebraska.

B. Order for Service in the Corps d'Afrique

Following is John Chamberlin's order detailing him for service in the Corps d'Afrique, August 31, 1863 (original in the possession of John Bisbee).

Appendix C

C. Engineering Instructions, Duane's Manual

Following is a transcription of parts of Duane's Manual, highlighting the engineering instructions that would have been used by Chamberlin (Duane, *Manual for Engineer Troops*, 55, 67, 80–1).

II. Rules for Making Fascines.

6. FASCINES DESCRIBED.

Fascines are a superior kind of fagot, which being built in courses, with a moderate slope, and secured by pickets driven into an earthen parapet, form a revetment useful in field-works.

A *Fascine*, when the term is used without further specification, implies one about eighteen feet long and nine inches in diameter, such as is used in reveting batteries, &c., and which can be cut to any shorter length, as may be required, during the execution of the field-work in which it is used. To make fascines thicker than the above dimension would be a waste of materials.

34. OF HURDLES.

Hurdles consist of strong wicker-work, of a rectangular form, and as they may occasionally be useful in a siege, the mode of making them shall be described.

The best size for military purposes is six feet long, and two feet nine inches high. The same kind of pickets will therefore answer, as in making very strong gabions; and, generally speaking, the rods for hurdles should not be much less than an inch in diameter. An even number of pickets must always be used: and I consider ten a good proportion for a six-feet hurdle, although the woodmen in this neighborhood generally employ only eight for a hurdle of that length.

In preparing to make a hurdle, it is necessary to describe an arc of a circle on the ground, with a radius of about eight feet, making the length of the arc six feet. This space must be divided into nine equal parts. A picket is then driven into the ground at each end of it, and others into every intermediate point of division, making ten in all. Then the watling is begun, on the same principle nearly as in gabion making, excepting that you do not work round a circle, but in a continued line;

Appendices

and therefore when you come to one of the extreme pickets at either end, you must twist part of your rod like a withe, and bend it round the picket, after which you must work in the contrary direction.

In commencing a hurdle, the men work from the bottom upward, as in gabion making, but the first rod is not pressed down close to the ground, excepting in the centre. Both its ends are raised about nine inches above the ground, and there bent round the extreme pickets by twisting. Thus the first rods used form an arc of a circle, concave on the upper side. The second and third rods are bent round the extreme pickets, as close to the ground as possible, at each end of the hurdle, but in the centre they rise higher than the first rods used; and thus the first three or four rods, or rather courses of rods, composing the web of the hurdle, arc interlaced in such a manner, by crossing each other toward the centre, as to prevent the separation of that part of the web from the pickets.

III. Rules for Making: Gabions and Hurdles.
21. OF GABIONS.

Gabions are cylindrical hampers, open at top and bottom, which, being filled with earth, form a revetment useful in field-works, but more especially in a siege, in the construction of batteries, and in the operations called the regular and flying sap. Light gabions are a species of basket work, and it requires greater skill and care to make them than is necessary in making heavier ones, which may be compared to hurdle work.

22. DESCRIPTON AND DIMENSIONS OF GABIONS.

For many years past we have made all our gabions of the same size, namely, two feet in exterior diameter, and two feet nine inches high in the web, but averaging three feet in height when used for the revetment of a trench or fieldwork, in consequence of the projecting ends of the pickets. Hence when the term GABION is used, without further specification, it implies one of the above dimensions, and no other.

Appendix D

D. Fort Gaines Orders

Orders #51 for Capt. Chamberlin to be assistant engineer at Fort Gaines, September 21, 1864 (original in the possession of John Bisbee).

> Head-Quarters 97th U.S.C.I.
> Dauphine Island Septr 21.1864
>
> Special Orders
> No. 51.
>
> (Extract)
>
> 1. Until Captain Gilbert Hill is again returned to duty, Captain Jno H Chamberlain "E" company will act as Asst. Engineer in the repairs on Fort Gaines, reporting for orders to Lieut C. J. Allen. U.S. Engineers. Engr in charge.
>
> By order of Comdg Officer
> Wm Haight Jr
> Adjutant
>
> Capt Chamberlain

Appendices

E. Receipt for Clothing Issued in October 1864

Receipt-Roll of clothing issued in the month of October 1864, to "E" Co. 97th U.S.C.I. (original in the possession of John Bisbee).

Appendix F

F. Stores Lost in Action, December 18, 1864

This is a list of stores lost in action at Pine Barren Creek, Florida, on December 18, 1864. It formed part of John Chamberlin's Quarterly Return of Ordinance Stores, Deccember 31, 1864 (original in the possession of John Bisbee). (See next page.)

Appendices

Camp of the 97th U.S. Col. Inf. Infy
Barrancas Dec. 31st 1864.

I certify, on honor, that on the 18th day of Dec, 1864, at Pine Barren Creek Fla, the Stores enumerated below were lost, under the following circumstances.

The Regt. to which my Company belongs, was engaged with the enemy, and one Private was killed and one Private wounded in my Company. The arms and accoutrements of these men were left on the field, as the Regt. fell back immediately after the engagement, and they could not be recovered.

The following is the list of Stores so abandoned:

- 2 Springfield Rifled Muskets Cal. 5.77
- 2 Cartridge Boxes & Plates
- 2 Cartridge Box Belts & Plates
- 2 Waist Belts & Plates
- 2 Cap Pouches & Picks
- 2 Gun-Slings
- 2 Screw-Drivers & Wrenches
- 2 Tampions
- 2 Bayonet Scabbards

John N. Chamberlin
Capt. 97th U.S. Col. Inf. Infy
Comdg. Co. "E"

I certify, that the facts, as above set forth are correct to the best of my knowledge and belief.

Peter Thompson
2nd Lieut. 97th U.S.C.I.
Comdg. Co. "K"

Appendix G

G. Field Work Order, April 24, 1865

Orders for Captain Chamberlin to take charge of construction of the Field Work at Blakely, April 24, 1865 (original in the possession of John Bisbee).

Blakely Ala Apr 24 1865

Capt Chamberlain
97 USCI Captain

You will please take charge of the construction of the Field Work at this place in accordance with the Order of the C.O. USCI assigning Cos E & K of that Regt to duty, and construct the Work upon the plan generally indicated by the following Extract from instructions turned over to me.

Extract
x x x

You will also in purserance of G.F.O. charge dated Apr 12 1865 from these HdQs construct without delay a field work for three hundred (300) men & six (6) Smooth bore field guns, for the temporary protection of the Brick Yard landing at Blakely against land approaches of small parties of the enemy _ x x x x x _ & rifled trench placed in advance to command the crossing of the Shore road leading northward where it crosses the Swamp & Stockades or other Suitable lines of defense. Complete the enclosure of the landing with a gateway x x x x x _ Military obstacles should be arranged in connection with the swamp which nearly surrounds the site proposed.

x x x

Other details not covered by the above or the verbal instructions given you will be left to your own judgment.

A detail of 150 men has been ordered to report to you daily at 7 A.M. from the garrison of the Post

I desire the collection and guarding of Entrenching tools or other property to be done from the lines outside this place & the Materials &c brought to the landing for shipment.

The Commanding officer has orders to furnish details of officers & men & the Post Quartermaster will furnish Tools & Transportation upon your requisition.

Very Truly
Your Obdrserv [?]
A.M. Clark Maj Eng

Appendices

H. Chronology of John's and Anna's Letters

John Chamberlin's and Anna Bullock's letters, February 1864 to December 1865.

| *John Chamberlin's Letters* | *Anna Bullock's Letters* |

1864

Feb. 22   John's **1st letter** to Anna, from Berwick City, Louisiana

Mar. 31   Anna wrote John (**her 1st**)

Apr. 28   John rec. Anna's letter of Mar 31(**her 1st**)

May 2   John's **2nd letter** to Anna, from Alexandria, Louisiana

May 24   John's **3rd letter** to Anna, from Morganza, Louisiana

July 16   Anna wrote John (**her 2nd**)

July 28   John rec. Anna's letter of July16 (**her 2nd**)

Aug. 4   John's **4th letter** to Anna, from Bayou St. John, Louisiana

Sept. 30   Anna wrote John (**her 3rd**)

Oct. 17 *(approximately)*   John rec. Anna's letter of Sept 30 (**her 3rd**)

Oct. 23   John's **5th letter** to Anna, from Fort Gaines, Alabama

Nov. 20   Anna wrote John (**her 4th**)

1865

Jan. 10 or 13   John rec. Anna's letter of Nov 20 (**her 4th**)

Jan. 15   John's **6th letter** to Anna, from Barrancas, Florida

Feb. 22   Anna wrote John (**her 5th**)

Apr. 4   John's **7th letter** to Anna, from near Mobile

Appendix H

(John Chamberlin's Letters)	*(Anna Bullock's Letters)*
Apr. 19 Anna rec. John's **7th letter**	
May 25	Anna wrote John (**her 6th**)
June 2 John's **8th letter** to Anna, from Mobile, Alabama	
June 9	John rec. Anna's May 25 letter (**her 6th**)*
June 14 John's **9th letter** to Anna, from Mobile	John rec. Anna's Feb 22 letter (**her 5th**)
Aug. 20	Anna wrote John (**her 7th**)
Sept. ?	John rec. Anna's Aug 20 letter (**her 7th**)**
Sept. 10 John's **10th letter** to Anna, from Mobile	
Oct. 1	Anna wrote John (**her 8th**)
Oct. 10	John rec. Anna's Oct 1 letter (**her 8th**)
Nov. 13 John's **11th letter** to Anna, from Sennett, New York	
Nov. 26	Anna wrote John (**her 9th**)*
Dec. 15	John rec. Anna's Nov 26 letter (**her 9th**)†
Dec. 21 John's **12th letter** to Anna, from Mobile	

*The only letters of Anna's written in 1864 and 1865 that have been preserved.

**John returned to Mobile from Sparta, Alabama, ca. September 10 to find this letter waiting for him.

†John returned to Mobile from New York December 15 to find this letter waiting for him.

Appendices

I. Jennie Rogers *Orders*

Orders for Master of Steamer *Jennie Rogers* to be at Claiborne, Alabama, and report to Capt. John N. Chamberlin, Provost Marshal, Conecuh County, Alabama, September 4, 1865 (original in the possession of John Bisbee).

Appendices J and K

J. Leave of Absence, October 18, 1865

Orders for leave of absence for Captain John N. Chamberlin, October 18, 1865 (original in the possession of John Bisbee).

> HEADQUARTERS, DEPARTMENT OF ALABAMA,
>
> MOBILE, ALA., *October* 18*th*, 1865.
>
> SPECIAL ORDERS,
> No. 79.
> *(Extract.)*
>
> * * * *
>
> II.—In compliance with the privilege expressed in General Orders, No. 123, dated War Department, Adjutant Generals Office, July 20, 1865, Leave of Absence for twenty (20) days with permission to proceed beyond the limits of this Department, and to apply to the Commanding General Military Division of the Tennessee, for an extension of thirty days, is granted
> Captain *John N. Chamberlain*, Co. "E," 97th U. S. C. I.
>
> * * * *
>
> By order of Major General CHAS. R. WOODS,
>
> SAM. W. SNOW, A. A. G.
>
> Official :
>
> Assistant Adjutant General.

K. Soldiers in Black Companies Commanded by Capt. Chamberlin

This list was compiled from "Receipt-Roll of Clothing" reports filed by Chamberlin (originals in the possession of John Bisbee). September 1863–April 1864: soldiers in Co. E, 3rd Regiment Engineers, Corps d'Afrique. April 1864–April 1866: soldiers in Co. E, 97th Regiment, U.S.C.I. (Engineers). **Key:** - = not listed on report; corp = corporal; mus = musician; serg = sergeant; x = listed on report

173

Appendices

	2/'64	7/'64	9/'64	10/'64	1/'65	3/'65	6/'65	9/'65	12/'65	1/'66	4/'66
Arnold, Fate	x	-	x	x	x	x	x	x	x	x	x
Ayers, John	serg	x	serg	serg	serg	serg	serg	-	-	-	-
Battice, John	x	x	x	x	x	x	x	x	x	x	x
Baylor, Reuben	-	x	corp	corp	x	corp	corp	corp	corp	corp	corp
Brayee, Ziba	-	x	x	x	x	x	x	x	x	x	x
Cartz, William M.	x	-	-	-	-	-	-	-	-	-	-
Diggs, General	x	mus	mus	mus	mus	mus	mus	mus	mus	mus	mus
Ferguson, Anderson	x	x	x	-	-	-	-	-	-	-	-
Francis, John	x	x	x	x	x	x	x	x	x	-	x
Garrison, George	x	x	-	x	x	-	x	x	x	corp	corp
Gee, Joseph	-	-	-	-	-	-	x	x	x	x	x
Gillem, Willis	-	-	-	-	-	x	x	x	x	-	x
Hall, James	corp	corp	corp	corp	corp	-	corp	corp	corp	corp	corp
Harman, Nathaniel	-	x	x	x	x	-	x	-	x	-	x
Harrison, Henry	-	-	-	-	-	-	x	x	x	-	x
Henry, James	-	x	x	x	x	x	x	x	-	x	x
Horman, Nathaniel	x	-	-	-	-	x	-	x	-	x	-
Howard, Peter	-	-	-	-	-	-	x	x	x	x	x
Hudson, Charles	x	x	x	x	x	x	x	x	x	x	x
Hughes, Major	-	-	-	-	-	-	x	x	x	x	x
Humbard, Robert	-	-	-	-	-	-	x	x	x	x	x
Ingraham, Ranson	-	-	-	-	-	-	x	x	x	x	x
Jackson, Andrew	-	-	-	-	-	-	x	x	x	corp	corp
Jackson, Harry	-	x	x	x	-	corp	corp	-	corp	corp	-
Jackson, Henry	x	-	x	-	x	-	-	corp	x	-	corp
Jennings, January	-	-	-	-	-	x	-	-	-	-	-
Johnson, Albert	x	x	corp	corp	corp	corp	corp	corp	corp	-	-
Johnson, Alexander	-	-	-	-	-	-	x	x	x	x	x
Johnson, Amiel	-	-	-	-	-	-	x	x	x	x	x
Johnson, Frederick	-	-	-	-	-	-	x	x	x	x	x
Johnson, George	-	-	-	-	-	-	x	x	x	x	x
Johnson, Gillem	-	-	-	-	-	-	x	x	x	x	x
Johnson, John	-	-	-	-	-	-	x	x	x	x	x
Johnson, Joseph	x	x	x	x	x	x	x	x	x	-	x
Johnson, Thomas	x	x	x	x	x	x	x	x	x	x	x
Jones Robert	-	-	-	-	-	-	x	x	x	x	x
Jones, Edmund	x	x	x	x	-	-	x	x	-	-	-
Jones, Franklin	x	-	-	-	-	-	-	-	-	-	-
Jones, Peter	-	-	-	-	-	-	x	x	x	x	x
Jones, Savan	-	x	-	x	x	x	x	-	x	x	x
Jones, William	x	x	x	x	x	x	x	x	x	x	x
Junior, Thomas	-	-	-	-	-	-	x	x	x	x	x
Kenny, William	corp	serg	serg	serg	serg	serg	serg	serg	serg	serg	serg
Knox, Jordan	x	x	x	x	x	x	x	x	x	x	x
Knox, Marshall	x	x	x	x	x	-	x	x	x	x	x

Appendix K

	2/'64	7/'64	9/'64	10/'64	1/'65	3/'65	6/'65	9/'65	12/'65	1/'66	4/'66
Knox, Pleasant	x	x	-	x	x	x	x	x	x	x	x
Lear, John	x	-	-	-	-	-	-	-	-	-	-
Lemy, John	-	x	x	-	-	-	-	-	-	-	-
Leui or Levi, John	-	corp	corp	corp	corp	x	x	x	x	x	x
Levee, Felix	x	x	x	x	-	x	-	x	x	x	x
Lewis, Felix	-	x	x	-	-	-	-	-	x	-	-
Lewis, John	x	x	-	x	x	x	x	x	x	x	x
Major, Moses	x	x	x	x	-	-	-	-	-	-	-
Malone, Adam	-	x	x	x	x	x	x	x	x	x	x
Manuel, John	x	x	x	x	x	x	x	x	x	x	x
McCarty, William	-	x	x	-	x	x	x	x	-	-	x
Miner, Willaim	serg	x	serg	1 serg	1 serg	1 serg	1 serg	1 serg	1 serg	1 serg	1 serg
Monroe, General	-	x	x	x	x	x	x	x	-	x	x
Moore, George	corp	serg	serg	-	serg	serg	serg	serg	serg	serg	serg
Mow, Phillip	x	corp	corp	corp	corp	corp	x	corp	corp	corp	corp
Murphy, Stephen	x	x	x	x	x	corp	serg	serg	serg	serg	serg
Pierre, John	x	x	x	x	x	x	x	x	x	x	x
Proveaux, Alexis	x	x	x	x	x	x	x	x	x	x	x
Rama, Isham	x	x	x	x	x	x	x	x	x	x	x
Red, John	serg	x	x	x	x	x	x	x	x	-	x
Robinson, Harry	x	x	x	x	x	x	corp	serg	-	serg	-
Robinson, William	corp	x	x	x	x	x	x	x	x	x	x
Robinson, Thomas	x	x	x	x	-	-	-	-	-	-	-
Russ (or Rufs), Charles	-	x	x	x	x	x	x	x	x	x	x
Russ (or Rufs), Frederick	x	x	x	x	x	-	-	-	-	-	-
Rydal, Reuben	x	x	x	-	x	x	x	-	-	-	-
Sessions, David	-	x	x	x	x	x	x	x	x	-	x
Shaw, Oliver	x	x	x	x	x	x	x	x	x	x	x
Treadwell, Albert	serg	x	x	-	x	x	x	x	x	x	x
Washington, Isaac	-	mus	mus	mus	mus	mus	mus	mus	mus	mus	mus
Williams, James	1 serg	x	serg	serg	serg	serg	x	x	x	x	x
Williams, Thomas	x	corp	corp	corp	x	x	x	x	x	x	x
TOTAL SOLDIERS	44	53	51	47	47	45	65	63	60	54	60

Chapter Notes

Chapter 1

1. John Chamberlin was the son of Joel and Polly (Metcalf) Chamberlin, both born in Royalston, Massachusetts. The 1860 Cayuga County, New York, federal census lists Joel and Polly as each age 61, and their children: Charles, 29, Eleanor, 26, Newton J, 23, Harriett, 20, and a married brother George, 32. (Researched and written by Marilyn Young, a great, great-granddaughter of John N. Chamberlin.)

2. *The Annual Report of the Adjutant-General of the State of New York for the Year 1901* (Albany: J. B. Lyon, 1902), 27, hereafter referred to as AG for the year 1901. Military Service Records obtained from the National Archives, June 11, 2014. John Chamberlin was listed as a corporal from November 1861 to June 1863 and as a sergeant from July 1863 to September 1, 1863. Based on his comments in later chapters, apparently Chamberlin enlisted as a private in September 1861.

3. James Hall, *Cayuga in the Field: A Record of the 75th N.Y. Volunteers, Comprising an Account of Its Organization, Camp Life, Marches, Battles, Losses, Toils and Triumphs in the War for the Union, with Complete Rolls of Its Members*, vol. 2 (Auburn, New York, 1873), 18–22; *The War of the Rebellion: A Compilation of the Official Records of the Union and Confederate Armies* (Washington, D.C. Government Printing Office, 1880–1901), ser. 1, 26:363, hereafter referred to as OR. On June 30, 1862, Col. John A. Dodge was commander of the 75th N.Y.V. at Fort Pickens and Pensacola, Florida, under Brig. Gen. L. G. Arnold; *The War of the Rebellion: A Compilation of the Official Records of the Union and Confederate Navies* (Washington, D.C.: Government Printing Office, 1894–1922), ser. 1, 1:337, 342, and others, hereafter referred to as ORN. The *Baltic* was a steamer chartered for $1,500/day and used by the Union Navy up and down the Atlantic seaboard throughout the war.

4. Hall, *Cayuga in the Field*, 2:22.

5. *Ibid.*, 2: 26, 28.

6. John H. Eicher and David J. Eicher, *Civil War High Commands* (Stanford University Press, 2001), 146; OR, ser. 1, 6:666–7; 16:497. Col. Harvey Brown (1795–1874) of New Jersey served many places in the United States and Mexico throughout his lengthy military career. He was a Yankee commander at Ft. Pickens while Chamberlin was there.

7. "Warriors throughout history have considered all goods and property seized during a conflict to be contraband, if such items can aid and abet the enemy's ability to continue to make war. The Civil War is a unique conflict because the assets that were considered contraband often included human beings." Gen. Benjamin Butler (1819–1893) was the first general to treat the runaways in this way. Whether Chamberlin was using the term to refer to runaway slaves or white Rebel deserters is unknown. Junius P. Rodriguez, "Contrabands," in *Encyclopedia of the American Civil War: A Political, Social and Military History*, ed. David S. Heidler and Jeanne T. Heidler (New York: W.W. Norton, 2000), 491–3.

8. David J. Coles, "Santa Rosa Island," in Heidler and Heidler, *Ency. of the Am. Civil War*, 1704. John K. Jackson was one of the leaders of an unsuccessful Confederate attempt to capture Fort Pickens on Santa Rosa Island, October 9, 1861.

9. OR, ser. 1, 16:496.

10. Anita Palladino, ed., *Diary of a Yankee*

Chapter Notes—2

Engineer: The Civil War Story of John H. Westervelt, Engineer, 1st New York Volunteer Engineer Corps (New York: Fordham University Press, 1997), 13. Sutlers were officially authorized civilians who set up business at camps to sell miscellaneous items such as food, paper, and tobacco. Although prices were supposed to be regulated, many charged outrageously, resulting in frequent clashes between soldiers and sutlers.

11. AG for the Year 1901, 173. Hartwell A. Wilkins was Chamberlin's tent-mate. At the age of 18 he enlisted for three years in the 75th N.Y.V. at Sennett on September 24, 1861. He was mustered in as a corporal, Co. D, on November 26, 1861, and discharged September 19, 1863, for promotion to first lieutenant, Co. D, 88th U.S. Colored Troops.

12. AG for the Year 1901, 36; *The Annual Report of the Adjutant-General of the State of New York* (Albany: Comstock & Cassidy, 1863), 666, hereafter referred to as AG for the Year 1863. Andrew Corning was "mustered in as first lieutenant, Co. D," 75th N.Y.V., November 26, 1861, and was one of John Chamberlin's commanding officers during basic training in New York. Corning was promoted to captain December 17, 1862, and was discharged on November 20, 1863.

13. Spencer C. Tucker, "Phelps's Raid," in Heidler and Heidler, *Ency. of the Am. Civil War*, 1510. To avoid its being captured by the Union, the steamer *Time* was burned by the Confederates on the Tennessee River during Phelps's Raid, February 1862.

14. Mark M. Boatner III, *Civil War Dictionary* (New York: David McKay, 1987), s.v. "Arnold, Lewis." Lewis G. Arnold (1817–1871) was a commander in several places, including Fort Pickens on Santa Rosa Island, Florida, and briefly in New Orleans, until a stroke forced him to retire.

Chapter 2

1. David J. Coles, "Fort Pickens," in Heidler and Heidler, *Ency. of the Am. Civil War*, 744–5. Forts Pickens, McRee, and Barrancas guarded the entrance to Pensacola Bay and the valuable Pensacola Navy Yard. Fort Pickens was built on the western tip of Santa Rosa Island and was the only one of the three forts that remained in Union hands throughout the Civil War. Forts McRee and Barrancas were strengthened by the Confederates in early 1861, but later lost to the Union.

2. Joseph C. G. Kennedy, *Population of the United States in 1860; Compiled from the Original Returns of the Eighth Census* (Washington, DC: Government Printing Office), 54, accessed November 17, 2014, https://archive.org/details/populationofusin00kennrich.

3. *Encyclopedia Britannica Online*, s.v. "Pensacola," last updated March 25, 2013, http://www.britannica.com/EBchecked/topic/450266/Pensacola; William Dobak, *Freedom by the Sword: The U.S. Colored Troops, 1862–1867* (New York: Skyhorse, 2013), 139; Joe Knetsch, "Pensacola, Florida," in Heidler and Heidler, *Ency. of the Am. Civil War*, 1487–9.

4. OR, ser. 1, 6:658–9.

5. "Historic St. Michael's Cemetery in the Heart of Pensacola, FL," St. Michael's Cemetery Foundation of Pensacola, Inc., accessed January 25, 2015, www.stmichaelscemetery.org. Presumably this is the cemetery Chamberlin described. St. Michael's, the only cemetery established in Pensacola before the Civil War, was probably in use by the mid-to-late eighteenth century.

6. *Webster's Third New International Dictionary of the English Language*, Unabridged, s.v. "hemp." The archaic meaning of the word is a gallows rope, or a hanging.

7. "Second Inaugural Address, March 4, 1865," In *The Complete Works of Abraham Lincoln*, ed. Roy P. Basler, vol. 8, 1864–1865 (New Brunswick, NJ: Rutgers University Press, 1953), 333.

8. ORN, ser. 1, 6:62; ORN, ser. 2, 3:815, 817, 826. The Steamer *Rhode Island* was used extensively in the early part of the war as a supply boat. On May 31, 1863, in the British Bahamas, it attacked the *Margaret and Jessie*, a Confederate blockade runner carrying 730 bales of cotton.

9. Robert Saunders, Jr., "Benjamin, Judah Philip," in Heidler and Heidler, *Ency. of the Am. Civil War*, 209; Mark A. Lause, "Giddings, Joshua Reed," in *ibid.*, 839; R. Boyd Murphree, "Lopez, Narciso," in *ibid.*, 1218–20; ORN, ser. 1, 18:453. The *Creole* had a colorful history. Early in its life it was the site of a slave mutiny. In the 1840s it was the center of a legislative controversy involving Anglo-American negotiations. In 1850 its owner, Narciso Lopez, barely escaped Cuba in it after an attempt to get Cuba annexed to the United States. The Rebel steamer was finally captured by U.S. Army soldiers at Lakeport, Louisiana, on May 11, 1862; ORN, ser. 1, 18:481. The *General Meigs* was employed as a troop transport.

Chapter 3

1. David P. Eldridge, "New Orleans, Capture of," in Heidler and Heidler, *Ency. of the Am. Civil War*, 1412–3.
2. Dobak, *Freedom by the Sword*, 89, 91; OR, ser. 1, 15:556–7.
3. OR, ser. 1, vol. 39, pt. 2, p. 18; ser. 1, 18:134–48; ser. 1, 6:694–5, 705–6; Michael S. Davis, "Farragut, David Glascow," in Heidler and Heidler, *Ency. of the Am. Civil War*, 682–5. Ships under the command of Com. David G. Farragut (1801–1870) captured New Orleans in May 1862. In addition he participated in battles at Port Hudson, Red River, and Mobile Bay, as did Chamberlin. He was promoted to rear admiral for his services at Vicksburg; for more on the fall of New Orleans, see: C. P. Weaver, ed., *Thank God My Regiment an African One: The Civil War Diary of Colonel Nathan W. Daniels* (Baton Rouge: Louisiana State University Press, 1998), 1, 5; Dobak, *Freedom by the Sword*, 93. Maj. Gen. Benjamin F. Butler (1818–1893), lawyer and former politician from Massachusetts, led the infantry in the capture of New Orleans, and then became commander of the Dept. of the Gulf, which included the command of New Orleans.
4. Lincoln Bramwell, "Nashville, Tennessee," in Heidler and Heidler, *Ency. of the Am. Civil War*, 1388.
5. "Jackson Barracks," on the website for Louisiana Division/City Archives, New Orleans Public Library, accessed February 11, 2015, www.neworleanshistorical.org/items/show/267#.VNveOC4Ufct. The Marine Barracks, first known as the "New Orleans Barracks," were built in response to the War of 1812, as one of numerous defenses for coastal cities. In 1866, they were renamed for Andrew Jackson.
6. China trees are common "soap-berry trees of the southern U.S. They grow rapidly and make good firewood." Frederic G. Cassidy, Joan Houston Hall, and Luanne Von Schneidemesser, eds., *Dictionary of American Regional English*, vol. 1 (Cambridge, MA: Belknap Press of Harvard University Press, 1985), s.v. "china trees."
7. Frederick H. Dyer, *A Compendium of the War of the Rebellion*, vol. 3 (New York: Thomas Yoseloff, 1959), 1213–4. The 1st and 2nd Louisiana Regimental Infantry (Union) were organized at New Orleans on July 30, 1862, and September 29, 1862, respectively. Their initial duty was to defend New Orleans. They remained in Louisiana for the rest of the war, serving several places including at Port Hudson and in the Red River campaign.
8. *Appleton's Hand-Book of American Travel* (New York: D. Appleton, 1869), accessed January 24, 2015, from Perry-Castaneda Library Map Collection, on the website for the University of Texas Libraries, www.lib.utexas.edu/maps/historical/new_orleans_1869.jpg. Rampart and Dauphin Streets ran parallel so the house could not have been at a corner.
9. AG for the Year 1901, 49. Capt. Charles C. Dwight was one of Chamberlin's commanding officers during basic training in New York. At age 31, he enrolled in the 75th N.Y.V. on September 17, 1861, to serve three years. He was mustered in as captain, Co. D, on October 3, 1861. On July 10, 1862, he was promoted to "assistant adjutant-general of volunteers."
10. Rhett Breerwood, "Camp Parapet: The Union," in New Orleans Historical, accessed January 31, 2015, http://www.neworleanshistorical.org/items/show/658; Weaver, *Thank God My Regiment*, 6; Heidler and Heidler, "Phelps, John Wolcott," in Heidler and Heidler, *Ency. of the Am. Civil War*, 1508–9; for Butler, see Eric Foner, *The Fiery Trial: Abraham Lincoln and American Slavery* (New York: W.W. Norton, 2010), 169–70.
11. For Butler, see Weaver, *Thank God My Regiment*, 9; for Confederate black militia, see Dobak, *Freedom by the Sword*, 91–2; for regiments of native guards, see Lawrence Lee Hewitt, "An Ironic Route to Glory: Louisiana's Native Guards at Port Hudson," in *Black Soldiers in Blue: African American Troops in the Civil War Era*, ed. John David Smith (Chapel Hill: University of North Carolina Press, 2002), 79–80; for numbers of enlistees, see Dobak, *Freedom by the Sword*, 96.
12. Richard J. Sommers, *Richmond Redeemed: The Siege of Petersburg* (Garden City, NJ: Doubleday, 1981), 31; OR, ser. 1, 15:590.
13. Dobak, *Freedom by the Sword*, 21; OR, ser. 1, 15:590, 716–7. Gen. Nathaniel Banks (1816–1894), a former governor of Massachusetts, was one of the first three major generals of volunteers Lincoln appointed in 1861. He was defeated by the Confederates in Virginia in 1862. On November 9, 1862, he was ordered by the President to command

Chapter Notes—4

New Orleans and relieve General Butler. Banks ordered the establishment of the Corps d'Afrique on May 1, 1863. He also commanded the capture of Port Hudson in July 1863 and the disastrous Red River Campaign of 1864.

14. The result of the conferences between Banks and the planters was "an agreement to employ the negroes at wages." In the past, the wages that were paid "were as follows: $10 per month for mechanics, &c; $6 or $7 for field hands and $4 for women. In such cases, they were also fed, but had to find their own clothing." "Department of the Gulf: New Regulations with Planters," February 11, 1863, in *The New York Times Complete Civil War*, eds. Harold Holzer and Craig L. Symonds (New York: Black Dog & Leventhal, 2010), reprinted on DVD.

15. For the abuse of authority, see OR, ser. 3, 1:897; ser. 1, 15:611; ser. 1, 15:584–5; Dobak, *Freedom by the Sword*, 98–9.

16. "The Banks Expedition: Gens. Banks and Butler and the Slave Question," December 28, 1862, in Holzer and Symonds, *NYT Complete Civil War*, from DVD.

17. Eric Foner, *The Fiery Trial*, 250–1.

Chapter 4

1. David S. Heidler and Jeanne T. Heidler, "Port Hudson, Louisiana Campaign," in Heidler and Heidler, *Ency. of the Am. Civil War*, 1546.

2. John Coleman, "Flag at Brashear," quoted in *Morgan City Review*, March 23, 1927, website for the Young-Sanders Center for the Study of the War Between the States in Louisiana, accessed March 23, 2015, www.youngsanders.org/youngsandersflagbrashear.html. Bayou Beuff is listed on maps now as "Bayou Boeuf." Brashear City is now called Morgan City.

3. Holzer and Symonds, *NYT Complete Civil War*, 314. Confederate Maj. Gen. Richard Taylor (1826–1879), the son of former U.S. Pres. Zachary Taylor, was the youngest major general in the Rebel army.

4. ORN, ser. 1, 20:134–5.

5. Boatner, *Civil War Dict.*, s.v. "Weitzel, Godfrey." Godfrey Weitzel (1835–1884) was a major general in the Union Army, as well as the acting mayor of New Orleans during the federal occupation of the city. He commanded a division at the siege of Port Hudson and later commanded the expedition to Sabine Pass.

6. In this usage, invest means "to surround with troops or ships so as to prevent escape or entry, to lay siege to." *Webster's 3rd New Int. Dict.*, s.v. "invest."

7. OR, ser. 1, 15:290. The OR tells the same story, adding the fact that the total killed and wounded was 150.

8. Heidler and Heidler, "Emory, William Hemsley," in Heidler and Heidler, *Ency. of the Am. Civil War*, 653–4; John T. Hubbell and James W. Geary, *Biographical Dictionary of the Union* (Westport, CT: Greenwood, 1905), s.v. "Grover, Cuvier." Brig. Gen. William H. Emory (1811–1887) was commander of the Defenses of New Orleans from May until August 1863. Gen. Cuvier Grover (1828–1885) distinguished himself on the western front before the Civil War, and was noted for his bravery at Second Bull Run. As a commander under General Banks in Louisiana, he played an important role in the siege of Port Hudson.

9. American Battlefield Protection Program, "Fort Bisland," accessed July 8, 2015, www.nps.gov/abpp/battles/la006.htm.

10. American Battlefield Protection Program, "Irish Bend," accessed July 8, 2015, ibid.

11. ORN, ser. 1, 18:472; 20:113, 139, 699.

12. David J. Eicher, *The Longest Night: A Military History of the Civil War* (New York: Simon & Schuster, 2001), 444; Spencer C. Tucker, "Semmes, Raphael," in Heidler and Heidler, *Ency. of the Am. Civil War*, 1731; ORN, ser. 1, 20:823. Confederate Capt. Oliver J. Semmes was the son of Raphael Semmes, a Confederate naval officer who spent much of the war raiding merchant vessels as a means of hurting the North financially. "Semmes Battery" refers to Oliver's artillery men.

13. ORN, ser. 1, 19:335; 20:64. The Rebel *Hart* was used during the early part of the war to tow barges and transport equipment and munitions. General Banks wrote to Admiral Farragut in April 1863 that he had forced the Rebels to destroy the ship.

14. ORN, ser. 1, 20:134.

15. Dobak, *Freedom by the Sword*, 100; OR, ser. 1, 15:81, 804, 1000.

16. *Twelve Years a Slave: Narrative of Solomon Northup, a Citizen of New-York, Kidnapped in Washington City in 1841, and Rescued in 1853* (Auburn, Alabama, 1853). Solomon Northup, a free African American farmer and musician from New York, was

Chapter Notes—5

taken hostage and sold into slavery in 1841 in New Orleans. He was freed in 1853, aided by a man named Samuel Bass. The same year, Northup published the slave narrative/memoir *Twelve Years a Slave*. Northup spent 10 years of captivity and slavery on the Epps' plantation on Bayou Boeuf, about 25 miles southeast of Alexandria, Louisiana.

17. For Vicksburg, see John S. Bowman, ed., *The Civil War Almanac* (New York: World Almanac Publications, 1993), 148. For story of the battle at Port Hudson, see Dobak, *Freedom by the Sword*, 104–9; OR, ser. 1, vol. 26, pt. 1, pp. 12–4; Heidler and Heidler, "Port Hudson, Louisiana Campaign," in Heidler and Heidler, *Ency. of the Am. Civil War*, 1546–9; Hewitt, "An Ironic Route to Glory," in Smith, *Black Soldiers in Blue*, 83–99; Eicher and Eicher, *Civil War High Commands*, 485–6. Brig. Gen. Thomas Sherman (1839–1914) was a teacher from Boston. He served in the Army of the Potomac and at Gettysburg. *Ibid.*, 109. Brig. Gen. Christopher Auger (1821–1898), a career officer from Michigan, served primarily in Virginia before Port Hudson.

18. ORN, ser. 1, 18:503, 710, 726, 761, 781. The *Sallie Robinson* was a versatile boat. It was described at various times as an army transport, a prize steamer, and a river steamer. Several references tell about its pulling boats off the bank, including the *Rhode Island* at Algiers near New Orleans.

19. Rifle pits were holes "dug out by soldiers as a temporary protection while engaging the enemy." John D. Wright, *The Language of the Civil War* (Westport, CT: Oryx, 2001), 252.

20. David Eicher, *The Longest Night*, 472. Union casualties: 203 killed, 1401 wounded, and 188 missing.

21. Heidler and Heidler, "Port Hudson, Louisiana Campaign," in Heidler and Heidler, *Ency. of the Am. Civil War*, 1549.

22. OR, ser. 1, vol. 24, pt. 3, pp. 470–1.

23. Dobak, *Freedom by the Sword*, 109.

24. ORN, ser. 1, 18:535, 750. The *Laurel Hill* was used for transporting troops and towing boats.

25. Winston Groom, *Vicksburg, 1863* (New York: Alfred A. Knopf, 2009), 421; Gary Gallagher, Stephen Engle, Robert Krick, and Joseph Glatthar, *Civil War: Fort Sumter to Appomattox* (Oxford: Osprey, 2003), 142.

26. Noah A. Trudeau, *Like Men of War: Black Troops in the Civil War 1862–1865* (Boston: Little, Brown, 1998), 44, 467; John David Smith, "Let Us All Be Grateful," in Smith, *Black Soldiers in Blue*, 54.

Chapter 5

1. For Corps d'Afrique see OR, ser. 1, 15:716–7; Howard C. Westwood, *Black Troops White Commanders and Freedmen During the Civil War* (Carbondale: Southern Illinois University Press, 1992), 36. The designation "Corps d'Afrique" was not recognized by the War Department as an official army corps; for Robinson see OR, ser. 1, 34:169, 248–53; ser. 1, vol. 41, pt. 4, p. 930; ser. 1, 44:105. Col. George D. Robinson was commander of the 3rd Corps d'Afrique starting on September 1, 1863, and the 5th Corps d'Afrique at the Red River Campaign in the spring of 1864; for 3rd Regiment information see Dyer, *Compendium of the War of Rebellion*, 3:1718.

2. AG for the Year 1901, 16. This probably refers to Eugene F. Boughton, age 21, who enlisted October 14, 1861, at Genoa, to serve three years. He was mustered in as a private, Co. D, on November 26, 1861, and discharged September 12, 1863, for promotion in the 3rd Louisiana Engineers Corps d'Afrique. He died at Pine Barren Creek, December 17, 1864.

3. Keith P. Wilson, *Campfires of Freedom: The Camp Life of Black Soldiers During the Civil War* (Kent, OH: Kent State University Press, 2002), 142.

4. This may be an allusion to Herman Melville, *Typee: A Real Romance of the South Seas* (Boston, 1845).

5. Joseph T. Glatthaar, *Forged in Battle: The Civil War Alliance of Black Soldiers and White Officers* (New York: Free Press, 1990), 36, 177; Heidler and Heidler, "Thomas, Lorenzo," in Heidler and Heidler, *Ency. of the Am. Civil War*, 1945; Aaron Sheehan-Dean, ed., *The Civil War: The Final Year Told by Those Who Lived It* (New York: The Library of America, 2014), 169.

6. Smith, "Let Us All Be Grateful," in Smith, *Black Soldiers in Blue*, 37–9; Glatthaar, *Forged in Battle*, 38.

7. Glatthaar, *Forged in Battle*, 53, 59.

8. ORN, ser. 1, 7:433; 19:766. The *Nassau*, formerly the Rebel *Gordon*, was a seasoned blockade-runner. The Union forces captured it near Wilmington, North Carolina, in 1862,

and subsequently used it as a tugboat and towboat.

9. Capt. J. C. Duane, *Manual for Engineer Troops* (New York, 1864), 14–43 and related diagrams, accessed January 25, 2015, http://archive.org/stream/manualforenginee00duanrich#page/n5/mode/2up. In a war fought amid swamps and across many rivers and streams, quickly assembled bridges and rafts were essential. A pontoon bridge consisted of a row of small boats covered with planks. Complete instructions for transportation of supplies, set-up, and removal of these bridges are given in this manual.

10. Eicher and Eicher, *Civil War High Commands*, 243. Maj. Gen. William B. Franklin (1823–1903), a career officer from Pennsylvania, spent the major portion of his wartime service in the Army of the Potomac. OR, ser. 1. vol. 26, pt. 2, pp. 286, 288–92, 294–310; "CWSAC Battle Summaries: Sabine Pass II," by the American Battlefield Protection Program, in the Heritage Preservation Services, accessed July 8, 2015, www.nps.gov/abpp/battles/tx006.htm.

11. ORN, ser. 1, 12:523, 593, 764. This is probably the *Belvedere*, which was used extensively to transport troops and freight, and to tow other boats.

12. Eicher and Eicher, *Civil War High Commands*, 216. Col. Nathan Augustus Monroe Dudley (1825–1920), from Massachusetts, was actually the Assistant Inspector General of the Dept. of the Gulf at that time.

13. Glatthaar, *Forged in Battle*, 106. Major General Banks wanted U.S.C.T. companies to have fifty instead of the usual one hundred enlisted men. His rationale was that the rate of training in smaller companies could be improved with more individual and small-group instruction.

14. Abraham Lincoln, "Letter to Governor Johnson," in Basler, *Works of Abraham Lincoln*, 4:149; Glatthaar, *Forged in Battle*, after 146; Foner, *The Fiery Trial*, 249.

15. For background on Douglass, see Doris Kearns Goodwin, *Team of Rivals: The Political Genius of Abraham Lincoln* (New York: Simon & Schuster, 2005), 161, 207, 407, 470; Holzer and Symonds, *NYT Complete Civil War*, 137. Frederick Douglass (1818–1895), who was born a slave in Maryland and escaped to freedom, was an African American social reformer, abolitionist leader, Lincoln critic, and major spokesman for the anti-slavery movement; Philip S. Foner, *Life and Writings of Frederick Douglass: The Civil War, 1861–1865*, vol. 3 (New York: International, 1952), 365.

Chapter 6

1. Henry Wadsworth Longfellow, "A Psalm of Life," v. 6, from *The Complete Poetical Works of Henry Wadsworth Longfellow*, Household Ed. (Cambridge, MA: Riverside Press, 1902), 3.

2. Anna M. Bullock, born in Cayuga County, New York, on April 26, 1840, was the daughter of Nathan Bullock and Polly Howard, who were born and married in New York. Their four other children, all born in New York, were Howard Amos, Arad Gilbert (Gib), Albert E. (Bertie), and Sarah. About 1855, Nathan moved his family from Sennett, Cayuga County, New York, to Waterloo, Black Hawk County, Iowa, where he began a trade as a carpenter. His wife died about this time, and in March 1856, Nathan married Eunice (Field) Wykoff. They had two children, Frederick and Estelle (probably called Stella by Anna Bullock). (Researched and written by Marilyn Young, a great-great-granddaughter of John N. Chamberlin.)

3. Bullock described her reaction to Chamberlin's first letter in one she wrote much later, on June 25, 1866: "How I laughed over your uncertainty of the fate it might meet. Do you remember it? You thought if I were married, you were safe at least. I wondered then if you wrote to me merely for old acquaintance sake, but upon reading it the second time, could find nothing more than that."

4. This is the last verse of the hymn "God's Glory Is a Wondrous Thing," written by the English priest Frederick W. Faber (1814–1863). Source: *Jesus & Mary*, 1849, alt., accessed March 24, 2015, http://www.hymnary.org/hymn/CYBER/1909.

5. *Encyclopedia Britannica Online*, s.v. "Temperance Movement," last updated August 4, 2014, http://www.britannica.com/EBchecked/topic/586530/temperance-movement; David M. Fahey, *Temperance and Racism* (Frankfort: University Press of Kentucky, 1996), 5–20.

6. Samantha Jane Gaul, "Conscription, U.S.A.," in Heidler and Heidler, *Ency. of the Am. Civil War*, 487–8. The Draft Act of 1863

was the first instance of compulsory service in the federal military. All male citizens between the ages of 20 and 45, as well as aliens who had declared their intention of becoming citizens, were at risk of being drafted. No married man could be drafted until all unmarried men had been taken.

Chapter 7

1. Dobak, *Freedom by the Sword*, 122–3; Ludwell H. Johnson, *Red River Campaign: Politics and Cotton in the Civil War* (Kent, OH: Kent State University Press, 1993), 46–7; Sheehan-Dean, *The Civil War: The Final Year*, 24.
2. Eicher and Eicher, *Civil War High Commands*, 504. Presumably this is a reference to Leroy Augustus Stafford, a planter and a sheriff, who became a brigadier general in the C.S.A. He was born in 1822 near Cheneyville, Louisiana. In May 1864, he died in Richmond, Virginia, of wounds sustained in battle.
3. Johnson, *Red River Campaign*, 100.
4. Boatner, *Civil War Dict.*, s.v. "Ransom, Thomas." Thomas E. G. Ransom (1834–1864), a Union commander in the Red River Campaign, was wounded four times during the war, but always returned to fight. *Ibid.*, s.v. "Smith, Andrew Jackson." Andrew Jackson Smith (1815–1897) led a Union division in the Red River Campaign and later was a commander in the final campaign against Mobile, Alabama, in 1865.
5. This engagement was known as the "Battle of Monett's Ferry." From "CWSAC Battle Summaries," by the American Battlefield Protection Program, in the Heritage Preservation Services, accessed January 24, 2015, http:www.cr.nps.gov/hps/abpp/battles/la021.htm.
6. Richard H. Holloway of the Forts Randolph and Buhlow State Historic Site in Pineville, Louisiana, personal communication with editor, October 13, 2015; Holzer and Symonds, *NYT Complete Civil War*, April 30, 1864, 321–3; also, May 1, 1864, from DVD.
7. Heidler and Heidler, "Bailey, Joseph," in Heidler and Heidler, *Ency. of the Am. Civil War*, 158–9. Lt. Col. Joseph Bailey (1825–1867), a civil engineer, joined the 4th Wisconsin Cavalry at the start of the war and "served most of his time as an engineering officer." He worked in New Orleans, Port Hudson and Mobile Bay, and in the Red River Campaign.
8. OR, ser. 1, vol. 34, pt. 1, p. 251.
9. Johnson, *Red River Campaign*, 270.
10. Exodus 10:21–2 (AV). Egyptian darkness is a reference to one of the Egyptian plagues.
11. Richard H. Holloway, see n. 6. Robinson's official report mistakenly named this landmark Scraggy Point, instead of Snaggy Point.
12. See n. 8.
13. In a May 23, 1864, letter written from a steamer on the Mississippi River, Bert Bullock wrote to his sister Anna Bullock: "We lay four miles from the boats protecting Banks until he was safely across Bayou Achafalaya which he crossed on a pontoon composed of 20 steamboats. We had one quite severe fight while there loosing about 300 men. Our Regt lost only five & our Co none. We took over 300 prisoners besides killing & wounding a great many but as we did not take the trouble to bury them don't know how many. The rebs buried them next day under a flag of truce. The whole expedition has proved a fizzle. We have been skirmishing and fighting over half the time we were on Red River, and it is generally acknowledged that but for 'Smiths Guerrillas' [see n. 4 above] the whole thing would have been 'gobbled.'" Letter in possession of John Bisbee.
14. Howard Bullock wrote from Memphis on June 3, 1864: "Dear Sister, It is a long time since I have had pen in my hand to write home. We left camp on March the 9th for a trip up the Reed [sic] rivver [sic] with 30 days rations leaving our camp and extra clothes behind taking only one blanket and rubber with what clothes we wore, we are now on the way back to our things, which we need very much we have been without any shelter for the last three months taking the weather as it comes, we have all stood it first rate and are tough and hearty, it has been one of the worst managed things that I ever saw." Letter in possession of John Bisbee.
15. Dobak, *Freedom by the Sword*, 127; Sheehan-Dean, *The Civil War: The Final Year*, 147; Johnson, *Red River Campaign*, 279.
16. Dobak, *Freedom by the Sword*, 21; William Cowper, "God Moves in a Mysterious Way," 1733, in John Newton, *Twenty-Six Letters on Religious Subjects; to Which Are Added Hymns* (London, 1774). Discussed in Marilyn Kay Stulken, *Hymnal Companion to*

the Lutheran Book of Worship (Philadelphia: Fortress, 1981), 503. Complete hymn found in Lutheran Church in America, The American Lutheran Church, The Evangelical Lutheran Church of Canada, and The Lutheran Church—Missouri Synod, *Lutheran Book of Worship* (Minneapolis: Augsburg, 1978), 483. This is a parody of the hymn, which begins, "God moves in a mysterious way, his wonders to perform."

17. From 2 Samuel 3:33 (AV).

18. *Webster's 3rd New Int. Dict.,* s.v. "besom." A besom is a broom made with a bundle of twigs.

Chapter 8

1. Harriet Beecher Stowe, *Uncle Tom's Cabin or, Life among the Lowly* (Boston, 1852).

2. David J. Ulbrich, "Logistics," in Heidler and Heidler, *Ency. of the Am. Civil War,* 1208–10.

3. *Democracy in America* (1835–40) was written by French civil servant and political scientist Alexis de Tocqueville. Considering this choice of books, and his many quotations throughout the diaries and letters, Chamberlin seemed to be well-read.

4. Jayhawkers were Union guerrilla groups. "They ravaged entire towns suspected of aiding the Confederates. They stole everything from horses to silver from Confederate sympathizers, murdering several along the way." Wright, *Language of the Civil War,* 162.

5. The Rev. J. R. Dummelow, ed., *A Commentary on the Holy Bible* (New York: Macmillan, 1908), 223. The term *Baal,* meaning "lord" or "owner," was applicable to a number of deities in the Old Testament Hebrew world. Bowing to Baal was equivalent to turning your back on the "one true God," as in I Kings 16:31–2 (AV).

6. In a letter dated July 22, 1866, Bullock told Chamberlin, "Do you remember my writing to you once, that I did not think that many of Iowa girls would take up with any of the 'home guards.' I well remember your reply. That was nearly two years ago." That reply, which indicated a preference for Iowa, apparently gave Bullock some hope for their relationship.

7. AG for the Year 1901, 153. Peter Thompson enlisted in the 75th N.Y.V. February 26, 1862. He was discharged from that unit in 1863 to become an officer in the 3rd Engineers.

8. Fate Arnold is listed as a private in Chamberlin's Co. E, 3rd Regiment in February 1864 and July 1864. Roster of Co. E, 3rd Regiment Engineers Corps d'Afrique in "Camp and Garrison Equipage: Receipt Roll of Clothing," for February 27, 1864, and July 31, 1864. Original reports in possession of John Bisbee.

Chapter 9

1. OR, ser. 1, vol. 41, pt. 2, p. 118; ser. 1, 34:248–53; ser. 1, 34:169; ser. 1, vol. 41, pt. 4, p. 930; ser. 1, 49:105; ser. 1, 44:449.

2. OR, ser. 1, vol. 41, pt. 2, p. 119.

3. Goodwin, *Team of Rivals,* 550. If captured, every negro taken in arms and every white officer who commands negro troops faced death or slavery.

4. Duane, *Manual for Engineer Troops,* 147–8, 253. Sappers were soldiers employed in digging trenches and constructing fortifications.

5. Smith, "Let Us All Be Grateful," in Smith, *Black Soldiers in Blue,* 49.

6. *Ibid.,* 50.

7. "Bounties were payments made by the various governments of the Union and Confederacy to induce men to enlist in the military." Those bounties offered in July 1864 to new black volunteers were on the same scale as whites': $100 for one-year enlistments, $200 for two-year enlistments, and $300 for three-year enlistments. Dorothy O. Pratt, "Bounty System," in Heidler and Heidler, *Ency. of the Am. Civil War,* 256; OR, ser. 3, 5:658–60; see note 5 above, 51–2.

8. See n. 5, 52.

9. For traverses, see Ron Field, *American Civil War Fortifications,* vol. 2: *Land and Field Fortifications* (Oxford: Osprey, 2005), 17. A traverse is a raised mound of earth designed to obscure the interior spaces of field works from the view of the enemy; for bastions, see Webb Garrison Sr., *Webb Garrison's Civil War Dictionary: An Illustrated Guide to the Everyday Language of Soldiers and Civilians* (Nashville: Cumberland House, 2008), s.v. "bastion." "A bastion is a work projected toward the field at a salient angle with its apex pointing toward the enemy, constructed so that its defenders could fire on an attacking force even if it reached the walls." For parapets and embra-

Chapter Notes—10

sures, see note 4 above, 241–2. A parapet is a mound in front of a battery (an artillery platform), which serves as a protective covering for pieces (guns) and cannoniers. An embrasure is a slanted opening in the wall or parapet of a fortification, designed so that defenders could fire a cannon through it.

10. Duane, *Manual for Engineer Troops*, 55, 67, 80.

11. This is an abbreviation for *"instant,"* common usage in Chamberlin's time period for "of or occurring in the present month." *Webster's 3rd New Int. Dict.*, s.v. "instant."

12. Curtain refers to the "part of a bastioned front that connects two neighboring bastions"; a demi-lune, also called a ravelin, is a "detached work formerly used in fortifications and consisting of two embankments forming a salient angle in front of the curtain of the fortified position." *Webster's 3rd New Int. Dict.*, s.v. "curtain" and "ravelin."

13. Letter in possession of John Bisbee written to "Capt. Chamberlain" from "Engineer Office, Ft. Gaines, Sept 25, 1864," and signed by "Chas. J. Allen, 1st Lt. U.S. Corps Engineers." Charles. J. Allen was in charge of works in the repair of Fort Gaines (Appendix D reproduces original "Special Orders No. 51" dated Sept. 21, 1864). OR, ser. 1, 34:411–2 presents a report from M. D. McAlester, Chief Engineer, Military Division of Western Mississippi, and describes Lt. Allen's reconnaissance work on Fort Gaines after it surrendered to the Union on August 9, 1864. Later Allen was placed in charge of the planned work when McAlester had to be absent.

14. Chamberlin was with the 75th N.Y.V. at the siege of Port Hudson. In this letter he is referring to his new company, composed of soldiers who participated in assaults on Port Hudson as members of the 1st and 3rd Louisiana Native Guards on May 27 and June 14, 1863.

15. Richard N. Current, *Encyclopedia of the Confederacy* (New York: Simon & Schuster, 1993), s.v. "Copperheads." Copperheads was a "smear term" applied to northern Democrats critical of the Lincoln administration, who were also allied with the peace movement. These Democrats were likened to the venomous snake. Recent historians are kinder, labeling them as "conservative and partisan critics."

16. Eric Foner, *Reconstruction: America's Unfinished Revolution, 1863–1877*, 1st ed. (New York: Harper & Row, 1988), 9; Wilson, *Campfires of Freedom*, 71–102. Periodically Chamberlin reported that he was busy with paperwork. As Glatthaar notes, "It took one officer four days of constant work ... to prepare all the muster rolls and returns of clothing and camp and garrison equipage for his company, and he had to perform this work every three months. Training an enlisted man to do this work freed an officer to devote more time to the men." Glatthaar, *Forged in Battle*, 101. (Chamberlin never reported that anyone else in his company did this paperwork.)

17. Smith, "Let Us All Be Grateful," in Smith, *Black Soldiers in Blue*, 39; Glatthaar, *Forged in Battle*, 203.

18. OR, ser. 3, 3:252.

Chapter 10

1. Goodwin, *Team of Rivals*, 653–4. The 1864 Democratic National Convention was held in Chicago, Illinois, August 29–31. The Democratic Party "was rent by the anger between the War Democrats ... and the Peace Democrats" and compromised to nominate pro-war General George B. McClellan for president and anti-war Representative George H. Pendleton for vice-president. The convention adopted a peace platform, of which McClellan disapproved because he favored restoration of the Union.

2. "Mess of pottage" is a Biblical reference to Genesis 25:29–34, in which Esau "despised his birthright" and sold it to his twin, Jacob, for "pottage of lentils" (AV).

3. Bowman, *The Civil War Almanac*, 221. Atlanta fell to Sherman's forces on September 2, 1864.

4. "The State Canvass—the Seymour Party and the Rebellion," in Holzer and Symonds, *NYT*, October 6, 1862, *NYT Complete Civil War*, 189. Thomas H. Seymour (1807–1868) was considered the leader of the Seymour Party, which "organized their movement on the specific and exclusive ground of opposition to the Government," and encouraged the Rebels; "Where Shall Vallandigham Go?" May 13, 1863, *ibid.*, 237; "Vallangdigham in Dixie: His Transfer to the Rebel Lines," May 26, 1863, *ibid.*, 238. Clement Vallandigham (1820–1871) was an anti-war Democrat from Ohio. He publicly denounced "King Lincoln" and called for his removal from the presidency. In 1863 Val-

landigham was arrested, court-martialed, and deported to the Confederacy; John Garraty and Mark Carnes, eds., *American National Biography* (Oxford: Oxford University Press, 1999), 408, 751–2. Fernando Wood (1812–1881) served as mayor of New York City and later as a congressman from New York. He maintained pro-southern and pro-slavery associations, and became a Peace Democrat; Goodwin, *Team of Rivals*, 654. Goodwin names Fernando Wood, along with Thomas Seymour and Clement Vallindigham, as the leaders of the peace wing of the Democratic Party at the time of the 1864 Democratic convention; Bruce Tap, "Copperheads," in Heidler and Heidler, *Ency. of the Am. Civil War*, 498–9. Daniel Voorhees was a prominent Copperhead political leader.

5. "Have mercy on me, O God, according to your steadfast love; according to your abundant mercy blot out my transgressions. Wash me thoroughly from my iniquity, and cleanse me from my sin. For I know my transgressions, and my sin is ever before me. Against you, you alone, have I sinned, and done what is evil in your sight, so that you are justified in your sentence and blameless when you pass judgment. Indeed, I was born guilty, a sinner when my mother conceived me." From Psalm 51 (AV).

6. *American Heritage Dictionary of the English Language*, 5th ed. (Boston: Houghton Mifflin Harcourt, 2011), s.v. "pandemonium." Pandemonium was the capital of Hell in *Paradise Lost*, an epic poem by John Milton.

7. "Truth shall spring out of the earth; and righteousness shall look down from heaven." Psalm 85:11 (AV).

8. Goodwin, *Team of Rivals*, 699.

9. H. Lee Cheek Jr., "Stephens, Alexander Hamilton," in Heidler and Heidler, *Ency. of the Am. Civil War*, 1857–9. Alexander H. Stephens (1812–1883) was vice president of the Confederacy and helped shape the Confederate Constitution, although originally he opposed secession. He believed in the superiority of whites. Estranged from Jefferson Davis, by early 1862 he was "not intimately involved in the affairs of state."

Chapter 11

1. In his diary, **November 30, 1864,** Chamberlin described the "lighthouse near Fort McRae. It is 202 feet high from the foundation. It is 20 feet in diameter at the base which is circular. It is built of brick in the most substantial manner. A winding staircase of iron extends to the summit. At the top one has a very wide view of the surrounding country and far out to sea. Pine forests extend as far as the eye can reach."

2. ORN, ser. 1, 21:828, 854; 25:273–6. In July 1863 the *Clyde* was tied up on the Mississippi River 30 miles south of Memphis. Lt. Griswold, master of the Union gunboat *Hastings*, seized the *Clyde* for violating General Grant's order that no boats could land along the river unless they were under the cover of a gunboat. In addition, the government suspected that the boat had been used for smuggling. The owners of the *Clyde* denied the accusation and protested the seizure, and as U.S. citizens demanded a trial for seizure without cause. Eventually the navy turned the boat over to Brigadier General Phelps, who gave it to General Hurlbut for use as an army ferry.

3. Texas State Historical Association, "Brazos Island," *Handbook of Texas Online*, accessed August 5, 2013 (http://www.tshaonline.org/handbook/online/articles/rrb10). Brazos Island is a barrier island south of Padre Island, Texas. At different times during the Civil War the island's port was occupied by Union or Confederate forces. It was an important avenue of trade and supply. The last shot of the Civil War is reported to have been fired on Brazos Island on May 12, 1865. Most of the buildings on the island were destroyed by the hurricane of 1867, and the port and settlement have long ceased to exist.

4. Duane, *Manual for Engineer Troops*, 241–60. Revetments were earthwork bases for parapets, batteries, or any other fortification. They were built of fascines, earth, gabions, or sand.

5. Sods were used to sustain an embankment because they are strong and durable. "Sods should be cut from a well-clothed sward with the grass of a fine short blade, and thickly matted roots." D. H. Mahan, *A Treatise on Field Fortification*, 3rd ed. (New York, 1852), 36, accessed August 18, 2015, http://quod.lib.umich.edu/m/moa/AJR7399.0001.001/70?rgn=full+text;view=image.

6. OR, ser. 1, 44:449.

7. The town of Pollard was established in 1861 at the juncture of the Alabama & Florida and the Mobile & Great Northern

railroad lines. Because cargo could be brought in by steamboat on the Conecuh River, the town, in its heyday, was an important rail center. It was a vital Confederate military post during the Civil War, thus suffering much destruction in federal raids of December 1864 and March 1865. Patricia Hoskins Morton, Auburn University. Published August 29, 2007, last updated July 23, 2013, http://www.encyclopediaofalabama.org/face/Article.jsp?id=h-1321.

8. "With Mobile in Federal hands, the vital Mobile and Ohio Railroad across Mississippi became the principal means of transportation for supplies to Mobile, especially for war materials like arms, gunpowder, and iron. The Alabama and Florida Railroad running from Montgomery to the little town of Pollard 60 miles northeast of Mobile was extended to the Tensaw River, with goods either shipped by barge from there to Mobile or hauled overland." Sean Michael O'Brien, *Mobile, 1865: Last Stand of the Confederacy* (Westport, CT: Praeger, 2001), 23.

9. For Boughten, see chap. 5, n. 2; for Burnham, see website, accessed August 10, 2015, www.nps.gov/civilwar/search-soldiers-det. Lt. Frederick D. Burnham was a member of company K, 97th Reg., U.S.C.I.

10. Gen. St. John Liddell (1815–1870) was known as "a reliable, hard-hitting infantry commander for the Confederates. He fought in the Red River Campaign and completed his military service around Mobile in 1865." Patricia Faust, ed., *Historical Times Illustrated Encyclopedia of the Civil War* (New York: Harper & Row, 1986), s.v. "Liddell, Gen. St. John"; O'Brien, *Mobile, 1865*, 89.

11. Gerald Todd, "Civil War Cavalry Forum," March 4, 2004, last updated April 5, 2013, http://mainecav.org/history.htm#2ndMaine. Lt. Col. Andrew Spurling, of the 2nd Maine Cavalry, enlisted in the Union Army in 1861 and went to the Dept. of the Gulf in January 1864. Based on action in 1865, he received the Congressional Medal of Honor in 1897.

12. Ezra J. Warner, *Generals in Blue: Lives of Union Commanders* (Baton Rouge: Louisiana State University Press, 1964), 301; OR, ser. 1, 44:449. Brig. Gen. Thomas J. McKean, a native of Pennsylvania, graduated from West Point in 1831. He resigned his commission to become a civil engineer in 1834. During the war he commanded military districts in Louisiana, Mississippi, and Tennessee. In the fall of 1864 he was Chief of Cavalry of the Dept. of the Gulf; Laurent Ditmann, "Beauregard, Pierre Gustave Toutant," in Heidler and Heidler, *Ency. of the Am. Civil War*, 198–200; OR, ser. 1, 44:449. Pierre Gustave Toutant Beauregard (1818–1893) was born near New Orleans and was a graduate of West Point. He coordinated the siege of Fort Sumter, then went on to command the Confederate coastal defenses. He later participated in many of the most important battles of the war, but always seemed to be involved in conflict with other military leaders.

13. Arthur W. Bergeron, Jr., *Confederate Mobile* (Jackson: University Press of Mississippi, 1991), 165; OR, ser. 1, 44:449; Enoch K. Miller, "An Important Letter from a Chaplain," in *Christian Recorder*, February 2, 1865, accessed March 31, 2015, http://www.accessible.com/accessible/docButton?AAWhat=builtPage&AAWhere=THECHRISTIANRECORDER.FR1865020423.70996&AABeanName=toc3&AANextPage=/printBrowseBuiltPage.jsp.

14. Bruce Levine, *The Fall of the House of Dixie: The Civil War and the Social Revolution That Transformed the South* (New York: Random House Trade Paperbacks, 2013), 230–1, 240, 243.

15. For Liddell, see O'Brien, *Mobile, 1865*, 8; Sheehan-Dean, *The Civil War: The Final Year*, 553, 576; Levine, *The Fall of the House of Dixie*, 166–8; Gallagher et al., *Civil War*, 301.

Chapter 12

1. Current, *Ency. of the Confederacy*, 2: 737–8. William Hardee (1815–1873) helped organize the Confederate Army. He was nicknamed "Old Reliable," since he won most battles in which he participated.

2. Boatner, *Civil War Dict.*, s.v. "Atlanta, Battle of" and "Thomas, George Henry;" OR ser. 1, vol. 48, pt. 1, pp. 580, 781. George Henry Thomas (1816–1870) taught at West Point, then served with Hardee and Lee before the Civil War. Known as the "Rock of Chickamauga," he was a major player in the Atlanta Campaign and the March to the Sea.

3. OR, ser. 1, vol. 34, pt. 3, p. 665; ser. 1, vol. 26, pt. 1, pp. 638–9; ser. 1, vol. 34, pt. 1, pp. 209–58; ser. 1, 49:146, 149. Brig. Gen. John C. Palfrey (1836–1908) served in a number of campaigns in which Chamberlin served, including Port Hudson and the Red

River. He was also in charge of operations during the Siege of Fort Morgan. He is listed as "Captain of Engineers, U.S. Army."

4. Last two lines are a poorly remembered version of part of the poem "Mammoth Cave," by George Dennison Prentice; *The Poems of George D. Prentice*, ed. John James Piatt (Cincinnati, 1876), 96, accessed February 5, 2015, http://archive.org/stream/poemsofgeorgedpr00inpren/poemsofgeorgedpr00inpren_djvu.txt.

5. Wilson, *Campfires of Freedom*, 178–209.

6. Francis Meres in *Palladis Tamia: Wits Treasury* (London: 1598), 152, referred to *Love's Labors Won* as a comedy written by William Shakespeare, accessed February 9, 2015, www.archive.org/stream/ancientcriticale02hasluoft#page/152/mode/2up. According to Roselyn L. Knutson, the play was apparently lost after that and rediscovered in the mid–twentieth century. Several authors seem to think it was a precursor to various later works of Shakespeare. Current lists of his works do not list this play; www.lostplays.org/index.php/Love's_Labour's_Won, created by Roselyn L. Knutson, page 86 last updated April 24, 2014. (If this play had been lost, was Chamberlin really reading the other Shakespeare play, *Love's Labors Lost*?)

7. This is probably a reference to the novel *Life and Adventures of Martin Chuzzlewit*, by Charles Dickens (London, 1843), last updated August 3, 2014, http://www.gutenberg.org/files/968/968-h/968-h.html.

8. Baron Antoine Henri Jomini, *Life of Napoleon*, vol. 1, trans. H. W. Halleck (New York, 1864). From European Libraries, from the Collections of Oxford University, accessed February 5, 2015, https://archive.org/details/lifenapoleontrw01jomigoog.

9. Goodwin, *Team of Rivals*, 23, 690–4.

10. ORN, ser. 2, 1:30; ser. 1, 13:121, 343. The U.S.S. *Alabama* was part of the "Atlantic Blockading Squadron" and spent time near Charleston during the early part of the war.

Chapter 13

1. Dobak, *Freedom by the Sword*, 140–3.

2. Boatner, *Civil War Dict.*, s.v. "Granger, Gordon." Gordon Granger (1822–1876) commanded the land forces that captured Fort Gaines and Fort Morgan at Mobile Bay. He was also a commander during the Battle of Fort Blakely and later occupied Mobile.

3. Wright, *Language of the Civil War*, s.v. "Pontoniers"; Duane, *Manual for Engineer Troops*, 14–43 and related diagrams; OR, ser. 1, vol. 34, pt. 1, p. 248; OR, ser. 1, vol. 34, pt. 3, pp. 664–5. Pontoniers were soldiers who built pontoon bridges, an especially dangerous task as it was often done under enemy fire. Capt. John J. Smith had formerly served with the 97th U.S.C.I. regiment in Alexandria, Louisiana. At Mobile he commanded a white company of pontoniers. In a report from Simmsport, Louisiana, on May 19, 1864, Capt. John Palfrey reported: "The troops available for engineer operations in this department are one company of pontoniers (white) and five regiments (colored). The pontonier company, led by Capt. J. J. Smith, has been enlisted about two months. It has its own train, with tools and wagons and 180 feet of bateau bridge complete. It is under the orders of the chief engineer of the department. It is now with the army in the field."

4. Gene A. Smith, "Monitor," in Heidler and Heidler, *Ency. of the Am. Civil War*, 1346–7; Current, *Ency. of the Confederacy*, vol. 3. s.v. "Monitor." The *Monitor* was a prototype vessel designed by John Ericsson for the Union Navy to counter the Confederate ironclad *Virginia*. It was a relatively small ship with a shallow draft to "allow it to operate in virtually any harbor." *Monitor* also referred to a class of relatively small warships with large guns, modeled after the original *Monitor*. Wright, *Language of the Civil War*, s.v. "Tinclads." Tinclads were "warships whose wood was protected with a tin covering. This covering could stop only rifle and musket fire."

5. The steamer apparently survived the bad weather because Chamberlin used it after the war (see chap. 15 and app. I).

6. ORN, ser. 1, 16:386, 432; ser. 2, 1:144, 167. The *O'Sage* and *Milwaukee* were both built in the early years of the war. The *O'Sage* had a single turret, the *Milwaukee* a double turret. Both were destroyed by torpedoes on March 28, 1865, at the mouth of the Blakely River, during Admiral Farragut's attack on Mobile.

7. Current, *Ency. of the Confederacy*, vol. 1, s.v. "Army Ordinance," and "Weapons." The Parrott rifle was a muzzle-loading rifled artillery weapon with a shrunken reinforcing steel band at its breech to give it additional strength. It had a tendency to blow up in the field.

8. Accessed September 5, 2015, www.nps.

gov//civilwar/search-soldiers-det. Capt. James Gilbert Hill joined the war with the 42nd Massachusetts Volunteers. Later he served with the 1st Engineer Corps before joining the 97th U.S.C.I. Eicher and Eicher, *Civil War High Commands*, 507–8. Gen. Frederick Steele (1819–1868), from New York, spent much of his military career in Mexico and in various places in the West and Southwest. Shortly after the war he went to California.

9. Maxine Turner, "Torpedoes" in Current, see n. 7, vol. 4:1603–5; Russ. A. Pritchard, "Hand Grenades and Land Mines," in *ibid.*, vol. 2:734–5.

10. Charleston, South Carolina, was a "hot bed of secessionist sentiment," in the first state to secede from the Union, making it one of the most radical cities in the country. Gallagher et al., *Civil War*, 29; Levine, *Fall of the House of Dixie*, 262.

11. These are the last lines of the chorus for the popular song "Home Again," written by Marshal Spring Pike, "Historic American Sheet Music," Duke University Libraries: Digital Collection, accessed February 23, 2015, http://library.duke.edu/digitalcollections/hasm_n0945/.

12. A Brooke rifle was "an excellent heavy artillery piece, Confederate-invented and - manufactured; the Brooke rifle saw service both on Ironclads and in seacoast fortifications." Faust et al., eds., *Historical Times*, s.v. "Brooke rifle."

13. All of the following articles are from Heidler and Heidler, *Ency. of the Am. Civil War.* Heidler and Heidler, "Mobile Campaign," 1345. Batteries Tracy and Huger commanded the Tensas and Alabama rivers. For the surrender, see Lisa Lauterbach Laskin, "Appomattox Court House," 72. Heidler and Heidler, "Granger, Gordon," 862. Major General Granger (1822–1876), born in New York, was very successful in early campaigns of the war, so much so that the governor of Tennessee asked Lincoln not to transfer such "an aggressive soldier" to the Dept. of the Gulf. The request was ignored and Granger joined in the battle of Mobile Bay.

14. For spelling of the town name, see Norman A. Nicholson, *War Comes to Baldwin County!* Pamphlet published for Historic Blakeley State Park in Spanish Fort, Alabama. "Blakeley is the correct spelling of the town where Fort Blakely was situated. It was only spelled without the additional 'e' during the Civil War"; other information from personal communication with Stacey Gardner, Senior Ranger/Park Historian, Historic Blakely State Park, May 23, 2014. The original spelling of this river is Tensas, which was based on the old Native American tribe by the same name. Some old maps labeled the river as the Apalachee River, like the map in O'Brien, *Mobile, 1865*, after 136.

Chapter 14

1. Goodwin, *Team of Rivals*, 735–7. Sec. of State William Seward, although severely injured, survived the attack because, due to a carriage accident a few days earlier, he was wearing a "metal contraption" to hold his broken jaw in place, which deflected the knife aimed at his jugular vein.

2. Daniel Barr, "Canby, Edward Richard Sprigg," in Heidler and Heidler, *Ency. of the Am. Civil War*, 352–3. General Canby (1817–1873), born in Kentucky but raised in Indiana, graduated from West Point. His early career was spent primarily in the Southwest and Mexico. Transferred east, he was eventually instrumental in planning and implementing the Union assault on Mobile, where he was severely wounded.

3. James M. McPherson, *Battle Cry of Freedom: The Civil War Era* (Oxford: Oxford University Press, 1988), 853; William Tidwell, *Come Retribution: The Confederate Secret Service and the Assassination of Lincoln*, with James O. Hall and David Winfred Gaddy (Jackson: University Press of Mississippi, 1988), 3–8.

4. O'Brien, *Mobile, 1865*, 216.

5. Sheehan-Dean, *The Civil War: The Final Year*, 725; "The Greatest Military Display in the World," *New York Herald*, May 24, 1865, quoted in Sheehan-Dean, 725–7; Lois Bryan Adams, "Letter from Washington," *Detroit Advertiser and Tribune*, May 24, 1865, quoted in Sheehan-Dean, 728–30; "Letters from Washington," *Detroit Advertiser and Tribune*, May 27, 1865, quoted in Sheehan-Dean, 730–3.

6. Mollie (Mary) Pratt was the daughter of N. Lyman and Lucy Pratt, who were family friends of the Bullocks in Iowa (researched and written by Marilyn Young, a great-great-granddaughter of John N. Chamberlin).

7. McPherson, *Battle Cry of Freedom*, 853.

8. Jefferson Davis was captured by federal cavalry on May 10, 1865, near Irwinville,

Georgia. Surprised in the middle of the night, he threw on a cloak in the dark as he ran from his tent. It turned out to be his wife's cloak, which led to stories later that he was caught wearing women's clothes. "1865 Chronology," in Holzer and Symonds, *NYT Complete Civil War*, 501.

9. Jeremiah 31:15 (AV).

10. "Lincoln's Second Inaugural Address," *Works of A. Lincoln* (see chap. 2, n. 7).

11. McPherson, *Battle Cry of Freedom*, 6–7.

12. Robert William Fogel and Stanley L. Engerman, *Time on the Cross: The Economics of American Negro Slavery* (Boston: Little, Brown & Co., 1974), 166, accessed February 10, 2015, http://faculty.weber.edu/kmackay/economics%20of%20slavery.asp; Howard Dodson, *Jubilee: The Emergence of African-American Culture* (Washington, DC: National Geographic, 2002), 57; for New York, see Eric Foner, *Gateway to Freedom: The Hidden History of the Underground Railroad* (New York: W. W. Norton & Co., 2015), 9.

13. For the Missouri Compromise and the Dred Scott Case, see Gallagher et al., *Civil War: Fort Sumter to Appomattox*, 13–6; for Fugitive Slave Acts, see Junius P. Rodriguez, "Fugitive Slave Act of 1850," in Heidler and Heidler, *Ency. of the Am. Civil War*, 794; for the House Divided, see Eric Foner, *The Fiery Trial*, 99.

14. Charles Francis Adams, "Completing 'The Great Idea': London, June 1864," in Sheehan-Dean, *The Civil War: The Final Year*, 202.

15. Lincoln (see n. 10), 330.

16. This is probably a reference to Micah 4:3 (AV).

17. Romans 13:7 (AV).

Chapter 15

1. Samuel Taylor Coleridge, "Historical Sketch: Of the Manners and Religion of the Ancient Germans," in *The Watchman*, 1796. Reprinted in *Essays on His Own Times*, ed. by his daughter, 1850. First AMS ed., vol. 1 (New York: AMS, 1971), 130. The title "Queen of May" comes from an ancient pagan tradition of the goddess of fertility and peace. M. Jean Frisk, "The Queen of May," accessed January 30, 2015, www.tomorrowsworld.org/commentary/the-queen-of-may. Christianity incorporated the term into its rituals, in reference to the Virgin Mary. Many Roman Catholic churches and other institutions are named "Queen of Peace."

2. President Andrew Johnson issued an amnesty proclamation on May 29, 1865, to induce all persons to return to their loyalty to the United States of America. This proclamation "conferred amnesty and pardon, including restoration of all property rights except for [owning] slaves, upon participants in the rebellion who took an oath pledging loyalty to the Union and support for emancipation. Fourteen classes of Southerners, however, most notably major Confederate officials and owners of taxable property valued at more than $20,000, were required to apply individually for Presidential pardons." Eric Foner, *Reconstruction*, 183.

3. The *Evening Post, New York*, for July 19, 1865, reprinted the *Mobile Tribune's* editorial, "The Fourth in Mobile," 3, copy of article received from Megan Halsband, Reference Librarian, Serial & Government Publications Division, Library of Congress, November 18, 2014.

4. William Shakespeare, *Hamlet*, Act 3, Scene 4, line 74, G. R. Hibbard, ed. (Oxford: Clarendon Press, 1987).

5. Eric Walther, "Yancey, William Lowndes," in Heidler and Heidler, *Ency. of the Am. Civil War*, 2157–8. William Lowndes Yancey (1814–1863) was a secessionist and a C.S.A. senator and diplomat; Janet B. Hewett, ed., *The Roster of Confederate Soldiers, 1861–1865* (Wilmington, NC: Broadfoot, 1996), 8:328; J. H. Ingraham belonged to the Virginia 5th Cavalry, Company K.

6. "The Fourth in Mobile," in *Boston Liberator*, July 21, 1865, 115, copy of article received from Megan Halsband (see n. 3).

7. Thomas McAdory Owen, *History of Alabama and Dictionary of Alabama Biography* (Chicago: S. J. Clarke, 1921), last updated February 6, 2014, www.archives.state.al.us/counties/conecuh.html; Kennedy, *Population of the United States, 1860*, 9. Sparta, a town in southwest Alabama, was the county seat of Conecuh County from 1818 until 1868. The population of this county was 11,311 in 1860; this total included 4,882 slaves. Sparta is not listed in the 1860 census of "cities and towns," which lists only towns with a population of 1,000 or more.

8. Eric Foner, *The Fiery Trial*, xvii–xxi.

9. Maj. Gen. K. Garrard, "Special Orders No. 9," District of Mobile, August 25, 1865. Original document in possession of John Bisbee; Heidler and Heidler, "Garrard, Kenner," Heidler and Heidler, *Ency. of the Am. Civil War*, 814. Maj. Gen. Kenner Garrard

Chapter Notes—16 and 17

(1828–1879) was captured by the Confederates in Texas in 1861 and was exchanged in 1862; Warner, *Generals in Blue*, 167–8. He led troops in battles at Fredericksburg and Gettysburg, the campaign of Atlanta, and the capture of Mobile. After the war he was commander of the District of Mobile.

10. B. F. Riley, *History of Conecuh County, Alabama* (Columbus, Georgia, 1881), 189–91, accessed February 18, 2015, http://files.usgwarchives.net/al/conecuh/history/other/gms42historyo.txt, file contributed for use in US GenWeb Archives by Joy Fisher, May 25, 2004.

11. According to Anna Bullock's letter written to Chamberlin on February 13, 1866, Anna Field was Anna Bullock's mother's sister and "Principal of the Female Seminary" in Waterloo. Mary Beth Eldridge, *Brief Biographies of Early Residents of Waterloo, Black Hawk Co., Iowa*, 1993, accessed May 4, 2015, http://www.rootsweb.ancestry.com/~iabiog/blackhawk/h1993/h1993-al.htm. The school, called the Prairie Home Seminary, was founded in 1862 by Anna Field and her sister Elizabeth to teach young ladies.

Chapter 16

1. Evert A. Duyckinck and George L. Duyckinck, *The Cyclopedia of American Literature* (Philadelphia, 1880), 563. Quoted in "Strangers to Us All: Lawyers and Poetry," vol. 2, by James R. Elkins, first posted September 2, 2001, myweb.wvnet.edu/~jelkins/lp 2001/saxe.html. Website from "John Godfrey Saxe Papers," Bailey-Howe Memorial Library, University of Vermont, Burlington, Vermont. Saxe (1816–1887) was a Vermont lawyer, speaker, and poet.

2. Rom. 12:15 (AV).

3. Anna is quoting the song "Guard of Land and Sea: National Song & Chorus," words by T. E. Garrett with music by F. Woolcott (Saint Louis, 1861). In "Historic American Sheet Music," Duke University Libraries, accessed January 28, 2015, http://library.duke.edu/digitalcollections/hasm_a4996_a4996–1.

4. Edward James, ed., *Notable American Women 1607–1950: A Biographical Dictionary*, vol. 2 (Cambridge, Massachusetts: Belknap Press of Harvard University, 1971), s.v. "Heron, Matilda." Matilda Heron (1830–1877) was an Irish-born actress who began acting in Philadelphia in 1851 and received acclaim in the Midwest, South, and New York City by 1857. By the mid–1860s her reputation had begun to fade.

5. A different perspective is provided by a reader identified as "Wisconsin," who replied to a *Mobile Tribune* July 6, 1865, editorial: "At the present time the commissary is issuing to destitute white persons at the rate of five thousand five hundred rations daily ... to colored persons less than one-tenth of this amount." Letter to the editor, *Mobile Tribune*, July 7, 1865, reprinted in *Evening Post: New York*, July 19, 1865, copy of article received from Megan Halsband, Library of Congress.

6. Eric Foner, *The Fiery Trial*, 321–2. The Freedmen's Bureau (officially the Bureau of Refugees, Freedmen, and Abandoned Lands) was initiated by President Lincoln in March 1865, to function for one year after the Civil War. It served many purposes, most importantly providing assistance to tens of thousands of former slaves and white refugees in the South. In addition it regulated labor contracts, established schools, set up courts to protect blacks from violence, and rented confiscated lands to blacks and impoverished whites.

7. Repudiation was cancellation of war debt. "A section of the 14th Amendment voided all debts incurred in support of the Confederate effort and prohibited any compensation for lost slaves." As a result, thousands of people who had lent money to the Confederate government lost millions of dollars. Claudine L. Ferrell, *Reconstruction* (Westport, CT: Greenwood, 2003), 26.

Chapter 17

1. In 1865 the meaning of *arbitrament* was the "right or power of deciding or controlling." *Webster's 3rd New Int. Dict.*, s.v. "arbitrament."

2. The 3rd Louisiana Engineers Corps had been formed on September 1, 1863. The same men made up the 97th U.S.C.I., which was formed on April 19, 1864, making it twenty months old in January 1866. OR, ser. 1, vol. 34, pt. 3, correspondence, p. 222; the information about the individual soldiers is based on "CAMP AND GARRISON EQUIPAGE. Receipt Roll of Clothing of Capt. John N. Chamberlin." These were reports that Chamberlin filed with the War Department thirteen times in 1864–1866. These reports listed clothing issued to his

soldiers; presumably they were fairly complete records of their names. App. E shows an example of these reports. Chamberlin filled out these reports in triplicate, retaining one for himself. Thirteen of these original copies are in possession of John Bisbee.

3. See chap. 16, n. 6. The Freedman Bill was eventually extended over Johnson's veto in July 1866.

4. Brooks D. Simpson, *The Reconstruction Presidents* (Lawrence: University Press of Kansas, 1998), 96–8. Eric Foner, *Reconstruction*, 243, 250.

5. "Copartnership document," signed by John N. Chamberlin and Peter Thompson and witnessed by Geo. M Chamberlin in Mobile, Alabama, on Jan. 24, 1866. Original document in possession of John Bisbee.

6. A barouche is a "four-wheeled carriage with a driver's seat high in front, two double seats inside facing each other, and a folding top over the back seat." www.merriam-webster.com/dictionary/barouche, copyright 2015, accessed June 17, 2015.

7. Gretchen A. Adams, "Phillips, Wendell," in Heidler and Heidler, *Ency. of the Am. Civil War*, 1512–3. Phillips (1811–1884), of Boston, was a leading abolitionist crusader whose oratorical eloquence helped fire the antislavery cause during the period leading up to the Civil War.

8. Eric Foner, *Reconstruction*, xxiii, 132–3, 322.

9. Dobak, *Freedom by the Sword*, 475.

10. "QUARTERLY RETURN OF ORDNANCE AND ORDNANCE STORES RECEIVED, ISSUED, AND REMAINING ON HAND. Co. 'E' 97th Regiment U.S.C.I. Infantry, ... transmitted to the Chief of Ordnance, Washington, D.C., on the 12th day of April, 1866 by John N. Chamberlin." Original in possession of John Bisbee.

Chapter 18

1. See chap. 6, n. 2.
2. "Gentle Annie"

Thou wilt come no more, gentle Annie,
Like a flower thy spirit did depart;
Thou art gone, alas! Like the many
That have bloomed in the summer of my heart.
Shall we nevermore behold thee;
Never hear thy winning voice again—
When the Springtime comes, gentle Annie,
When the wild flowers are scattered o'er the plain?

We have roamed and loved mid the bowers
When thy downy cheeks were in their bloom;
Now I stand alone mid the flowers
While they mingle their perfumes o'er thy tomb.

Ah! the hours grow sad while I ponder
Near the silent spot where thou art laid,
And my heart bows down when I wander
By the streams and the meadows where we strayed.

"Gentle Annie" was a popular American song composed by Stephen Foster in 1856. John W. Beattie et al., eds., *The Gray Book of Favorite Songs*, 4th ed. (Chicago: Hall & McCreary, 1941), 80.

3. This could be a reference to Ruth 1:16 (AV), a Biblical passage often used at weddings.

4. Song of Solomon 8:7 (AV).

Epilogue

1. During the war, John Chamberlin had sent money to George Chamberlin to invest in land. George had bought a joint farm and after the war didn't have the cash to buy John Chamberlin's share.

2. Affidavit in John N. Chamberlin's pension file from Elias Lestor, a surgeon of his regiment (97th U.S.C.I.), who also knew him while he was in the 75th N.Y.V.

3. Teaching Certificate, November 26, 1870, signed by Leonard Hardy; real estate agreement signed by George, Charles, and John Chamberlin, Elbridge, New York, May 1, 1871. Original copies of both documents in possession of John Bisbee.

4. Affidavit in John N. Chamberlin's pension file from Geo. H. Parsell, the family doctor who cared for John at Weedsport, New York, between the time of his mustering out and his death.

Bibliography

Government Documents

American Battlefield Protection Program. "CWSAC Battle Summaries." Heritage Preservation Services. Accessed January 24, 2015. http:www.cr.nps.gov/hps/abpp/battles/la021.htm, and accessed July 8, 2015, www.nps.gov/abpp/battles/tx006.htm.

Annual Report of the Adjutant-General of the State of New York. Albany: Comstock & Cassidy, 1863.

Annual Report of the Adjutant-General of the State of New York for the Year 1901. Albany: J. B. Lyon, 1902.

Duane, Capt. J. C. *Manual for Engineer Troops.* New York, 1864. Accessed January 25, 2015. http://archive.org/stream/manualforenginee00duanrich#page/n5/mode/2up.

Kennedy, Joseph C. G. *Population of the United States in 1860. Compiled from the Original Returns of the Eighth Census.* Washington, D.C.: Government Printing Office. Accessed November 17, 2014. https://archive.org/details/population fusin00kennrich.

Louisiana Division/City Archives. "Jackson Barracks." New Orleans Public Library. Accessed February 11, 2015. www.neworleanshistorical.org/items/show/267#.VNveOC4Ufct.

Owen, Thomas McAdory. *History of Alabama and Dictionary of Alabama Biography.* Chicago: S. J. Clarke, 1921. Last updated February 6, 2014. www.archives.state.al.us/counties/conecuh.html.

Riley, B. F. *History of Conecuh County, Alabama.* Columbus, GA, 1881. File contributed for use in USGenWeb Archives by Joy Fisher. Accessed February 18, 2015. http://files.usgwarchives.net/al/conecuh/history/other/gms42historyo.txt.

U.S. Government. *The War of the Rebellion: A Compilation of the Official Records of the Union and Confederate Armies.* 70 vols. in 128 pts. Washington, D.C.: Government Printing Office, 1880–1901.

―――. *The War of the Rebellion: A Compilation of the Official Records of the Union and Confederate Navies.* 30 vols. Washington, D.C.: Government Printing Office, 1894–1922.

Other Sources

Adams, Gretchen A. "Phillips, Wendell." In Heidler and Heidler, *Ency. of the Am. Civil War*, 1512–3.

Appleton's Hand-Book of American Travel. New York: D. Appleton, 1869. Perry-

Bibliography

Castaneda Library Map Collection. Website for the University of Texas Libraries. Accessed January 24, 2015. www.lib.utexas.edu/maps/historical/new_orleans_1869.jpg.

Barr, Daniel. "Canby, Edward Richard Sprigg." In Heidler and Heidler, *Ency. of the Am. Civil War*, 352–4.

Beattie, John W., William Breach, Mabelle Glenn, Walter Goodell, Edgar B. Gordon, Norman H. Hall, Ernest G. Hesser, E. Jane Wisenall, and Florence Martin, eds. *The Gray Book of Favorite Songs*. 4th ed. Chicago: Hall & McCreary, 1941.

Beckman, W. Robert. "Sickles, Daniel Edgar." In Heidler and Heidler, *Ency. of the Am. Civil War*, 1784–6.

Bergeron, Arthur W., Jr. *Confederate Mobile*. Jackson: University Press of Mississippi, 1991.

Berlin, Ira, Joseph P. Reidy, and Leslie S. Rowland, eds. *The Black Military Experience*. Cambridge: Cambridge University Press, 1982.

Boatner, Mark Mayo, III. *Civil War Dictionary*. New York: David McKay, 1987.

Boston Liberator. July 21, 1865. "The Fourth in Mobile." Copy of article received from Megan Halsband, Reference Librarian, Serial & Government Publications Division, Library of Congress, on November 18, 2014.

Bowman, John S., ed. *The Civil War Almanac*. New York: World Almanac, 1983.

Bramwell, Lincoln. "Nashville, Tennessee." In Heidler and Heidler, *Ency. of the Am. Civil War*, 1387–90.

Breerwood, Rhett. "Camp Parapet: The Union." *New Orleans Historical*. Accessed January 31, 2015. http://www.neworleanshistorical.org/items/show/658.

Cassidy, Frederic G., Joan Houston Hall, and Luanne Von Schneidemesser, eds. *Dictionary of American Regional English*. Vol. 1. Cambridge, MA: Belknap Press of Harvard University Press, 1985.

Catton, Bruce. *Picture History of the Civil War*. 1982 ed. New York: Bonanza Books, 1982.

Cheek, H. Lee, Jr. "Stephens, Alexander Hamilton." In Heidler and Heidler, *Ency. of the Am. Civil War*, 1857–9.

Cimbala, Paul A. "Freedmen's Bureau." In Heidler and Heidler, *Ency. of the Am. Civil War*, 783–4.

Coleman, John. "Flag at Brashear." In *Morgan City Review*, March 23, 1927. Website for the Young-Sanders Center for the Study of the War Between the States in Louisiana. Accessed March 23, 2015. www.youngsanders.org/youngsandersflagbrashear.html.

Coleridge, Samuel Taylor. "Historical Sketch: Of the Manners and Religion of the Ancient Germans." From *The Watchman*. March 17, 1796; 130. In *Essays on His Own Times*. Vol. 1. Edited by his daughter. New York, 1850. First AMS ed. New York: AM, 1971.

Coles, David J. "Fort Pickens." In Heidler and Heidler, *Ency. of the Am. Civil War*, 744–5.

———. "Santa Rosa Island." In Heidler and Heidler, *Ency. of the Am. Civil War*, 1704.

Cowper, William. "God Moves in a Mysterious Way," 1733. In John Newton, *Twenty-Six Letters on Religious Subjects; to Which Are Added Hymns*. London, 1774. Discussed in Marilyn Kay Stulken, *Hymnal Companion to the Lutheran Book of Worship*. Philadelphia: Fortress, 1981. Complete hymn in Lutheran Church in America, The American Lutheran Church, The Evangelical Lutheran Church of Canada, and The Lutheran Church—Missouri Synod. *Lutheran Book of Worship*. Minneapolis: Augsburg, 1978.

Bibliography

Current, Richard N., ed. *Encyclopedia of the Confederacy*. 4 vols. New York: Simon & Schuster, 1993.
Davis, Michael S. "Farragut, David Glascow." In Heidler and Heidler, *Ency. of the Am. Civil War*, 682–5.
Dickens, Charles. *The Life and Adventures of Martin Chuzzlewit*. London, 1843. Last updated August 3, 2014. http://www.gutenberg.org/files/968/968-h/968-h.html.
Ditmann, Laurent. "Beauregard, Pierre Gustave Toutant." In Heidler and Heidler, *Ency. of the Am. Civil War*, 198–200.
Dobak, William. *Freedom by the Sword: The U.S. Colored Troops, 1862–1867*. New York: Skyhorse, 2013.
Dodson, Howard. *Jubilee: The Emergence of African-American Culture*. Washington, D.C.: National Geographic, 2002.
Dummelow, The Rev. J. R., ed. *A Commentary on the Holy Bible*. New York: Macmillan, 1908.
Duyckinck, Evert A., and George L. Duyckinick. *The Cyclopedia of American Literature*. Philadelphia, 1880. Quoted by James R. Elkins in "Strangers to Us All: Lawyers and Poetry." Vol. 2. Website first posted September 2, 2001. myweb.wvnet.edu/~jelkins/lp-2001/saxe.html. From "John Godfrey Saxe Papers." Bailey-Howe Memorial Library, University of Vermont, Burlington.
Dyer, Frederick H. *A Compendium of the War of the Rebellion*. Vol. 3. New York: Thomas Yoseloff, 1959.
Eicher, David J. *The Longest Night: A Military History of the Civil War*. New York: Simon & Schuster, 2001.
Eicher, John H., and David J. Eicher. *Civil War High Commands*. Stanford: Stanford University Press, 2001.
Eldridge, David P. "New Orleans, Capture of." In Heidler and Heidler, *Ency. of the Am. Civil War*, 1412–3.
Eldridge, Mary Beth. *Brief Biographies of Early Residents of Waterloo, Black Hawk Co., Iowa*. 1993. Accessed May 4, 2015. http://www.rootsweb.ancestry.com/~iabiog/blackhawk/h1993/h1993-al.htm.
Faber, Frederick W. "God's Glory Is a Wondrous Thing." Source: *Jesus & Mary*, 1849, alt. Accessed March 24, 2015. http://www.hymnary.org/hymn/CYBER/1909.
Fahey, David M. *Temperance and Racism*. Frankfort: University Press of Kentucky, 1996.
Faust, Patricia, ed. *Historical Times Illustrated Encyclopedia of the Civil War*. New York: Harper & Row, 1986.
Ferrell, Claudine L. *Reconstruction*. Westport, CT: Greenwood Press, 2003.
Field, Ron. *American Civil War Fortification*. Vol. 2, *Land and Field Fortifications*. Oxford: Osprey, 2005.
Fisher, Steven. "Lincoln Assassination." In Heidler and Heidler, *Ency. of the Am. Civil War*, 1192–6.
Fogel, Robert William, and Stanley L. Engerman. *Time on the Cross: The Economics of American Negro Slavery*. Boston: Little, Brown, 1974. Accessed February 10, 2015. http://faculty.weber.edu/kmackay/economics%20of%20slavery.asp.
Folmar, John Kent, ed. *From That Terrible Field: Civil War Letters of James M. Williams, Twenty-First Alabama Infantry Volunteers*. Tuscaloosa: University of Alabama Press, 1981.
Foner, Eric. *The Fiery Trial: Abraham Lincoln and American Slavery*. New York: W.W. Norton, 2010.
_____. *Gateway to Freedom: The Hidden History of the Underground Railroad*. New York: W.W. Norton, 2015.

Bibliography

———. *Reconstruction: America's Unfinished Revolution, 1863–1877*. New York: Harper & Row, 1988.
Foner, Philip S., ed. *Life and Writings of Frederick Douglass*. Vol. 3, *The Civil War, 1861–1865*. New York: International, 1952.
Foster, Stephen. "Gentle Annie." 1856. *The Gray Book of Favorite Songs*. Edited by John W. Beattie et al. Chicago: Hall & McCreary, 1919.
Frisk, M. Jean. "The Queen of May." Accessed January 30, 2015. www.tomorrowsworld.org/commentary/the-queen-of-may.
Gallagher, Gary, Stephen Engle, Robert Krick, and Joseph Glatthar. *Civil War: Fort Sumter to Appomattox*. Oxford: Osprey, 2003.
Garraty, John, and Mark Carnes, eds. *American National Biography*. Oxford: Oxford University Press, 1999.
Garrett, T. E. "Guard of Land and Sea." Saint Louis, 1861. From "Historic American Sheet Music." Accessed January 28, 2015. Duke University Libraries. http://library.duke.edu/digitalcollections/hasm_a4996_a4996-1.
Garrison, Webb, Sr. *Webb Garrison's Civil War Dictionary: An Illustrated Guide to the Everyday Language of Soldiers and Civilians*. Nashville: Cumberland House, 2008.
Gaul, Samantha Jane. "Conscription, U.S.A." In Heidler and Heidler, *Ency. of the Am. Civil War*, 487–8.
Glatthaar, Joseph T. *Forged in Battle: The Civil War Alliance of Black Soldiers and White Officers*. New York: Free Press, 1990.
Goodwin, Doris Kearns. *Team of Rivals: The Political Genius of Abraham Lincoln*. New York: Simon & Schuster, 2005.
Groom, Winston. *Vicksburg, 1863*. New York: Alfred A. Knopf, 2009.
Guerrisi, Bryan. Introduction to *Civil War Love Stories*, by Gill Paul. New York: Metro Books, 2013, 7–19.
Hall, James. *Cayuga in the Field: A Record of the 75th N.Y. Volunteers, Comprising an Account of Its Organization, Camp Life, Marches, Battles, Losses, Toils and Triumphs in the War for the Union, with Complete Rolls of Its Members*. Vol. 2. Auburn, NY, 1873.
Heidler, David S., and Jeanne T. Heidler. "Bailey, Joseph." In Heidler and Heidler, *Ency. of the Am. Civil War*, 158–9.
——— and ———. "Emory, William Hemsley," in Heidler and Heidler, *Ency. of the Am. Civil War*, 653–4.
——— and ———. "Mobile Campaign." In Heidler and Heidler, *Ency. of the Am. Civil War*, 1345.
——— and ———. "Phelps, John Wolcott." In Heidler and Heidler, *Ency. of the Am. Civil War*, 1508–9.
——— and ———. "Port Hudson, Louisiana Campaign." In Heidler and Heidler, *Ency. of the Am. Civil War*, 1546–9.
——— and ———. "Thomas, Lorenz. " In Heidler and Heidler, *Ency. of the Am. Civil War*, 1945.
——— and ———, eds. *Encyclopedia of the American Civil War: A Political, Social, and Military History*. New York: W.W. Norton, 2000.
Hewitt, Janet B., ed. *The Roster of Confederate Soldiers, 1861–1865*. Vol. 8. Wilmington, NC: Broadfoot, 1996.
Hewitt, Lawrence Lee. "An Ironic Route to Glory: Louisiana's Native Guards at Port Hudson." In Smith, *Black Soldiers in Blue*, 78–106.
Holzer, Harold, and Craig L. Symonds, eds. *The New York Times Complete Civil War*. New York: Black Dog & Leventhal, 2010.

Bibliography

Hubbell, John T., and James W. Geary. *Biographical Dictionary of the Union*. Westport, CT: Greenwood, 1905.
James, Edward, ed. "Heron, Matilda." *Notable American Women 1607–1950: A Biographical Dictionary*. Vol. 2. Cambridge, MA: Belknap Press of Harvard University, 1971.
Johnson, Ludwell H. *Red River Campaign: Politics and Cotton in the Civil War*. Kent, OH: Kent State University Press, 1993.
Jomini, Baron Antoine Henri. *Life of Napoleon*. Translated by H. W. Halleck. Vol. 1. New York, 1864. European Libraries from the Collections of Oxford University. Accessed February 5, 2015. https://archive.org/details/lifenapoleontrw01jomigoog.
Knetsch, Joe. "Pensacola, Florida." In Heidler and Heidler, *Ency. of the Am. Civil War*, 1487–9.
Knutson, Roslyn L. Last updated April 24, 2014. www.lostplays.org/index.php/Love's_Labour's_Won.
Laskin, Lisa Lauterbach. "Appomattox Court House." In Heidler and Heidler, *Ency. of the Am. Civil War*, 67–72.
Lause, Mark A. "Giddings, Joshua Reed." In Heidler and Heidler, *Ency. of the Am. Civil War*, 839.
Levin, Kevin M. "Mobile Bay." In Heidler and Heidler, *Ency. of the Am. Civil War*, 1342–4.
Levine, Bruce. *The Fall of the House of Dixie: The Civil War and the Social Revolution That Transformed the South*. Random House Trade Paperback Ed. New York: Random House Trade Paperbacks, 2014.
Lincoln, Abraham. *The Complete Works of Abraham Lincoln*. Edited by Roy P. Basler. 6 vols. New Brunswick, NJ: Rutgers University Press, 1953.
———. *The Writings of Abraham Lincoln*. Edited by Arthur B. Lapsley. Centennial Edition. Vol. 6, *1862–1863*. Vol. 7, *1863–1865*. New York: P. F. Collier, n.d., ca. 1906.
Longfellow, Henry Wadsworth. *The Complete Poetical Works of Henry Wadsworth Longfellow*. Household Ed. Cambridge: Riverside, 1902.
Lowe, John D. "Battle on the Levee," in Smith, *Black Soldiers in Blue*, 107–29.
Mahan, D. H. *A Treatise on Field Fortification*, 3rd ed. New York, 1852. Accessed August 18, 2015. http://quod.lib.umich.edu/m/moa/AJR7399.0001.001/70?rgn=full+text;view=image.
McPherson, James M. *Battle Cry of Freedom: The Civil War Era*. Oxford: Oxford University Press, 1988.
Melville, Herman. *Typee: A Real Romance of the South Sea*. Boston, 1845.
Meres, Francis. *Palladis Tamia, Wits Treasury*. London, 1598. Accessed February 9, 2015. www.archive.org/stream/ancientcriticale02hasluoft#page/152/mode/2up.
Miller, Enoch K. "An Important Letter from a Chaplain." In *Christian Recorder*. February 2, 1865. Accessed March 31, 2015. Accessible only with fee. http://www.accessible.com/accessible/docButton?AAWhat=builtPage&AAWhere=THE CHRISTIANRECORDER.FR1865020423.70996&AABeanName=toc3&AANext Page=/printBrowseBuiltPage.jsp.
Milton, John. "*Paradise Lost*." In *American Heritage Dictionary of the English Language*. 5th ed. Boston: Houghton Mifflin Harcourt, 2011.
Mobile Tribune. "The Fourth in Mobile." Editorial reprinted in *Evening Post, New York*. July 19, 1865. Copy of article received from Megan Halsband, Reference Librarian, Serial & Government Publications Division, Library of Congress, on November 18, 2014.
Morton, Patricia Hoskins. "Escambia County." August 29, 2007. Last updated July 23, 2013. http://www.encyclopediaofalabama.org/face/Article.jsp?id=h-1321.

Bibliography

Murphree, R. Boyd. "Lopez, Narciso." In Heidler and Heidler, *Ency. of the Am. Civil War*, 1218–20.
Nicholson, Norman A. *War Comes to Baldwin County!* Pamphlet published for Historic Blakeley State Park in Spanish Fort, AL., n.d.
Northup, Solomon. *Twelve Years a Slave: Narrative of Solomon Northup, a Citizen of New-York, Kidnapped in Washington City in 1841, and Rescued in 1853*. Auburn, NY, 1853.
O'Brien, Sean Michael. *Mobile, 1865: Last Stand of the Confederacy*. Westport, CT: Praeger, 2001.
Palladino, Anita, ed. *Diary of a Yankee Engineer: The Civil War Story of John H. Westervelt, Engineer, 1st New York Volunteer Engineer Corps*. New York: Fordham University Press, 1997.
Pike, Marshall S. "Home Again." Boston, 1850. From "Historic American Sheet Music." Duke University Libraries: Digital Collection. Accessed February 23, 2015. http://library.duke.edu/digitalcollections/hasm_n0945/.
Pratt, Dorothy O. "Bounty System." In Heidler and Heidler, *Ency. of the Am. Civil War*, 256–7.
Prentice, George Dennison. *The Poems of George D. Prentice*. Edited by John James Piatt. Cincinnati, 1876. Accessed February 5, 2015. http://archive.org/stream/poemsofgeorgedpr00inpren/poemsofgeorgedpr00inpren_djvu.txt.
Pritchard, Russ. A. "Hand Grenades and Land Mines." In Current, *Ency. of the Confederacy*. 2:734–5.
Rodriguez, Junius P. "Contrabands." In Heidler and Heidler, *Ency. of the Am. Civil War*, 491–3.
———. "Fugitive Slave Act of 1850." In Heidler and Heidler, *Ency. of the Am. Civil War*, 794–6.
St. Michael's Cemetery Foundation of Pensacola, Inc. Accessed January 25, 2015. www.stmichaelscemetery.org.
Saunders, Robert, Jr. "Benjamin, Judah Philip." In Heidler and Heidler, *Ency. of the Am. Civil War*, 209–11.
Shakespeare, William. *Hamlet*. Edited by G. R. Hibbard. Oxford: Clarendon, 1987.
Sheehan-Dean, Aaron, ed. *The Civil War: The Final Year Told by Those Who Lived It*. New York: The Library of America, 2014.
Simpson, Brooks D. *The Reconstruction Presidents*. Lawrence: University Press of Kansas, 1998.
Smith, Adam I. P. "Seward, William Henry," in Heidler and Heidler, *Ency. of the Am. Civil War*, 1736–40.
Smith, Gene A. "Monitor." In Heidler and Heidler. *Ency. of the Am. Civil War*, 1346–7.
Smith, John David, ed. *Black Soldiers in Blue: African American Troops in the Civil War Era*. Chapel Hill: University of North Carolina Press, 2002.
Smith, John David. "Let Us All Be Grateful That We Have Colored Troops That Will Fight." In Smith, *Black Soldiers in Blue*, 1–64.
Sommers, Richard J. *Richmond Redeemed: The Siege of Petersburg*. Garden City, NJ: Doubleday, 1981.
Stowe, Harriet Beecher. *Uncle Tom's Cabin or, Life among the Lowly*. Boston, 1852.
Stulken, Marilyn Kay. *Hymnal Companion to the Lutheran Book of Worship*. Philadelphia: Fortress, 1981.
Tap, Bruce. "Copperheads." In Heidler and Heidler, *Ency. of the Am. Civil War*, 498–9.
Texas State Historical Association. "Brazos Island." *Handbook of Texas Online*.

Bibliography

Accessed August 5, 2013. http://www.tshaonline.org/handbook/online/articles/rrb10.

Tidwell, William. *Come Retribution: The Confederate Secret Service and the Assassination of Lincoln.* With James O. Hall and David Winfrey Gaddy. Jackson: University Press of Mississippi, 1988.

Todd, Gerald. "Civil War Cavalry Forum." March 4, 2004. Last updated April 5, 2013. http://mainecav.org/history.htm#2ndMaine.

Trudeau, Noah A. *Like Men of War: Black Troops in the Civil War 1862–1865.* Boston: Little, Brown, 1998.

Tucker, Spencer C. "Phelps's Raid." In Heidler and Heidler, *Ency. of the Am. Civil War*, 1509–10.

———. "Semmes, Raphael." In Heidler and Heidler, *Ency. of the Am. Civil War*, 1730–32.

Turner, Maxine. "Torpedoes." In Current, *Ency. of the Confederacy.* 4:1603–4.

Ulbrich, David J. "Logistics." In Heidler and Heidler. *Ency. of the Am. Civil War*, 1207–10.

Walther, Eric H. "Yancey, William Lowndes." In Heidler and Heidler, *Ency. of the Am. Civil War*, 2157–8.

Warner, Ezra J. *Generals in Blue: Lives of Union Commanders.* Baton Rouge: Louisiana State University Press, 1964.

Weaver, C. P., ed. *Thank God My Regiment an African One: The Civil War Diary of Colonel Nathan W. Daniels.* Baton Rouge: Louisiana State University Press, 1998.

Westwood, Howard C. *Black Troops, White Commanders, and Freedmen During the Civil War.* Carbondale: Southern Illinois University Press, 1992.

Wilson, Keith P. *Campfires of Freedom: The Camp Life of Black Soldiers During the Civil War.* Kent, OH: Kent State University Press, 2002.

Wright, John D. *The Language of the Civil War.* Westport, CT: Oryx, 2001.

Index

Numbers in **_bold italics_** refer to pages with illustrations.

Abolitionist 50, 55, 79
Adams, Charles Francis 122
Alabama (U.S. steamer) 106
Alexandria, LA 33, **_35_**, 39, 64–66; fire 67
Allen, Lt. C.J. 38, 82
Amnesty Proclamation 126; oath 129–130
Army Corps: 13th 64; 16th 111; 19th 33, 39
Arnold, Brig. Gen. Lewis G. 13, 26
Atchafalaya River, LA 34, **_35_**, 37–38, 40, 68
Atlanta, GA 68, 99
Attakapas country, LA 34
Auburn, NY 7
Augur, Gen. Christopher C. 41

Bailey, Lt. Col. Joseph 66
Baltic (U.S. transport) 7, 8
Banks, Maj. Gen. Nathaniel 29, **_30_**, 31, 36–37, 39, 41–42, 46, 63, 66, 68–69; his soldiers 33, 39–40, 63
Baton Rouge, LA 23, **_35_**
Battery Tracy, AL **_9_**, 111
Battle of Irish Bend, LA 38
Battle of Pine Barren Creek, FL 97–99
Bayou Boeuf (central LA) 40
Bayou Boeuf (southern LA) 33–34, **_35_**, 36
Bayou St. John, LA 79
Bayou Teche, LA 33–34, **_35_**, 37–39
Beauregard, Gen. G.T. 99
Belvedere (U.S. steamer) 53
Berwick Bay, LA 33, **_35_**, 36, 55, 57, 60, 63
black soldiers 29, 32, 45–46, 50–51, 53–54, 80, 98, 100; consolidation of regiments 77; education of 82, 84; numbered U.S. regimental designations 55; pay equalization 78–80; recruitment of 32, 51, 53–55, 71, 100; *see also* white officers of black soldiers

Black-Water River, FL **_9_**, 22
Blair, Francis Preston 105–106
Blakely, AL **_9_**, 99, 108, 110–111, 114
Booth, J. Wilkes 114–115
Boston Liberator 128
Boughton, 1st Lt. Eugene F. 46–47, 97
Bragg, Gen. Braxton 44
Brashear City, LA 33–34, **_35_**, 38
Brown (U.S. steamer) 53
Brown, Col. Harvey 8, 12
Bullock, Albert (Bert) 68, 135, 159
Bullock, Gilbert (Gib) 73, 135
Bullock, Howard 58, 68, 73, **_132_**, 135
Bullock, Nathan 57, 59
Bureau of Colored Troops 51, 55
Bureau of Refugees, Freedman, and Abandoned Lands *see* Freedmen's Bureau
Butler, Gen. Benjamin F. 23, 25–26, 28–29, 31, 50

Camp Arnold, FL 16, 20
Camp Bisland, LA 37
Camp Carrolton, LA 80
Camp Cayuga, NY 7
Camp Hubbard, LA 33
Camp Parapet, LA 28
Camp Seward, FL 8–9, 11
Canby, Maj. Gen. E.R. S. 7, 114
Cane River, LA **_35_**, 64–65, 76
Carrolton, LA 25, 77
Cayuga County, NY 7
Chamberlin, Charles 56, 60, 144–145, 148, 157
Chamberlin, George 140, 143–144, 157
Chamberlin, Harriet 58
Chamberlin, Joel 7
Chamberlin, Johnny R. **_89_**
Chamberlin, Polly 7

199

Index

Chamberlin, Sarah 88, 157
Charleston, SC 101, 109
Chattanooga, TN 100
Chicago Convention (Democratic) 87
Choctaw Bayou, LA *35*, 67–68
Civil Rights Bill of 1866 142; veto of 195
Cleburne, Gen. Patrick 100
Clifton (U. S. gunboat) 52
Clyde (U.S. steamer) 93
Columbia, SC 109
Conecuh County, AL 129
Confederate Congress 100
Connecticut Units: 13th Cavalry 24
Constitution, U.S. 121–122
contrabands, Rebel 10, 20; slaves 28
copperheads 83, 118, 145
Corning, Capt. Andrew 12, 36, 41, 46, 48
Corps d'Afrique 46, 58; 3rd Regt. Engineers 46, 52, 54–55, 63, 66; 5th Regt. Engineers 66
Cotton (Rebel transport) 3, 9
Cowper, William 69
Creole (U.S. steamer) 22, 56

Dauphine Island, AL *9*, 75, 81
Davis, Jefferson 20, 100, 105–106, 111, 115–116
Declaration of Independence 58, 128
Detroit Advertiser and Tribune 117
Diana (Rebel gunboat) 37–38
Diana (U.S. gunboat) 34–36
Dodge, Col. John A. 7, 11
Douglass, Frederick 55, 79
Draft Act of 1863 62
Dred Scott case 121
Dudley, Col. 54
Dwight, Capt. Charles C. 26

Elbridge, NY 147, 157
emancipation 130
Emancipation Proclamation 31, 101, 130
Emory, Gen. William H. 36
Escambia Creek, AL 97
Estrella (U.S. gunboat) 38
Europe 59, 61

Farragut, Adm. David G. 23–24, 35
Fish River, AL *9*, 108
Florida 7, *9*, 15, 18, 93
Fort Barrancas, FL *9*, 16, 93, 96
Fort Bisland, LA 36–37
Fort Gaines, AL *9*, 81–82, 102, 106
Fort Griffin, TX 52
Fort Griswold, NY 8
Fort Hamilton, NY 8
Fort Huger, LA *9*, 111

Fort Lafayette, NY 8
Fort McAllister, GA 101
Fort McRee, FL *9*, 15, 93
Fort Morgan, AL *9*, 81, 107
Fort Pickens, FL 8, *9*, 10–11, 15, 20, 93
Fort Sumter, SC 29
Fort Wagner, SC 32, 54
France 31, 63
Franklin, Maj. Gen. William B. 52
Franklin, LA *35*, 38
Freedmen's Bureau 137, 141; veto of bill for 142–143
Fugitive Slave Acts 121

Garnie (Rebel steamer) 38
Governor Island, NY 7
Grand Ecore, LA *35*, 65–66, 69
Grand Lake, LA 34, *35*, 36, 38, 66
Granger, Gen. Gordon 107, 111
Grant, Gen. Ulysses S. 33, 45, 63, 111, 139
Great Britain 31
Grover, Gen. Cuvier 36, 66; his soldiers 37–38, 41
Gulf of Mexico *9*, *35*, 44

Hardee, Gen. William Joseph 101
Hart (Rebel gunboat) 38, 53
Hazeltine, 1st Lt. Charles P. 94
Heron, Matilda 137
Hill, Capt. James Gilbert 108

Industrial Revolution 121
Ingraham, Capt. J.H. 129
Iowa 74
Iowa 82nd Regt. Co. C 118, 133

Jackson, Andrew 106
Jackson, Col. John K. 10
Jacksonville, FL 32, 54
jayhawkers 71
Jenny Rogers (U.S. steamer) 108, 129
Johnson, Andrew 114, 118, 139, 141–142, 145
July 4th 43–44, 127

Laurel Hill (U.S. steamer) 44, 51–52
Lee, Gen. Robert E. 44, 100, 111, 114–115
Lestor, Dr. Elias 157
Liddell, Gen. St. John 98–99
Lincoln, Abraham 19, 29, 32, 44–45, 50, 54, 63, 79, 87–88, 91–92, 99, 106, 118, 130; assassination 114–116, 118; Second Inaugural Address 19, 59, 91
Longfellow, Henry Wadsworth 56–57
Louisiana 31–32, *35*, 56, 60–61, 74
Louisiana Native Guards (Confederate) 29

200

Index

Louisiana Native Guards: 1st Regt. 24, 28–29, 41, 50; 2nd Regt. 24, 28–29, 45, 50; 3rd Regt. 28–29, 41, 45, 50; 4th Regt. 28–29

Maine 121
Mansfield, LA *35*, 64
Marine Barracks, New Orleans, LA 24
McClellan, Maj. Gen. George B. 87, 89–90
McKean, Brig. Gen. Thomas J. 99
Meigs (U.S. steamer) 22
Mexican War 24
Mexico 63
Militia Act of July 1862 79
Miller, Enoch 99
Milliken's Bend, LA 32, 54
Milwaukee (U.S. monitor) 108
Mississippi 8th Cavalry (Confederate) 16
Mississippi River 23, 33, *35*, 41, 44
Missouri 121
Missouri Compromise of 1820 121
Mobile, AL *9*, 108–119, 127–129, 131, 145
Mobile Bay, AL *9*, 10, 81, 107, 109
Mobile Tribune 128
Morganza, LA *35*, 66, 80

Napoleon, Emperor 105
Nashville, TN 24
Nassau (U.S. steamer) 52
Navy Yard, Pensacola, FL 10, 12, 15, 102
Negroes 28–29, 58, 141, 143; *see also* racial prejudice
New Iberia, LA *35*, 53–54
New Market Heights, VA 45
New Orleans, LA 23, 26, 28–29, 31, *35*, 46; Canal St. 25
New Orleans Tribune 128
New York 56, 74
New York City, NY 7, 25, 121
New York Herald 117
New York Times 31, 65–66
New York Units: 75th Volunteers 7, 10, 16, 21–22, 33–34, 36–37, 39–44, 46–48, 52, 119
Northup, Solomon 40

Okolonce (U.S. schooner) 52
Opelousas, LA *35*, 39–40
Osage (U.S. monitor) 108

Palfrey, Capt. John 102
Pensacola, FL *9*, 11–12, 15–18, 93, 102; cemetery 17–18
Pensacola Bay, FL 8, *9*, 10, 12, 21
Phelps, Brig. Gen. John Wolcott 28
Pilot Town, AL 107

Pine Barren Creek, FL 97–99
Pleasant Hill, LA *35*, 64–65
Pollard, FL *9*, 97, 99
pontoon bridge 52–54, 57, 64–68, 78, 107–108
Port Hudson, LA 33, *35*, 39, 45–46; siege of 40–44
presidential election of 1864 86–88, 90
provost marshall 63, 66, 129

Queen of the West (Rebel gun-boat) 34, 38–39

racial prejudice 50, 84, 144
Ransom, Gen. Thomas Edward 64
Red Chief (U.S. steamer) 53
Red River, LA *35*, 39, 64–66, 68; Campaign 63, 68–69; dam 66
review of Eastern troops 118
Rhode-Island (U.S. steamer) 19
Richmond, VA 20, 106, 122
Robinson, Maj. George D. 46–47, 66–68, 97–99

Sabine Pass, TX 52–53
Sachem (U.S. gunboat) 52
Sallie Robinson (U.S. steamer) 41
Salt Works 39
Santa Rosa Island, FL 8, *9*, 10–11
Saratoga, NY 61
Savannah, GA 101
Secretary of War 31, 79
Semmes, Capt. Oliver J. 38
Semmes Battery 38
Sennett, NY 7, 57, 58–59, 73–74, 90
Seward, William Henry 114
Seymour, Thomas H. 88
Shakespeare, William 71
Sherman, Gen. Thomas W. 41
Sherman, Gen. William Tecumseh 68, 101, 109
Ship Island, AL 81
Shreveport, LA 63
slavery: cause of War 11–12, 19; economic impact 95, 121; escape from 28–29; government and 11, 32, 40, 59, 120–122, 130
Smith, Maj. Gen. A.J. 64–65, 108
Smith, Capt. John J. 107–108
Snaggy Point, Red River, LA 68
South Carolina Units 32
Spanish Consul 17
Spanish Fort, AL *9*, 108, 110
Sparta, AL 129
Spurling, Lt. Col. Andrew B. 98
Starks Landing, AL 111
Staten Island, NY 8

201

Index

Steele, Gen. Fredrick 108
Stephens, Alexander H. 92
Stevens, Capt. Thomas 115
Stowe, Harriet Beecher 70

Taylor, Gen. Dick 34, 37, 67
temperance societies 61
Tennessee 15
Tensaw River, AL *9*, 111, *112*
Texas 44, 51–52, 63, 71, 94
Thomas, Gen. George Henry 101
Thomas, Brig. Gen. Lorenzo 50
Thompson, Lt. 75
Time (Rebel steamer) 12
torpedoes (mines) 109–110, 120
Truesdale, Maj. George 85

Uncle Tom's Cabin 122
Union (U.S. steamer) 39
United States Colored Troops (U.S.C.T.) 45, 51; 25th Regt. 101; 82nd Regt. 77–78, 97–99; 96th Regt. 128; 97th Regt. 77–78, 97–99, 108, 123, 128, 131, 140; 97th Regt., Co. E 67, 83, 85, 10; 99th Regt. 77, 79
Utica, NY 61

Vallandigham, Clement 88
Vermillion Bayou, LA 53
Vicksburg, MS 33, 39–41, 44
Voorhees, Daniel 88

Walton, Mrs. George 17
War Department 28–32, 46, 79–80
Washington, DC 113, 117
Washington, LA *35*, 39
Waterloo, IA 57, 140, 147
Weitzel, Gen. Godfrey 34, 38, 41, 50, 52
white officers of black soldiers 50–51, 83; examinations for 51, 77–78
Wood, Fernando 88
Woodman, Col. Andrew J. 101

Yancey, W.L. 129
Yankee Blade (U.S. transport) 13

www.ingramcontent.com/pod-product-compliance
Ingram Content Group UK Ltd.
Pitfield, Milton Keynes, MK11 3LW, UK
UKHW031836280125
454351UK00006B/188